Alfred Hitchcock and the British Cinema

Alfred Hitchcock and the British Cinema

with a new introduction

TOM RYALL

ATHLONE
London & Atlantic Highlands, NJ

First published 1986 by
Croom Helm Ltd

This edition published 1996 by
THE ATHLONE PRESS LTD
1 Park Drive, London NW11 7SG
and 165 First Avenue,
Atlantic Highlands, NJ 07716

© 1996 Tom Ryall

British Library Cataloguing in Publication Data
*A catalogue record for this book is available
from the British Library*

ISBN 0 485 12122 0

Library of Congress Cataloging-in-Publication Data
(registered)

Printed and bound in Great Britain by
Biddles Ltd, Guildford, Surrey GU1 1DA

Contents

Acknowledgements

My thanks are due to various colleagues in the School of Cultural Studies, Sheffield Hallam University, for providing the stimulating working environment in which this study took shape. I should also like to acknowledge the general influence of many individuals within the film education 'movement' and especially those associated with the Education Department of the British Film Institute both past and present. Special thanks are due to Alan Lovell for his help and encouragement particularly during the earlier stages of this project. Finally, I should like to thank my wife, Helen, for her support during the preparation of this book, and my children, Amy, Matthew and Kitty for their less conscious but no less valued support. This book is dedicated to them.

Introduction

Alfred Hitchcock and the British Cinema although originally published in 1986 still remains one of only two books devoted specifically to the director's crucial formative years as Britain's premier film maker.[1] It is also one of a small handful of books that deal with the British cinema during the interwar period[2] and these two dimensions – author and context – were the focus of the book generating its two interrelated aims. The first was to redress the balance in Hitchcock scholarship that had tended to neglect and, on occasion, dismiss the early part of Hitchcock's career in favour of his American films. Whilst the considerable achievement of Hollywood films such as *Notorious*, *Rear Window* and *Vertigo* had been acknowledged by numerous critics and formed the basis of Hitchcock's considerable critical reputation, the earlier British films such as *The Lodger*, *Blackmail* and *The Thirty-Nine Steps* had not really received the attention they merited as significant films in the history of cinema as well as important elements of the Hitchcock *œuvre*. The second aim was broader but possibly somewhat disguised by the book's title. 'The British cinema' was intended to have equal prominence in the study as the set of interrelated structures within which Hitchcock worked and by which his artistic horizons were both formed and constrained. Accordingly the book examines both the structure of the British film industry of the period with its system of stars and genres and characteristic stylistic features together with the specifics of the film culture which shaped the intellectual environment within which Hitchcock's films were made and received by audiences of various kinds. In terms of conceptual stance, the study is based upon two assumptions. Firstly, that an understanding of Hitchcock was derivable from a study of the film industry and culture within which he worked; secondly, and equally important to the book, that an understanding of the British cinema of the interwar period was derivable from a scrutiny of the ways in which Hitchcock negotiated its evolving and changing structures. As a recent writer on British cinema has observed,[3] the book can be seen as a contribution to the revision of 'orthodox' British film history, an intended corrective to those many influential accounts of British cinema which stress 'realism' and documentary above genre cinema and fantasy, and an account of Hitchcock's British films which sought to align them with what Charles Barr has identified as the 'strong under-life' of British cinema focused on sexuality and violence.[4]

The original text is presented here unrevised. However, since its publication there have been a number of books and articles both on Hitchcock in particular and on British cinema in general which relate to the concerns of the book including further work of my own on *Blackmail* and *The Thirty-Nine Steps*.[5] Some of this work is textually based and concerned with Hitchcock as an author, embedding critical commentary on the British films within specifically focused critical analyses of his work in general. For example, discussion of selected British films has been incorporated into Lesley Brill's study of Hitchcock as director of 'romance' films and into a feminist analysis of his work by Tania Modleski.[6] However, the major episode in Hitchcock studies in the late 1980s was undoubtedly the appearance of a new edition of Robin Wood's influential and pioneering book *Hitchcock's Films* under the title *Hitchcock's Films Revisited*.[7] Wood's book, first published in 1965, was a critical reading of selected American Hitchcock films and although the 1989 edition printed the original text unrevised it also included new material from the 1980s amongst which were essays on some of the British films. One of the new essays – 'The Murderous Gays: Hitchcock's Homophobia' – dealt with the presence of homosexual themes in the director's work and this dimension is the subject of an exhaustive study by Theodore Price – *Hitchcock and Homosexuality* – which traces such elements back to the British silent films.[8] British Hitchcock was also given significant space in *A Hitchcock Reader*, a substantial collection of essays which includes studies of *The Lodger*, *Blackmail* and the 1936 version of *The Man Who Knew Too Much*.[9] The major academic journals also reflected this growing interest in British Hitchcock with *Screen*, the influential British journal, publishing a lengthy essay on *Blackmail*, positioning it in relation to postmodernism,[10] and the American *Cinema Journal* carrying a piece on politics in Hitchcock focused on *The Man Who Knew Too Much* and *The Thirty-Nine Steps*.[11] Finally, in terms of critical work, *Hitchcock The Making of a Reputation* by Robert Kapsis[12] merits attention as an impressively argued thesis presenting a painstakingly detailed history of the director's 'biographical legend' which traces the ways in which Hitchcock has been constructed critically as an author and serious artist reaching back to his early days as a film maker in 1920s Britain.

Two things are worth picking out from this range of critical interpretation. Firstly, Robin Wood's book included a number of reflections on his original text and, of particular interest in this context, a revision of his original judgement of Hitchcock's British films as 'little more than 'prentice work, interesting chiefly because they are Hitchcock's'.[13]

Hitchcock's Films Revisited included a self-critique of this virtual dismissal of British Hitchcock together with an acknowledgement that 'the major elements of Hitchcock's mature style are already present in the British work'.[14] The new material included essays on *Blackmail*, *The Thirty-Nine Steps* and *Young and Innocent* written from a much more sympathetic standpoint compared to that of the original book. Secondly, one of Wood's key concerns was to rethink Hitchcock's work in the context of feminist film criticism and to challenge the post-Mulvey reading of his films as *simply* patriarchal and misogynist. This interweaves with Tania Modleski's *The Women Who Knew Too Much* which analyses a selection of films including *Blackmail* and *Murder!* from a feminist perspective. Her arguments sought a middle ground between critics who wrote Hitchcock off as a misogynist and those for whom Hitchcock's films presented a critique of patriarchy. Both Wood and Modleski treat Hitchcock's work from both periods of his career with a certain parity of esteem for the purposes of critical analysis and this contrasts with the previous critical relegation of the British work.

Alfred Hitchcock and the British Cinema contains incidental passages of critical interpretation but is predominantly concerned with positioning Hitchcock and his films in an historical and cultural context and developing a detailed profile of that context. In that sense it relates more closely to some of the recent writing on the history of British cinema rather than the interpretative criticism cited above. Work on the history of British cinema is only at a relatively infant stage in the sense that the basic empirical contours of that history are still being assembled and the hidden precepts that have governed attitudes to that cinema are still being excavated, understood and replaced by more nuanced positions. In both areas – the empirical and conceptual – the work of Charles Barr stands out and his edited essay collection – *All Our Yesterdays*[15] – published in the same year as *Alfred Hitchcock and the British Cinema* indicates the intellectual context in which the latter was written. It is a book that mixes critical interpretation and empirical history, with many of the contributors sharing the 'revisionist' position on British film history that is broadly anti-realist and pro-a cinema of fantasy. Such a position owes much to the work of the editor and Barr's various writings on British cinema constitute a formidable and evolving set of conceptual frameworks within which most of the interesting research on British cinema is now conducted. His introductory essay to *All Our Yesterdays* synthesises and develops the ways of thinking about British film history adumbrated in his previous work.[16] Hitchcock's films had slid easily into conventional accounts of British cinema as the work of a talented director capable of technical flourishes and stylistic 'touches' but lacking in seriousness and despite incidental 'realist' qualities not really part of the orthodox realist/documentary traditions which embodied, to quote critic Richard Winnington, 'the true business of the British movie'.[17] Barr's essay proposed alternative strands and tendencies in

British cinema and particularly those which highlighted the cinema's capacity for interiorisation, fantasy and self-reflexivity i.e. a modernist strand of meta-cinema to set beside the realist tendencies venerated by orthodox film historians. It is within that strand that Hitchcock's British films achieve a considerable significance though firmly within generic and cultural traditions that link his work with that of other British film makers.

Finally, with the publication of Jane E. Sloan's *Alfred Hitchcock: a filmography and bibliography*[18] students of Hitchcock's work have acquired a substantial guide to his work containing extensive and detailed information on both films and bibliographic resources and covering his British as well as his American career.

Notes

1. The other is Maurice Yacowar's *Hitchcock's British Films* (Archon Books, Connecticut, 1977). However, a number of general works on Hitchcock including Rohmer and Chabrol, Durgnat and Spoto incorporate comprehensive accounts of the British films.

2. Others would include M. Landy, *British Genres Cinema and Society, 1930-1960* (Princeton University Press, New Jersey, 1991) and R. Low, *Film Making in 1930s Britain* (Allen & Unwin, London, 1985).

3. A. Higson, *Waving the Flag: Constructing a National Cinema in Britain* (Clarendon Press, Oxford, 1995), p. 18.

4. C. Barr, 'A Conundrum for England', *Monthly Film Bulletin*, Aug. 1984, p. 235.

5. T. Ryall, *Blackmail* (British Film Institute, London, 1993); 'One Hundred and Seventeen Steps Towards Masculinity', in P. Kirkham & J. Thumim (eds.), *You Tarzan* (Lawrence and Wishart, London, 1993).

6. L. Brill, *The Hitchcock Romance* (Princeton University Press, New Jersey, 1988); T. Modleski, *The Women Who Knew Too Much* (Methuen, London, 1988).

7. Wood, R., *Hitchcock's Films Revisited* (Columbia University Press, New York, 1989).

8. T. Price, *Hitchcock and Homosexuality* (The Scarecrow Press, Inc., Metuchen, N.J., 1992).

9. M. Deutelbaum & L. Poague, *A Hitchcock Reader* (Iowa State University Press, Ames, 1986).

10. S. Eyüboglu, 'The authorial text and postmodernism: Hitchcock's *Blackmail*', Screen, 32:1, Spring, 1991.

11. I. R. Hark, 'Keeping Your Amateur Standing: Audience Participation and Good Citizenship in Hitchcock's Political Films', *Cinema Journal*, Vol. 29, No. 2, Winter, 1990.

12. R. E. Kapsis, *Hitchcock The Making of a Reputation* (University of Chicago Press, Chicago, 1992).

13. Wood, *Hitchcock's Films Revisited*, p. 73.

14. Ibid., p. 240.

15. C. Barr (ed.), *All Our Yesterdays* (British Film Institute, London, 1986).

16. See Barr, *Ealing Studios* (Cameron and Tayleur, London, 1977) and 'A Conundrum for England', *Monthly Film Bulletin*, Vol. 51, No. 607, 1984.

17. Quoted in Barr, *All Our Yesterdays*, p. 15.

18. Sloan, J. E., *Alfred Hitchcock a filmography and bibliography* (University of California Press, Berkeley, 1995).

Chapter One

Introduction –
Hitchcock and Criticism

Any study of Hitchcock has as its departure point the substantial textual entity — 'Hitchcock' — produced by the numerous critical studies of the director that have appeared since his films were accorded a privileged place in the revaluation of the American cinema initiated by the *Cahiers du Cinéma* critics of the 1950s. Much of this criticism has concentrated upon defining the stylistic and thematic identity of Hitchcock as an *auteur* but many recent critics and writers more concerned with theoretical problems than with authorial identity have used Hitchcock's films as reference points for studies of cinematic narration and psychoanalytical film criticism.[1] A diversity of Hitchcocks has emerged from the last three decades of critical activity and these will inevitably leave their mark on the present study. One of the study's aims is to supplement existing work on the director by examining the films of his British period, which have usually been neglected in favour of his American work. However, another aim is the construction of a contextual framework for the British films to allow of their analysis from an historically sensitive vantage point. The 'historicising of textual analysis'[2], as David Bordwell has called it, is an urgent task for criticism if textual study is to break free from the endless process of open reading based upon 'the sterile notion of the self-sufficient text'.[3] *Auteur* criticism has wrenched films and their directors from the historical circumstances of production and has defined the expression of the author's consciousness as responsible for the shape, form and meaning of a text. The individuality and uniqueness of the authorial *oeuvre* has often been an assumption based upon a self-contained study of a director's work rather than a quality requiring demonstration through comparison with, for example, the norms and conventions of film making during the period of the author. If Hitchcock's British work does display such qualities of individuality the activity of returning the films to their historical context will reveal this more certainly. This study whilst focusing on a film author with a substantially defined identity also depends upon a range of contextual critical terms, in particular, 'film culture' and 'national cinema'. It is the purpose of this introductory chapter to indicate the numerous nuances

1

of such terms which will be taken up during the course of the study.

'Film culture' entered the critical vocabulary of cinema in the early 1970s as a term referring to the limited and specifiable sphere of intellectual and cultural activity centred on the production of films. A film culture — 'an intermingling of ideas and institutions into recognisable formations'[4] — is constituted by the ideologies of film that circulate and compete in a given historical period and the forms in which such ideologies are institutionalised. The ensemble of practices captured by the idea provides a crucial determining framework for the production and consumption of films. The term embraces the immediate contexts in which films are made and circulated such as studios, cinemas and film journals, and those contexts which have to be constructed from the material network of the culture, the philosophies and ideologies of film. The various elements of a film culture constitute a complex non-monolithic entity containing within itself a set of practices and institutions, some of which interact in a mutually supportive fashion, some of which provide alternatives to each other, and some of which operate in a self-consciously oppositional fashion.

The notion of a 'film culture' provides the critic with an overarching sense of a context for cinema, an indication of the options available in principle to a film maker at a particular point in time. A more immediate context is that of 'national cinema', a common term in critical discussion but again one with a range of nuances. It can be thought of in at least two distinct though interrelated ways. Firstly, the term can connote the institutional framework within which a body of films is produced including patterns of production, distribution and exhibition and the significance of the industry to the social, political and economic life of a country. Secondly, and perhaps more usually, the connotation is the body of films produced by a national film industry, or the critical construction of those films as some kind of a coherency in terms of subject matter and theme. There is a long tradition of looking at films as a 'reflection' or 'expression' of a nation's preoccupations based on the idea that films, especially popular commercial films, are connected with the national psyche in rather more intimate ways than are other artistic and cultural forms. Siegfried Kracauer, for example, suggests that this is so because the collective character of film production provides a check on 'individual peculiarities in favor of traits common to many people'[5] and because films are directed at a large undifferentiated audience they can be 'supposed to satisfy existing mass desires'.[6] Approaches such as Kracauer's have been heavily criticised for their reductionism and their disregard of form and style yet the relationship between the social and ideological character of a nation and its cinematic output must constitute part of the definition of a national cinema.

Recent film theory has located the discussion of film in the social and national context within larger debates about ideology and its role as a source of social cohesion. Ideas of direct and simple 'reflection' or 'expression' have been discarded and there has been an acknowledgement of the active role that cinema can play both in the construction of ideology and in the critical dismantling of dominant ideological tendencies. The terminology of 'reflection' and 'expression' implies a channelling function for the cinema in relation to ideology whereas recent discussion has stressed the dynamic role of cultural production in the arena of ideology. A central concept is 'representation' and although one important sense of the word corresponds to Kracauer's notion of 'reflection', another of its senses stresses the activity of representation as an important element in the ideological work of social definition. Richard Dyer has pinpointed these distinctive senses in the following terms:

> Thus representation may mean the representing — the presenting over again — of reality, or it may be presenting-as, making reality out to be such-and-such. In the first definition, reality is taken as being unproblematically known, whereas the second definition stresses the construction of a sense or image of reality whose relationship to reality itself is always problematic.[7]

The film and ideology relationship is especially relevant to the discussion of British cinema because ideological considerations have played a major role in government attitudes towards the cinema since the introduction of state protection for the industry in the late 1920s and in the 'arm's length' system of censorship employed by the state as a means of controlling the social potential of the medium.

National cinemas have also been defined in ways other than those of social reflection. Some writers have used traditional critical approaches such as authorship and genre to construct a 'critical profile' of a national film industry. On the face of it, an approach based upon authorship and a concern with the individual and the unique is at odds with the logic of a national cinema study with its search for common qualities linking films on the basis of a shared national origin. Yet, critics such as Andrew Sarris and Roy Armes have written valuable accounts of the American and British cinemas respectively from such a perspective.[8] Sarris, indeed, has characterised the '*auteur* theory' as 'a critical device for recording the history of the American cinema'.[9] It was, however, the perceived shortcomings of an authorship approach to writing about American cinema that led a number of critics to investigate the concept of genre as an alternative to, or an important modifier of, the definitions of Hollywood films offered by *auteur* critics. In the late 1960s, critics such as Jim Kitses and Colin McArthur wrote about the major generic traditions in the American cinema in order to provide a more detailed context for the analysis of Hollywood films and as a method which drew attention to the genuinely national characteristics and traditions of Hollywood film making which remained untouched by *auteur* critics.[10] It was argued that the idea of genre enabled a more precise and accurate appraisal of the work of American film makers to be made, and this study will suggest the relevance of the idea of genre for the British cinema in similar terms. Another approach to the problem of defining a national cinema concerns matters of form and style in film. Indeed, a cursory glance at the conventional compendium histories of cinema confirms the frequency with which stylistic trends have been used to mark off one national cinema from another. For example, the German cinema of the 1920s is often discussed in terms of its characteristic *mise en scène* and cinematography, its visual style, whilst the Soviet cinema of the same period is discussed in terms of its particular form of editing — the 'montage' style. Although the precise definitions of the narrative and stylistic norms that might constitute national cinematic tendencies is not a well-developed area of film studies, it does seem correct, in principle, to assume that highly organised national film industries will develop conventions of form and style as they develop the thematic and iconographic conventions of a genre system. In terms of the British cinema during the interwar years when American films dominated the British screen, it was the classical narrative system that exercised a major influence on the stylistic evolution of the British film.

The above discussion has indicated the extent to which the field of reference conventionally termed 'the contextual' in relation to a film maker is both extensive and complex, endlessly ramified and abutting a variety of distinct areas of study such as economics, politics, aesthetics and so on. 'The British cinema' can mean a number of distinct though interrelated things. The other dimension of the study — Alfred Hitchcock, film maker — poses similar problems of definition. Again, some degree of sub-division is necessary for when we utter the words 'Alfred Hitchcock', we can intend different things. On the one hand there is the real human being, now deceased but still a biographical fact — the commonsense Hitchcock of everyday discourse. On the other hand, there is the critical construct, the 'Alfred Hitchcock' mentioned earlier as a product of the analysis and criticism of the films directed by the biographical individual. Much of this critical activity emerged from a framework of traditional *auteurism* with its sense of film maker as creator, as visionary and as moralist. In this way the biographical Hitchcock plays an important role in the critical activity which can be construed as a tracing of textual evidence back to its biographical source, working from the film to find out something about the person. Claude Chabrol wrote of a 'Hitchcockian universe' which the director made public through his films and through his responses to interviewers. In fact, *Cahiers du Cinéma* and its followers attached great importance to supplementing the work of critical analysis — the main focus of the journal — with extensive interviewing of film authors in order to corroborate the critical readings. The most straightforward and uncomplicated version of auteurism crosses freely from biography (the life of Alfred Hitchcock) to text (the films of Alfred Hitchcock) on the assumption that the latter were channels through which the particular preoccupations of the film maker — 'the Hitchcockian universe' — were communicated to the audience.

4

There is another side to the *auteurist* project which, though still dependent to some extent upon the creative consciousness of Romantic aesthetics, nevertheless defines the artistic universe in terms of the public world of the film text rather than the private world of the artistic mind. The stress in this dimension of auteurism is on the 'objective analysis of distinguished thematics and traits of style' and 'the hard core of basic and often recondite motifs which, united in various combinations, constitute the true specificity of an author's work'.[11] The stress on close textual analysis, on cinematic mise en scène, has been described by John Caughie as:

> the most important positive contributions of auteurism to the development of a precise and detailed film criticism, engaging with the specific mechanisms of visual discourse, freeing it from literary models, and from the liberal commitments which were prepared to validate films on the basis of their themes alone.[12]

And, it was such a stress on 'objective analysis' of the film text that brought the anti-Romantic intellectual influences of structuralism and semiology into the discussion of film authorship. Peter Wollen, for example, has argued for a radical separation between biography and text, suggesting that 'Fuller or Hawks or Hitchcock, the directors are quite separate from "Fuller" or "Hawks" or "Hitchcock", the structures named after them, and should not be methodologically confused'.[13] With this structuralist version of authorship the biographical individual is left behind and the artistic universe is presented as a product of the analytical encounter between critic and text. Yet, it is a difficult move to make resting upon a distinction which is not easy to sustain in the course of critical practice. As Geoffrey Nowell-Smith has pointed out, the two poles of the *auteur* theory are frequently difficult to disentangle in critical discussion:

> In practice, however, some sort of intentionality is always assumed, and *auteur* criticism tends to veer uneasily between the two poles of a statement of what the author, as self-reflecting consciousness, is supposed to have put into the film and the analysis of what can be shown to be objectively present in the form proper to the work of a particular artistic personality.[14]

Structuralist versions of authorship attempt, albeit unsuccessfully, to more or less jettison biography in order to make coherence and unity of the authorial oeuvre a function of critical analysis. Yet, for a critical practice which wishes to maintain some hold on history and context, the excision of biography is a problem. As John Caughie has put it, the author is 'the most accessible point at which a text is tied to its own social and historical outside'.[15] The notion of the 'biographical legend' developed within Russian Formalist criticism has been proposed as a way of considering relationships between text, author and biography with its suggestion that

5

'the authorial personality be considered a construct, created not only by the art works themselves but also by other historical forces'.[16] The 'biographical legend' mediates between the empirical life history of an artist or film maker and the artistic texts themselves. The artistic image of a film maker can have a key role in decisions about production and can explain the particular trajectory of an artistic career. It can also function as a guide for audiences in their reading of individual works. Such an image is the end product of a range of 'historical forces' which include the public utterances of the artist concerned together with a variety of discourses such as those of journalism, academic criticism, publicity and marketing, all of which work together to produce 'the biographical legend'.

This study of Alfred Hitchcock's British films is concerned with critical analysis and definition but it is also concerned with history and context as a grounding for such analysis. In taking the basic terms of the study — a national cinema and a film author — and subdividing them into a range of connotations, my intention was to indicate the complexity of a field of determinations for any given film or body of films. The remainder of the study is devoted to an examination of several different contexts for the films that Hitchcock made in Britain during the interwar period prior to his departure to Hollywood in 1939 including the minority film culture of the 1920s, the British film industry and its films, and the artistic contexts of genre and classical film form.

Notes

1. For example, the work of Raymond Bellour, Stephen Heath, Laura Mulvey and Peter Wollen.

2. D. Bordwell, 'Textual Analysis etc.', *Enclitic*, no. 10-11 (1981/82), p. 125.

3. Ibid., p. 135.

4. A. Lovell, 'Notes on British Film Culture', *Screen*, vol. 13, no. 2 (1972), p. 13.

5. S. Kracauer, *From Caligari to Hitler* (Princeton University Press, Princeton, New Jersey, 1947), p. 5.

6. Ibid.

7. R. Dyer, 'Introduction' in R. Dyer *et al. Coronation Street* (British Film Institute, London, 1981), p. 6.

8. A. Sarris, *The American Cinema* (Dutton, New York, 1968); R. Armes, *A Critical History of British Cinema* (Secker and Warburg, London, 1978).

9. A. Sarris, *The Primal Screen* (Simon and Schuster, New York, 1973), p. 48.

10. J. Kitses, *Horizons West* (Thames and Hudson, London, 1969); C. McArthur, *Underworld USA* (Secker and Warburg, London, 1972).

11. G. Nowell-Smith, 'Cinema and Structuralism', *Twentieth Century Studies*, no. 3 (1970), p. 133.

12. J. Caughie, *Theories of Authorship* (Routledge and Kegan Paul, London, 1981), p. 13.

13. P. Wollen, *Signs and Meaning in the Cinema*, 3rd edn (Secker and Warburg, London, 1972), p. 168.

14. Nowell-Smith, 'Cinema and Structuralism', p. 132.

15. Caughie, *Theories*, p. 3.

16. D. Bordwell, *The Films of Carl-Theodor Dreyer* (University of California Press, California, 1981), p. 4.

Chapter Two

British Film Culture in the Interwar Period

Hitchcock worked within the entertainment film industry making pictures which were aimed at a mass audience. Yet many of his films, particularly those of the 1920s, display clear relationships with the European 'art' cinemas of the period which constituted the focus of interest for the minority film culture in Britain that was centred on the film society movement and the specialised journal. This chapter offers an anatomy of the intellectual film culture of the 1920s and, in particular, draws attention to the influential role of the documentary film movement. It also examines two of Hitchcock's films from the 1920s — *The Lodger* (1926) and *Blackmail* (1929) — from the point of view of their specific links with the 'art' films of the minority film culture.

Film Art in Europe

The 1920s was a crucial decade in the development of specialised minority film cultures in the major European film-producing countries as well as in Britain. It was a period of self-conscious artistic experiment in the cinema in which the key artistic revolutions of the early twentieth century — Expressionism, Cubism, Futurism, Dadaism and so on — found an outlet in the cinematic experiments of film makers in Germany, France and the Soviet Union. Whereas the development of the cinema previously had been dominated by the concerns of a popular narrative art, the 1920s see the emergence of cinemas which bear the imprint of 'art' and 'high culture' attracting the attention of the educated classes who had previously scorned the medium. There had been, prior to this, some attempts to create a form of 'art' cinema in France and Italy. Firms such as the French Le Film d'Art and the Italian Série d'Or had been formed just before the First World War to film adaptations of stage classics and historical epics, and condensed versions of Shakespeare and Dante, with a view to attracting an educated middle class audience into the cinema. This familiar attitude towards the cinema, which treats it as a convenient reproductive channel for the presentation of the established cultural media of literature and drama, however, must be firmly distinguished from the attitudes towards cinema of the emerging film cultures of the 1920s. Film makers and theorists alike began to reflect upon the medium as an art form in its own right. Indeed, one marked tendency in this context was the urge of many film makers to disassociate their films from the conventions of literary and dramatic art forms and to ground their practices in the specific qualities of film alone — a form of aesthetic purism. The German film maker F.W. Murnau declared that film 'ought, through its unique properties, to tell a complete story by means of images alone; the ideal film does not need titles'.[1] And, in addition, the 1920s also witnessed an interest in 'pure cinema' represented by the experiments of artists such as Hans Richter, Viking Eggeling and Marcel Duchamp in which total abstraction was seen as freeing the film from what were sometimes perceived as the artistically debilitating constraints of narrative. The relationship between traditional art forms and the cinema had previously been confined to considerations of the suitability of the medium for the translation of literary and dramatic works and the 1920s saw the development of a more introspective attitude towards film. It was a period marked by intense reflection on the very nature of cinema as an art form and a period in which many film makers sought to explore the possibilities of film form in the richly experimental context of artistic modernism. Such theorising and film making, however, were not conducted in a spirit of scientific neutrality for these were also the years of the film manifesto, the period of committed film makers and theorists whose observations and practices implied conclusions about the ways in which films should be made and, by the same token, the ways in which films should not be made. Soviet film makers such as Kuleshov, Pudovkin, Eisenstein and Vertov, French film makers such as Epstein and Delluc published analytical and theoretical speculations on cinema, they made films and proclaimed aesthetic allegiances to this or that type of film. Film societies and cine clubs of one sort or another sprang up in one European country after another, facilitating the spread of ideas about cinema and film making on an international rather than a regional basis.

Such a fermentation of film culture did not occur in a vacuum. One of the primary determinants of the development of the various national film cultures of the 1920s was the American cinema which had moved into a position of dominance in the international film market. As Chapter 3 examines in more detail, the First World War saw the interruption of the European film industries and the rapid development of Hollywood as a mass producer of the long feature film which had only just begun to appear in the immediate pre-war years. By the 1920s the cinemas of Britain in particular but also of France, Germany, the Soviet Union and the Scandinavian countries were dominated by the American films of companies such as Paramount, First National and Fox which had set up distribution agencies in many of these European countries. The development of the European 'art' cinemas can be seen as a form of cultural defence against the hegemony of the Hollywood cinema. This defensive posture had both an economic and an artistic face. The European countries developed forms of film funding that differed in certain respects from the orthodox commercial financial methods through banks and investment companies that were developing in capitalist America. In 1915 a judgement in the American Supreme Court had defined motion pictures as a 'business, pure and simple, originated and conducted for profit'[2] and the development of Hollywood reflected the market economy of the United States. In Europe, business considerations whilst still important were accompanied by an interest in the artistic and propagandist possibilities of cinema which led to several countries enacting legislation to protect the development of their indigenous cinema. In Germany, for example, the state intervened in a number of ways. The best known and the biggest of the German film companies, the gigantic UFA company, was set up towards the end of the First World War with a mixture of government and private capital. Although 'the golden age of German cinema' was based on the efforts of a number of private companies and although the government relinquished its holding in UFA at the end of the war, the presence of the state signalled a rather different attitude towards the medium than was the case in America. Perhaps a more significant move by the German government was the introduction of quota legislation to limit the import of foreign, especially American, films and thus protect the German film industry. The state also passed legislation which granted tax concessions to exhibitors who screened films which were deemed to possess artistic and cultural merit and thus stimulated the development of an 'art' cinema and of producing units such as Decla-Bioscop which specialised in 'art' films. The development of an indigenous 'art' cinema was seen as an important weapon in the battle for a share of the growing international film market. The Americans were clearly leading the field in terms of a popular cinema addressed to an international mass audience but it was thought that there might also be an international audience who were not particularly interested in the typical Hollywood film but who might be interested in an internationally marketed 'art' cinema defined precisely by its difference from the typical Hollywood film. Perhaps an index of the success of the German cinema of the period and a vindication of the encouragement of 'art' film lies in the fact that Hollywood began to invest in the German cinema during the middle of the decade and then proceeded to lure the cream of German talent, actors, directors and technical personnel to Hollywood. The Soviet cinema was, of course, run by the state as a propaganda machine and film makers were recruited to work on behalf of the newly established socialist society. This did not preclude artistic experiment and indeed the 1920s is a period in the history of Soviet cinema that is marked by a diversity of aesthetic and political responses to film conceived of as a documentary and propagandist medium capable of playing a key role in the political and cultural development of a socialist state. In France, the avant garde film makers were dependent to some extent upon private finance although the modest ambitions of many of the film makers meant that self-financed projects were a possibility. L'Herbier and Renoir both financed their own films whilst Bunuel and Cocteau were both supported by the private patronage of the wealthy Comte de Noailles. Some of the large French commercial films such as Pathé and Gaumont followed the example of their German counterparts and fostered artistic wings within which some of the French 'impressionist' film makers of the time worked. In terms of aesthetics, the opposition to American cinema was reflected in the ways in which many European film makers deviated from the evolving conventions of the classical narrative cinema as it was developing in the hands of American film makers. German films such as *The Cabinet of Dr Caligari* (Weine, 1919) and *Waxworks* (Leni, 1924) experimented with an anti-illusionist mise en scène whilst the Soviet exploration of editing led to the non-classical montage patterns of Eisenstein's *October* (1928). The Dadaist and Surrealist film makers in France developed films with narrative structures which were loose, associative and dream-like as opposed to the tight logical narrative patterns of classical cinema. It is important, however, to acknowledge that these were currents of aesthetic opposition within national cinemas which contained many varieties of film style including those which conformed to the classical pattern. Indeed, Noel Burch has drawn attention to the important role played by the German films of Fritz Lang in the evolution of the classical system of narrative and Pudovkin's famous works of film theory contain much that is standard and 'classical' in its analysis of film form.

By contrast, the development of a specialised film culture in Britain in the 1920s does not appear to have been accompanied by any sustained production activity. There was not much in the way of a feature film industry in Britain before the 1927 legislation but the intense interest in experimental film forms as evidenced in the journal *Close Up* might have been expected to foster some kind of an avant garde movement. Some films were made by the *Close Up* writers Kenneth MacPherson and Oswell Blakeston and film society activist Ivor Montagu made a few short films based upon H.G. Wells' stories towards the end of the decade.[3] It would be difficult, however, to compare this handful of offerings to the substantial 'art' cinemas that had flourished in the rest of Europe.

Britain — the Film Society

The Film Society — frequently known as the London Film Society — was set up in 1925 in order 'to show a group of films which are in some degree interesting and which represent the work which has been done, or is being done experimentally in various parts of the world'.[4] The domination by Hollywood of the British screen meant that few examples of the developing international cinemas were available to British audiences. Some German films were screened in the early 1920s but the American film provided the

10

staple diet for the filmgoer, supplemented occasionally by a British film. In such circumstances, the perception of alternative forms of cinema, the awareness of developments in Germany, France, the Soviet Union and the Scandinavian countries, was inevitably confined to rather limited and specialised groups such as professional film workers and the affluent intelligentsia. Indeed, it was a confluence of figures such as Sidney Bernstein and Adrian Brunel from the film industry, and Ivor Montagu, the Cambridge-educated aristocrat, that led to the setting up of the Film Society.

The society had a precedent in the world of drama. The Stage Society had been formed in 1899 in order to allow the production of plays that would find difficulty in securing a production in the commercial theatre of the time. Its repertoire included the works of a number of foreign dramatists such as Wedekind, Pirandello, Cocteau, Gorki and Odets and it also introduced the works of Shaw to the public. It specialised, that is, in the experimental and the politically and socially committed drama of the day. The Film Society, like its theatrical predecessor, was financed by member subscription and it drew together a number of like-minded individuals from the film culture, both majority and minority, who shared a desire to broaden the provision of cinema in Britain. Ivor Montagu can fairly be regarded as the animating spirit behind the society both in terms of its actual formation and also in terms of a relatively clear perception of its educational and cultural significance. As far as he was concerned the society was not simply an alternative source of highbrow entertainment for an educated minority but it was to function as an important intervention in the course of British film. It was founded at a time when the British cinema was in a very fragile state with production dwindling towards the bleak record of 1926 yet it was also a time when government protection was clearly and confidently expected by many within the industry. Montagu regarded the society as providing an opportunity for the stimulation of interest in British production as he made clear in an interview in the early 1970s. As he said:

> We thought there are such a lot of films that we are interested in that are being made abroad, that we would like to fertilise British film ideas by seeing some of them. ...
> In this way we could draw into film artists, sculptors, writers, who up to then disdained films ... Also, we would be drawing new people into the cinema, new talent ...[5]

The impact of general artistic movements upon the cinemas of Germany, France and the Soviet Union has already been noted and Montagu's comments suggest that the potential interaction between film and the modernist mainstream of artistic development required demonstration to the British artistic community. Montagu approaches the society from the point of view of the film artist and intellectual but it is important to recognise that the original governing body of the society — the council — also

11

contained people from the commercial film industry. In that sense it represented an attempt to align the developing interest in the art of the film with the growth of the commercial industry itself. However, the division between the minority film culture represented by the society and the majority film culture of the commercial cinema is clearly indicated by the general attitude of film industry to the society which was one of outright hostility. Indeed, the film exhibitors actively opposed its very operation and put considerable pressure on Adrian Brunel who worked in the commercial industry to sever his connections with the society. The exhibitor Sidney Bernstein, the other key figure from the industry to play an active role in the society, was also placed in a difficult position because of his support. As Montagu has pointed out, Bernstein's support was crucial to the society:

> What made it possible was Bernstein's backing because he had influence with the trade and helped us a great deal. Although the trade also somehow despised him because they said he was trying to live in two worlds, the intellectual and the commercial, and they were very jealous of someone who was an egghead and a successful financier.[6]

Film as art and film as commerce were clearly construed as distinct and different spheres of activity and interest, and although there were a number of figures from the industry who took some sort of an interest in the society, Montagu's optimistic hopes for fruitful and creative interaction were not really fulfilled. The society gradually came to be tolerated by an industry which realised that it posed no serious threat, a fact which in itself emphasises the split between the art of the film and the commercial cinema in British film culture. Far from influencing the course of British film, the society might be regarded as having siphoned off potentially creative influences from the commercial cinema and directed them towards the documentary.

During the early years of its existence, the society introduced its narrowly based audience to the 'art' cinemas of Europe screening a variety of films including *The Cabinet of Dr Caligari*, *The Joyless Street* (Pabst, 1925) and *Nosferatu* (Murnau, 1921) from Germany; and *Mother* (Pudovkin, 1926), *The End of St Petersburg* (Pudovkin, 1927) and *The General Line* (Eisenstein, 1929) from the Soviet Union. It also screened many of the French avant garde films of the time but its programmes were not confined to the international 'art' cinema; they included documentaries, the scientific *Secrets of Nature* series of films, and films which illustrated technical developments in the medium. Another important reason for its existence was the screening of films which had been banned by the Board of Film Censors particularly those which were prohibited on political grounds. For example, *Battleship Potemkin* (Eisenstein, 1925) which the society screened during its 1928/9 season had previously been banned by the Board 'on the general ground that it deals with recent controversial events'.[7] The exam-

12

ple set by the society was taken up by others in different ways. The interest in alternative cinema stimulated the formation of film societies in various parts of the country based upon the subscription principle and operating as private clubs with self-selected audiences. In addition, the interest in the non-commercial film developed in more orthodox commercial ways towards the end of the 1920s with the setting up of what now are known as 'art' cinemas. In 1927 the Shaftesbury Avenue Pavilion began to screen foreign films after the fashion of the Film Society but with the important difference that these performances were open to the general public and did not require the formalities and expense of club membership. Subsequently this example was followed by the opening of the Regent Street Polytechnic in 1929, and during the 1930s several more 'art' cinemas opened in London including the Curzon in Mayfair, the Everyman in Hampstead, and the most famous of British 'art' cinemas, the Academy in Oxford Street. Together these cinemas constituted a developing art circuit capable of providing that wider perspective on the cinema that Montagu had hoped for with the inception of the Film Society. Although the society continued to present programmes until 1939 it gradually became a less important force in the film culture with the advent of a small alternative circuit based in London.

Critical and Theoretical Perspectives

Although Britain lacked its own 'art' cinema, at the close of the silent era it had become an important centre for the intellectual discussion of film and for the promotion of the new 'art' cinemas of Europe. Indeed, writing some years later, the American critic Richard Griffith suggested that the leadership of the film intellectuals of the period 'came mainly from Britain, which though it had produced few films and no good ones, seems to have been a fertile field for the ideal of cinematic perfectionism'.[8] A serious critical and theoretical literature of cinema began to emerge to complement the increasing attention being paid to the cinema by the serious press in which important figures from the Film Society such as Montagu, Iris Barry and Walter Mycroft had started to contribute to newspapers and journals such as the *Observer*, the *Sunday Times* and the *Spectator*. Other landmarks in this increasing intellectual interest in the cinema were the appearance of the journal *Close Up* in 1927 and the publication of Paul Rotha's *The Film Till Now* in 1930. The film society movement which gathered momentum towards the end of the decade, the development of a small metropolitan repertory cinema network, and a growing literature of the medium together constituted a minority film culture articulated in opposition to the majority culture based upon the commercial cinema. The perspectives offered by the original Film Society together with those that emerge from the serious critical writing of the late 1920s intermesh to produce a radical divide in the overall film culture involving a critical dismissal of the popular American cinema which dominated British screens and, its critical concomitant, the championing of the new 'art' cinemas of Germany, France and the Soviet Union.

The publication of the first issue of *Close Up* in July 1927 marks the first attempt to provide a theoretical forum for the cinema in the English language. The journal provided a platform for the intellectuals who attended the Film Society to express their views on the developing art of the cinema. Montagu has suggested a degree of distance between the Film Society and the journal yet it is clear that *Close Up* was similarly concerned with fostering an interest in the new, different cinemas that were emerging abroad. The attitude of the journal to the new European 'art' cinemas paralleled that of the Film Society. Great praise was lavished upon the German cinema, especially the director G.W. Pabst whose film *Joyless Street* had been screened by the society in 1926, and developments in French and Soviet cinema were reviewed with similar enthusiasm. By contrast, the American cinema was vilified, with one contributor referring to 'Hollywood poison'. There were exceptions such as the approval given to Erich Von Stroheim's *Greed* (1924) which also appeared on the programme of the Film Society, but the tone of the journal was predominantly hostile to American films. The following declaration from the second issue sums up the view of the cinema and the cinema audience that permeates the journal's writing:

> ... broadly speaking anything up to 75 per cent of modern films are at a certain level; they have moments, they reach a vast majority, they satisfy. But there is a minority of several million people to whom these films are tiresome, a minority that loves the film, but has too much perception, too much intelligence to swallow the dismal and paltry stories and acting set up week by week before it on the screen. This minority has got to have films it can enjoy, films with psychology, soundness, intelligence. Nobody wants (as a matter of fact a great many *do*) to rob the masses of their entertainment, and as long as they desire eye-wash and bunk they must have it.[9]

In such a context the journal construed its task as one of cultural education in order to alert cinema audiences to the various alternatives to Hollywood cinema coming especially from the prominent European film making countries but also from other parts of the world. To this end and in addition to the numerous articles extolling the virtues of the European 'art' cinemas, the journal also covered developments in a variety of less well known cinemas. During its six years of publication it carried articles on the cinemas of Argentina, Belgium, Czechoslovakia, the Netherlands, India, Japan, Portugal, Switzerland and Turkey, providing background information and critical analysis of a variety of films. Such an educational role parallels the avowed intentions of the Film Society which were to broaden the British perspective on cinemas other than the American. The Film

Society, as we have seen, also wished to stimulate British film production by demonstrating to British film makers the artistic possibilities of the medium. *Close Up* shared this concern with the national cinema but its view of the British film was even more jaundiced than its view of the American cinema. In an editorial in the first issue, Kenneth MacPherson referred to the British cinema as a 'laughing stock' compared to other national cinemas.[10] The journal frequently printed pieces devoted to the state of the domestic industry, many of which are marked by a tone of despairing ridicule. It did, however, point to a number of problems which beset British film production including the American domination of the British screen established during the First World War, the allegedly 'haphazard' approach to film making by British producers, and the misguided ambition of the industry to compete with the globally dominant American cinema by imitating the Hollywood film. In addition to the documentation of a selection of world cinema, the journal was also closely involved with the development of film theory and criticism. Its leading writers, MacPherson, Bryher, Oswell Blakeston, offered their conceptions of the art of film and, of considerable importance to the developing minority film culture, the journal also published translations of key writing on the cinema from abroad. It published a number of articles by Eisenstein including 'The Principles of Film Form', 'The Dynamic Square' and the important manifesto on sound film which Eisenstein co-wrote with Pudovkin and Alexandrov.[11] These writings undoubtedly reinforced the growing influence of the Soviet film makers on the minority film culture in Britain, an influence which was also reflected by Eisenstein, Pudovkin and Vertov's visiting and speaking to Film Society members in the late 1920s and early 1930s and by various screenings of the classic Soviet films such as *Battleship Potemkin, Mother, The Man with the Movie Camera* (Vertov, 1929), and *Enthusiasm* (Vertov, 1930).

The most comprehensive and influential summary of the state of film art from the British point of view in the late 1920s came with the publication of Paul Rotha's *The Film Till Now* in 1930. The book provided a survey of the development of world cinema to the early years of sound and it also contained a declaration of aesthetic principles in relation to the medium, a philosophy of film. It was both a history and a theory of the cinema and its influence upon subsequent thought about the cinema in Britain has been considerable. Although written more than 50 years ago its status as a framework text defining the parameters of debate within British film culture was not seriously challenged until the 1960s. Although its central tenets were developed in the rather special circumstances of the 1920s they have proved to be extremely durable, providing the basis for much subsequent film theory and criticism. The work of Roger Manvell, Ernest Lindgren, *The Penguin Film Review* and *Sight and Sound* can all be positioned in relation to the approach to cinema outlined in *The Film Till Now*.[12] Two points from the book are worth looking at in some detail as indicative of the film culture of the time. The first is the general condemnation of American cinema which became an ingrained feature of British film culture and the second is the aesthetic argument which underpins the high valuation of the European 'art' cinemas.

Rotha's sceptical attitude towards the American cinema was based on a number of ideas and assumptions. The industrial structure of Hollywood, the commercial intentions of the producers and the volume production policies which meant that studios were turning out almost a film every week, led to 'standardised pictures for a standardised audience'[13], according to Rotha. He defined Hollywood as 'a factory, managed and owned by a number of astute businessmen, who seek only large financial returns from the goods they manufacture'.[14] In many respects Rotha was correct, for the American cinema he was writing about had changed from the cottage industry of the pioneering days and was gradually becoming an arm of big business. The sound revolution had consolidated the involvement of Wall Street in the financial government of the industry so that by 1930, when *The Film Till Now* was published, all of the major American companies with the possible exception of Warner Brothers were owned ultimately by the two major banking concerns of Morgan and Rockefeller. Yet the assumption that the commercial structure of the film industry necessarily corrupts its products is one that requires demonstration. Indeed, the cinema that succeeded in mounting an artistic challenge to Hollywood, according to Rotha, was also a commercial cinema. The major films of 'the golden age of German cinema' emerged from large-scale companies producing films on a volume basis, standardising their output through the genre system and, like Hollywood, using actors who could accurately be described as 'stars'. Rotha displays a contempt for the intelligence of the mass audience and in this respect he echoes the condescending tone of the *Close Up* team as exemplified in the editorial quoted earlier. He characterises the average moviegoer of the period as passive, manipulable and incapable of true discrimination. Indeed, it was the indiscriminate quality of film viewing, he argues, that enabled Hollywood to move into its position of dominance in the international film market. In his own words:

> the very marvelling of the general public, watching every new film with mouths agape was sufficient for studios to become established on a practical basis, capable of mass production.[15]

As in the case of *Close Up* there was an unfortunate snobbishness, a tone of intellectual superiority, a series of assumptions about the largely working class audiences for the Hollywood picture. Perhaps Rotha's major concern about the Hollywood studio system of film production was the supposed threat to individual creativity and freedom of expression posed by the constraints of commerce. This assumption remained unquestioned as part of the commonsense thinking about the American cinema until the late 1940s and early 1950s when the *Sequence* critics in Britain and the *Cahiers du Cinéma* critics in France began to look rather more closely at the American cinema and began the task of its critical rehabilitation. Rotha did recognise that certain Hollywood film makers did produce worthwhile work although figures such as Stroheim and Chaplin, whom he admired, provided ammunition for his arguments about the system in the light of their problematic professional careers.

Rotha's analysis of film aesthetics was based primarily upon the achievements of the Soviet and German cinemas of the 1920s and was an implicit critique of the development of the classical narrative system in the American silent film. Following Soviet film theorists such as Kuleshov, Eisenstein and Pudovkin, Rotha identified editing as the crucial activity that elevated film from being mere mechanical duplication to the status of a creative art form. Indeed, the capacity of film to offer a credible representation of the physical world or, in Rotha's own words, 'the camera's misleading faculty of being able to record the actual'[16] constituted the major obstacle to the development of film art or 'film proper'. The task of the film maker was to depart from photographic realism as obviously as possible and, in terms of the Rotha aesthetic, films were evaluated according to their degree of departure from the inherent naturalism of the medium. Accordingly, in a hierarchy of cinematic forms, Rotha placed the abstract films of Richter and Eggeling at the head and the narrative fiction film — the typical Hollywood product — near the bottom. The Soviet cinema had a privileged place in Rotha's system in so far as the actual photographic material, the film shot, was regarded by film makers such as Eisenstein and Pudovkin as simply raw material to be brought to artistic life by the processes of montage. However, editing, although of crucial importance, was not the only route to aesthetic salvation available to film makers. Rotha also regarded certain trends in the German cinema of the time as important contributions to the artistic progress of the medium. *The Cabinet of Dr Caligari* was, according to Rotha, 'the first significant attempt at the expression of a creative mind in the new medium of cinematography'[17] and (together with *Battleship Potemkin*) 'one of the two most momentous advances in the history and development of cinema till now'.[18] Just as the Soviet film makers, particularly Eisenstein, explored anti-illusionist editing strategies so the films of the German silent cinema explored anti-illusionist forms of mise en scène and cinematography thus adding another dimension to the break with 'realism on the screen'[19] which was a key factor in the progress of cinema for Rotha. Just as Rotha's dismissal of the American cinema and his high estimation of the European 'art' cinema became part of the orthodox framework of film theory and criticism, so his high regard for non-realist film styles was to influence subsequent writers. The Rotha position contrasts in an interesting way with the realist position developed by André Bazin which serves as a kind of inversion of the orthodoxy. For Bazin, the silent cinemas of Germany and the Soviet Union deflected cinema away from its realist vocation. The montage experiments of the Russians and the plastic manipulations of the Germans worked against the capacity for realism which Bazin saw as defining the uniqueness of the cinema as an art form. Bazin regarded technological developments such as sound and deep focus cinematography as important innovations which steered the cinema along its correct evolutionary path towards greater and greater realism. Rotha, on the other hand, along with many theorists of the silent era, tended to view technological developments as an obstacle, as a threat. In the context of a discussion about the impact of colour cinematography and stereoscopic film he predicted that their adoption by film makers would lead to 'a tendency to hold the duration of a scene on the screen longer and longer, already the pre-eminent characteristic of dialogue films'.[20] In time, he continued, 'the powerful resources of cutting and editing will be forgotten and instead there will be long scenes lasting for minutes'.[21] This is an astute prediction of, for example, the famous kitchen sequence in *The Magnificent Ambersons* (Welles, 1942) in which a conversation sequence lasting in excess of four minutes is presented in a single shot with a couple of reframing camera movements. Rotha's remarks also anticipate the tradition of cinema admired by Bazin running from the work of Stroheim and Murnau in the silent period, through the films of Renoir and Welles in the 1930s and 1940s and implicitly embracing the wide screen colour cinema of Kazan, Minnelli and Preminger in the 1950s. Such a tradition is drastically at variance with Rotha's aesthetic based as it was upon the extended take and the optical realism of the deep space image rather than on the principles of montage and plastic manipulation of the image.[22]

The Documentary Impulse

Although the British documentary movement can be regarded as having begun with the appearance of John Grierson's film *Drifters* made in the late 1920s it is worth noting that there was some evidence of a documentary impulse within the British commercial cinema before that time. Of particular interest is the company British Instructional Films which was set up in 1919 by Harry Bruce Woolfe, one of the new crop of producers who entered the British film industry just after the end of the First World War. The kinds of films which Woolfe's company specialised in offer an alternative direction for the British cinema and one which prefigures the documentary directions of the 1930s and 1940s. Woolfe's earliest endeavours were film reconstructions, based upon important events of the war, that used a variety of techniques including documentary compilation, animated maps and diagrams. The first of these, *The Battle of Jutland*, was screened to the trade in 1921 and it became both a critical and a commercial success. It was followed by *Armageddon* (1923), based upon Allenby's campaign in Palestine, *Zeebrugge* (1924) and *Ypres* (1925), and later in the decade *The Battle for the Coronel and Falkland Islands* (1927). In addition to this series of reconstruction films, the company also embarked upon a programme of natural history films in 1922. The *Secrets of Nature* series, which was to last until the early 1930s, consisted of short films lasting no longer than ten minutes which were exhibited in ordinary cinemas as part of the normal programme. They were very successful and, in the words of Rachael Low, constituted 'one of the few bright features of the British film industry in the 1920s'.[23] British Instructional went through a number of ownership changes in the 1920s. It was bought by the Stoll company in 1924 with Woolfe remaining in control and in 1925 it was bought by E.A. Bundy and turned into a public company. Woolfe was to stay on as managing director but the company decided to move entirely into the fiction film realm with plans which included films to be written by the novelist John Buchan who was also a member of the board. This change of direction can be understood in the context of the anticipated legislation to protect and, indeed, to generate a British feature film industry which led to the formation of numerous companies even before the passage of the Cinematograph Films Act in 1927. Despite the move towards fiction, however, Woolfe's presence in the company preserved something of the documentary spirit. As Rachael Low puts it:

> Beginning as an actual film maker, he was afterwards drawn into the business and administration of the firm, distribution deals and take-overs, and later still the production of fiction films. But he retained his concern over what films were about, and even his hold on reality, which can be discerned even in the later purely story films, and which contrasted with the hectic Hollywood dream world seen, for example, in the many BIP films of the same period.[24]

The most notable feature produced by the company was a film which, like the earlier reconstructions, was drawn from an episode in the First World War, the Gallipoli campaign. *Tell England* (1931) produced by Woolfe and directed by Anthony Asquith was a fictional narrative although it did contain a number of documentary style reconstruction sequences. Subsequently, Woolfe returned to documentary and the instructional nature film with Gaumont British Instructional but it is interesting to note that this little-known figure in the British cinema of the period was working in a fashion which blended documentary and fiction in a way that was later to become commonplace in British cinema. Indeed, such a blend is often credited with producing the 'golden age of British cinema' during the war years of the 1940s. Woolfe is an interesting forerunner of that development.

John Grierson's *Drifters* (1929) was screened by the Film Society in November 1929. The film was made for a government agency, the Empire Marketing Board, and it set the pattern for the subsequent flowering of documentary film making under the aegis of state sponsorship that is the central feature of British documentary cinema during this period. The Empire Marketing Board had also produced a feature length fantasy film *One Family* (Creighton, 1930) which was intended to provide a dramatised account of the economic interdependence of the countries within the British Empire. It was, however, Grierson's film with its commitment to actuality filming derived from the example of Robert Flaherty, the American film maker, and its editing techniques influenced by the Soviet film makers, that provided the definitive cinematic model for the movement. Grierson was fundamentally a social propagandist committed to the notion that the full development of mass political democracy necessitated the full exploitation of the modern means of mass communication to educate and inform the electorate. He had spent time in the United States during the 1920s and had fallen under the influence of the writer Walter Lippmann who was pessimistic about the workings of democracy and the problems of an ill-informed electorate. Grierson did not share Lippmann's pessimism and he saw the cinema and especially the documentary film as a major means of providing a mass electorate with the kind of education necessary for the working of the system.[25] Grierson's basic commitment was to the liberal democratic version of society embodied in the British system and thus, under his guidance, the documentary film makers were unlikely to produce a radical critique of those aspects of Britain in the 1930s which formed the subject matter of films such as *Coal Face* (Cavalcanti, 1935) and *Song of Ceylon* (Wright, 1934). As Stuart Hood has pointed out, the former, although addressing the subject of coal mining, avoids mentioning the General Strike of 1926 and the legacy of bitterness derived from the starving back to work of the miners; and *Song of Ceylon* which is about the production of tea totally avoids questions of colonial labour and economic exploitation.[26]

Films such as these produced in conditions of state bureaucratic sponsorship, although offering opportunities for film makers to represent a different Britain on the screen, were subject to carefully defined limitations on the extent of their social comment, yet despite that, many film makers gravitated towards the movement in order to express their social and political views. It would be wrong, however, to picture the documentarists as social propagandists, pure and simple, as many of them had developed an interest in the cinema during the 1920s — the period of the 'art' film. Grierson himself, although in certain respects an instrumentalist where film was concerned, was also an astute film critic with an awareness of a wide range of cinema and an interest in directors such as Sternberg, Hitchcock and Ford whose work lies outside the documentary province and inside that form of cinema which attracted the opprobrium of many of the film intellectuals of the period.[27] The 'official' documentary movement, however, does not exhaust the scope of actuality film making in Britain during the 1930s despite the prominence given to it by most histories of the period. Recent research has drawn attention to a working-class-based documentary movement centred upon institutions such as the Progressive Film Institute and the Workers' Film and Photo-League which circulated alternative documentary films and newsreels through a variety of outlets including Co-operative Halls, Labour Party branches and trade unions.[28]

The Character of British Film Culture

In examining the alternative exhibition networks, the film societies and the 'art' cinemas, the critical and theoretical work of *Close Up* and Paul Rotha, and the documentary movement, we can note a common concern with and interest in the 'art' cinemas of Europe and frequently a complementary critical attitude towards the American cinema. A variety of linked conceptual polarities such as 'art versus commerce', 'entertainment versus art', 'individual creativity versus factory production', 'fiction versus documentary' unite the various different strands of the minority film culture in their support for certain kinds of cinema and their condemnation of the popular cinema of the day, both American and British. These positions are expressed most clearly in the somewhat elitist writing of the *Close Up* critics and Rotha, but such stances also can be regarded as underpinning the Film Society and the movement that it inaugurated. Indeed, although many newspaper film critics supported the foundation of the society in 1925 and attended its performances, C.A. Lejeune, writing at that time for the *Manchester Guardian*, was opposed to such a development because of its exclusive and elitist character.

Many figures associated with institutions from the minority film culture such as the Film Society did manage to pursue careers in the commercial film industry, the base of the majority film culture, and these included Anthony Asquith, Thorold Dickinson and Ivor Montagu. Yet many potential recruits to entertainment film gravitated towards Grierson and the documentary film. One of the major aims of the Film Society had been to attract artists of various types into the British film industry by clearly demonstrating the artistic potential of cinema as exemplified by the work of the leading European film makers of the day. However, it was the documentary movement which succeeded in doing exactly this with figures such as the painter William Coldstream, the composer Benjamin Britten and the poet W.H. Auden contributing to some of the most notable documentaries of the 1930s. Alan Lovell has argued that the interest in cinema as an art form which was fostered by the film societies and by film journals was, in fact, captured by the documentary movement so that individuals such as Basil Wright who ended up as a documentary film maker might, in a different cultural climate, have looked to the feature film industry for a career. 'Art' was deflected away from the commercial cinema and 'the documentary film became the British art film'.[29] The radical separation of 'art' cinema from its commercial counterpart prevented any interaction between the two that might have helped to create a more aesthetically interesting entertainment cinema in Britain during the interwar years. It may also be argued that because socially aware film making was associated with the various documentary strands of the time, the commercial cinema of the 1930s tended not to produce socially aware entertainment films. Hollywood, after all, had produced film makers such as Frank Capra and John Ford whose films often displayed social values in addition to those of

21

entertainment but a familiar comment on the British cinema of the period is that it virtually ignored social preoccupations and concerns.

The gravitation towards documentary is also signalled in the career of Paul Rotha whose interest in the cinema of the 1920s was catholic and embraced the various experiments in narrative fictional cinema. Grierson's move into documentary is comprehensible in the context of his social propagandist stance which led him to take a partly instrumentalist view of the medium. Rotha, by contrast, presents a different face in the 1920s with his deep interest in the formal aspects of the medium and his highly developed sense of film aesthetics. He had studied design and graphics at the Slade School of Fine Art in London and in 1928 he got a job in the props department at Elstree studios. Although he graduated to art direction and script writing within the commercial cinema, by the early 1930s he had moved over to documentary film making and although he did subsequently work in the feature film area, the bulk of his film making career was as a documentary director. After a brief association with Grierson he spent most of the 1930s making documentary films for Gaumont British Instructional and the Strand Film Company amongst others and he continued to write and comment upon cinema, contributing to journals such as *Cinema Quarterly* and publishing further books such as his *Documentary Film* which appeared in 1936.[30]

The documentary impulse is also perceptible in the film journal sphere. *Close Up* had ceased publication in 1932 perhaps because of the severe blow dealt to experimental and avant garde cinema by the enormous costs of the sound picture. Its place in the film culture was taken by *Cinema Quarterly* which initially defined its perspectives on cinema in terms quite similar to those of *Close Up*. An early issue, for example, celebrated 'the comparative success of such films as *Le Million, Mädchen in Uniform* and *Kameradschaft* despite their foreign dialogue and lack of organised publicity',[31] and the journal was an important publicity organ for the growing film society movement which was committed to the wider dissemination of 'art' cinema. Yet, in the course of its life, the journal gradually moved closer to the documentary movement. It began to publicise the work of documentary film makers as well as publishing articles by leading figures from the movement such as Grierson himself. By the summer of 1934, *Cinema Quarterly* had aligned itself wholeheartedly with the movement as is indicated by the following extract from one of its editorials:

> It is significant that men like Grierson, Flaherty, Rotha, have chosen documentary in preference to studio work. Because it is produced under saner and freer conditions and is generally the conception of a single mind, documentary is the one species of film which achieves a unity approaching artistic satisfaction.[32]

When *Cinema Quarterly* ceased publication in 1936 it was replaced by *World Film News* which was also closely linked to the documentarists. Like its predecessors, *World Film News*, whose name indicates a more straight-forward journalistic enterprise, continued to take an interest in the state of the commercial film industry. It published the famous economic analysis of the British film industry of the 1930s by Francis Klingender and Stuart Legg in 1936 which revealed the pattern of ownership and the chaotic financial structure of the industry. The detailed financial analysis upon which the article was based was subsequently published in 1937 as a pamphlet entitled *Money Behind the Screen* and this work has been credited by some writers with helping to precipitate the crisis in the industry of the late 1930s.[33]

Hitchcock and the Minority Film Culture

The profile of minority film culture in the interwar period is represented by the coterie cinema or film society as opposed to the Gaumont or the ABCs, film as art rather than film as popular entertainment, the European 'art' cinema instead of the popular American or British cinema, and an increasing tendency amongst those with a serious interest in film to cluster around documentary film making and, in particular, its Griersonian wing. Hitchcock's relationship to this branch of the film culture will be examined primarily in relation to the films he made in the 1920s and their links with the cinematic focal points of the minority film culture but, before this, a few remarks will be made about Hitchcock and the social network of the film culture.

Although much of the film industry was suspicious of developments such as the Film Society and its concern with the art of film, there were film makers and producers who did take an interest and did attend the society's screenings. Michael Balcon has referred to the society as 'the Mecca of all cineastes'[34] and his regular attendance plus that of figures such as Adrian Brunel, Thorold Dickinson, Anthony Asquith, writer Angus MacPhail and exhibitor Sidney Bernstein, indicated that there was some degree of interest in developments in the international cinema by some who were working in the commercial industry. The British film production industry was a fairly small enterprise in the 1920s and it may be surmised that there was a certain degree of fluidity between what became the minority and majority wings of the film culture. The small world of cinema in Britain when the Film Society was set up was perhaps not so neatly divided as later on when the cleavage between 'art' and commercial cinema, the superior claims of documentary film and so on were more precisely defined in print by Rotha and *Close Up*. Many of the Film Society people were friends or professional associates of Hitchcock and he was drawn into those circles of the film culture in which film as an art form was taken most seriously.

Hitchcock was working at the Islington Studios in the early 1920s when they were acquired by Balcon and he remained with Balcon's company until 1927. He had met Bernstein whilst working on *Woman to Woman* (Cutts, 1923) and Ivor Montagu, the leading figure in the society, had been brought in to work on Hitchcock's third feature *The Lodger* (1926) as director, after the distributor C.M. Woolf had rejected it. Yet, in terms of social background and experience, Hitchcock differed markedly from the aristocrats and university educated cineastes who became interested in cinema during this period. And, although he was interested in films such as *The Cabinet of Dr Caligari* and *The Last Laugh* (Murnau, 1924), he had become interested in the cinema by way of the Hollywood films that the minority film culture reviled. Some of his films display a grasp and understanding of documentary technique yet it is difficult to imagine Hitchcock following the university educated intellectuals into the government film units run by Grierson. The film analyses which follow will indicate the ways in which Hitchcock's early films can be related to the different cinemas which were the focal points of the minority film culture.

The Lodger (1926)

William Rothman has pointed out that when 'film's "Golden Age" is celebrated, Hitchcock's films are never given their due'.[35] He goes on to suggest that 'as I understand it, Hitchcock occupies a central place in the history of film, a place secured by *The Lodger* and the small but remarkable body of silent films that followed'.[36] Indeed, the film is not mentioned in Eric Rhode's *A History of World Cinema* and where it is mentioned in the large histories it is usually only to signal the antecedents of the Hitchcock thriller. Yet the trade reviews of the time noted its distinctiveness and its attempt to differentiate itself from American films which, as has been suggested, was one of the hallmarks of the 'art' cinemas of the period. As *Kine Weekly* put it:

'The Lodger', and other new productions give promise of a genuine reaction against the deeply-rooted Wardour Street superstition that America will only buy pictures similar to her own.[37]

Whilst such a comment does not indicate the presence in the British cinema of the time of a distinctive 'art' film movement along continental lines, it does at least indicate that there were trends in the work of some British film makers which might be regarded as different from the Hollywood example including, of course, the work of Hitchcock himself.

Conventional comment upon *The Lodger* locates it within the traditions of German Expressionist cinema and, indeed, Hitchcock has spoken of the film as 'the first picture possibly influenced by my period in Germany'.[38] Yet too much can be made of this 'influence'. Barry Salt has suggested that what is usually referred to as 'German Expressionist cinema' embraces only a handful of the films produced in Germany during the 1920s and that many of the effects associated with cinematic expressionism such as chiaroscuro lighting styles and pronounced camera angles 'had already appeared and begun to develop well before the 20s in American and Danish cinema, and had no real connection with the rise of Expressionist art'.[39] Also, the German directors such as Murnau and Lang whose work was known to Hitchcock were not, according to Salt, significantly involved with Expressionism. However, a combination of factors does suggest a German connection of sorts. *The Lodger* was made after Hitchcock had spent a period in Germany at the UFA studios in Berlin and at the Emelka studios in Munich where he worked on three pictures. The film is based upon the story of 'Jack the Ripper' which had provided the German director, Paul Leni, with an episode for his Expressionist film *Waxworks* (1924) which Hitchcock would have had the opportunity to see when it was screened by the Film Society in 1925. In certain respects, the mise en scène of the film recalls the use of shadows in German films such as *Nosferatu* and *The Cabinet of Dr Caligari*. Examples from the film which suggest its affinities with contemporary German film would include the early sequence in which the lodger (Ivor Novello) arrives at the Bunting house and is introduced to the audience by his shadow falling across the door; and, later in the film, the artificial spiral lighting pattern in the courtyard where Daisy (June) meets the lodger after his escape from the police. *The Lodger* also contains some striking examples of high angled shots down the stairwell as the lodger is making one of his late night detective forays and as Mrs Bunting follows him downstairs to search his room. This technique, however, may be better related to the experimentation with extreme high angle and direct overhead shots which Barry Salt has ascribed to the French cinema of the time.[40] On the other hand these shots do utilise the staircase motif which many critics have seen as a key figure in German silent cinema.[41] Hitchcock had an elaborate four-storied staircase set constructed for *The Lodger* and the staircase motif is one that crops up in a number of subsequent Hitchcock pictures including *Blackmail* and *Number Seventeen* from his British work and *Vertigo*, *Psycho* and *The Birds* from his American films.

The Lodger, however, is something more than striking lighting effects, unusual camera angles, staircase motifs and a terror theme. Indeed, the film can be linked on the basis of style and treatment to a number of directions in the cinema during the experimental period of the 1920s. A sequence frequently referred to is that in which the Bunting family become aware of the lodger pacing nervously around his room which is directly above them. The point-of-view of the suspicious family group is rendered by an artificial 'artistic' shot from underneath a ceiling made of plate glass through which the lodger's pacings can be seen. The shot is reminiscent of a sequence in the avant garde film *Entr'Acte* (René Clair, 1924) in which a male ballet dancer dressed as a woman is shot from directly underneath as he pirouettes on a pane of clear glass. The shots in *The Lodger* are not literal point-of-view shots but rather they represent mental impressions. It was this problem of depicting the interior life of the mind that marked out the French avant garde film makers of the day and in a film made soon after *The Lodger* Hitchcock included a lengthy stream-of-conciousness sequence which, in Raymond Durgnat's words, is constituted by '(s)uper-imposed tracks, pans and shots of streetscapes and traffic'.[42] The film, *Downhill* (1927), he suggests, produces 'a visual bewilderment not unworthy of *Entr 'Acte*'.[43] The Clair film was screened by the Film Society in January 1926 and again, as with the German films, Hitchcock had the opportunity to see it. However, the key point to establish is the visual stylistic association of *The Lodger* with the subjective and impressionist trends in film style coming from the French Surrealist and Dadaist film makers.

If the mise en scène and the cinematography of *The Lodger* point to German and French stylistic traditions, the editing of the film has more in common with trends in the American and Soviet cinema. The sequence in which Joe, Daisy's policeman boy friend, flirts with her contains some Griffith-like associative editing. Joe cuts out two pastry hearts then 'breaks' one of them when Daisy appears to scorn him. Such a use of the details of the mise en scène symbolically organised through the editing relates to the developing classical style of narration associated particularly with the American cinema. Conversely, the sequence in which the lodger is playing chess with Daisy seems to draw on the editing techniques of the Soviet cinema. Shots of the game are intercut with shots of a poker in the fireplace and whilst eventually the lodger innocently uses the poker to stir the fire, the montage of the sequence is organised to promote suspense by suggesting that it will be used to batter Daisy over the head. To use the terminology of André Bazin, Hitchcock 'alludes' to an impending assault through successive close-ups of the poker and of Daisy's 'golden curls'. Such an ominous meaning 'lies much more in the organisation of these elements rather than in their objective content'[44] although it should be pointed out that the film up to that point has created a web of suspicion around the lodger upon which the allusive montage feeds for its full impact. Finally, the film even displays links with documentary cinema in the opening sequence in which the various media of communication — the press, the electric display sign, the radio — are shown spreading to the public the news of the murder that occurs at the beginning of the film. As Barry Salt has noted, 'the documentary montage sequence' was not uncommon in films of the 1920s and was usually used to contribute general atmosphere to a narrative without having specific links with the actual story.[45] In the case of the opening of *The Lodger*, the sequence effectively suggests the spreading of fear and panic amongst the public, a theme which is concretised and individualised in the narrative which follows.

Blackmail (1929)

Just as *The Lodger* dominates Hitchcock's early career in terms of critical attention so *Blackmail* dominates accounts of his period with British International Pictures, the Hollywood-style company established at Elstree studios. Its position as Britain's first 'talkie' and the creative use of the soundtrack as in the celebrated 'knife' sequence have deflected attention

26

away from other stylistic qualities which link it to the main traditions of silent cinema.

The opening sequence, in particular, points in various stylistic directions and clearly indicates the silent origins of Britain's first 'talkie'. The sequence opens on a detail, a spinning hub cap, which is followed by a number of shots of a lorry speeding through the streets including a subjective travelling shot from the point of view of the driver. Interwoven with these are shots from inside the lorry which show the radio equipment that the police are using. The montage of images and the musical soundtrack convey an urgency that is underscored by a graphic insert which shows the address of the suspect they are chasing. There is no dialogue and the event is alluded to in the manner of a silent film with the single insert shot making clear what the images suggest. Moving further into the sequence, we can see the dependence upon a variety of silent film traditions. When the two policemen approach the suspect's room the stylistic reference becomes the German silent cinema with the faces of the policemen crossed by a series of narrow shadows, their ominous presence and the sense of menace and tension conveyed by framing and lighting in an expressionist manner. On the other hand, the complex interplay of point-of-view shots which follows owes more to the classical cinema and, in particular to the use of cross-cutting to create suspense which derives from the Griffith tradition. The sequence continues with the interrogation of the suspect back at the police station and the extended time scale of this operation is conveyed again in 'pure' silent cinema terms with a shot of an ashtray containing a couple of cigarettes dissolving into a shot of the same ashtray containing several cigarette butts. The suspect is then locked in a cell and the details of his imprisonment are handled in a similar fashion with an array of close ups of significant detail together with some explanatory 'title' shots such as a door bearing the word 'cells', a shot of a document which outlines the identification parade procedure and so on. The events are constructed from numerous small details according to the rules of narrative construction in the silent cinema as codified by theorists such as Pudovkin.[46] At the very end of the sequence when the two policemen are going off duty, snatches of dialogue are gradually introduced and the montage style of the earlier parts of the film disappears abruptly to be replaced by a number of lengthy shots which simply present characters in conversation or, to use Hitchcock's own words, 'photographs of people talking'.[47] It might be suggested that the opening sequence as a whole is a neat symbol of the British film industry at the time in its wavering state of mind about the talking picture in so far as the dialogue sequences make a belated and tentative entry at the end of a very solid and accomplished piece of silent film construction.

The opening sequence can also be related to documentary cinema. The careful exposition of the mechanics of detection (especially the detail of the wireless equipment which is used to guide the police to their quarry) gives way to the presentation of the procedures of arrest and imprisonment with documentary-like attention given to the details of finger-printing, the taking of 'mug' shots and the identification parade. The 'documentary' aspect is also present in the arrest itself with the seedy context of criminal life, the drab grey environment in which the suspect lives, being presented with a considerable degree of attention to what might be called 'realistic' detail. It is worth analysing this part of the film closely and describing the images that are used to depict the criminal environment. The police are shown arriving at an archway through which can be seen a number of men hanging around talking, some children playing and a horse and cart. The images are full of residual detail, elements which serve simply to provide a certain surface authenticity for the image. A subsequent image shows the children playing together with women talking to each other whilst hanging out washing and cleaning windows. Images such as these have little to do with the progress of the narrative and appear to be digressions into some sort of social realism which touches upon matters such as the particular context from which crime emerges. In addition, there is a hint of sympathy with the criminal suspect when a stone is hurled through a window at the police. A 'social commentary' barely but noticeably punctures the some-what cold, objective presentation of the preliminary chase, on the one hand, and the interrogation and imprisonment on the other. It was elements such as these which caught the attention of 'realist' critics such as John Grierson and Lindsay Anderson. Grierson, for example, referred to Hitchcock as 'the only English director who can put the English poor on the screen with any verisimilitude'[48] in a contemporary review of *Murder!* (1930) whilst Anderson, writing in the late 1940s, was impressed by the 'conscientious realism . . . of locales and characters'[49] in the British films as a whole. Raymond Durgnat has commented on the presence of such 'realistic vignettes' in Hitchcock's British films in the following terms:

. . . it must be remembered that realism in the '30s was a rarer and more difficult achievement, that the director couldn't just point a TV camera in the street. He had first to notice certain details, love them enough to remember and recreate them, and lastly to slide them deftly into the thriller context.[50]

The 'realist' aspects of the sequence, the use of location shots, picks up the use of semi-documentary sequences, which are to be found at the begin-nings of previous Hitchcock pictures. The openings of *The Lodger, The Ring* (1927) and *The Manxman* (1928) are like brief documentaries about the dissemination of news, fairground life and the fishing industry respect-ively. They also prefigure the documentary style of *The Wrong Man* (1957) from Hitchcock's American period.

The opening sequence of *Blackmail*, then, can be discussed in the context of the various traditions of European and American cinema developed during the silent era and it has some links with documentary cinema. By contrast, the sequence in which Frank (John Longden) and Alice (Anny Ondra) go for tea to a Lyons Corner House, brings the 'talkie' dimension of the film to the fore and provides the first opportunity in the film to examine the impact of dialogue shooting upon scenic construction during this early phase of sound cinema. The scene in the dining room is made up of 20 shots and lasts just over $4^1/2$ minutes. The dominant impression is of 'photographs of people talking' and a detailed analysis of the sequence confirms this. Almost $3^1/2$ minutes of screen time are taken up by four shots of Frank and Alice talking at their table in a profile two-shot. The remaining 16 shots, all quite brief, include a number of shots as the couple walk to their table, an insert of Alice's note to her artist friend (Cyril Ritchard), and the exchange of 'meaningful' close-ups when he arrives to meet her. The fluid cross-cutting of these close-ups contrasts with the static theatrical set-up for the dialogue shots, and here we are confronted with the impact of the primitive sound recording technology of the time which meant that dialogue which had to be lip-synchronised had to be recorded at the same time as the image. In addition, at this point before the development of the self-blimped camera, the shooting had to be done with the camera enclosed in a soundproof booth. This dictated a narrow range of camera positions and restricted both camera and actor movement in scenes involving dialogue. In this particular case, Hitchcock was faced with an additional problem of working with a Polish-born actress, Anny Ondra, whose accent would not have been appropriate to the English subject matter of the film. In the absence of post-synchronisation facilities, an English actress (Joan Barry) stood just out of camera range speaking the dialogue whilst Anny Ondra mimed the words for the camera. Subsequent dialogue sequences confirm the limitations imposed upon the fluid visual language of silent cinema with its mobile cinematography and its flexible cutting styles. However, as every film history book reminds us, *Blackmail* in one sequence at least does cope with the technological and aesthetic addition of speech in a novel way. This is the celebrated sequence in which the chatter of a minor character talking about the stabbing of the artist is distorted to highlight the word 'knife'. It is one of most-quoted sequences in the entire history of cinema and contemporary comment certainly picked it out as worthy of attention.

Hugh Castle, writing in *Close Up*, went as far as to suggest that 'that particular sequence is about the only one which we have on record in which sound has been definitely instrumental in the development of the drama'.[51] Kenneth MacPherson, editor of the journal, echoed Castle's global judgement and devoted the whole of an editorial to a consideration of the significance of *Blackmail* to the development of the sound picture. He wrote that the film was 'far and away the most significant determinant to the unification of sound-sight deliberately and sustainedly that we have yet had'.[52] *Blackmail* was greeted as the most important sound picture to date. The 'knife' sequence seemed to demonstrate the possibilities of a departure from the 'photographs of people talking' that dialogue films seemed to invite, with its expressionist distortion of the soundtrack. It also counter-points sound and image with the dialogue from off-screen space matched to a large close up of Alice. Counterpointing sound and image instead of synchronising them was favoured as the artistic path for the sound picture by the film intellectuals of the day. It was a way of overcoming the sound recorder's even more 'misleading faculty of being able to record the actual', to borrow Paul Rotha's words. Such a position had been given considerable prestige by the publication in *Close Up* in 1928 of the manifesto on sound film written by Eisenstein, Pudovkin and Alexandrov.[53] The Soviet statement which, according to Jay Leyda,[54] was actually written by Eisenstein and endorsed by the others, argued that the 'first experimental work with sound must be directed along the lines of its distinct non-synchronisation with the visual images'.[55] It went on to discuss the techniques of counterpointing sound and image and argued against the simple use of sound to achieve 'photographed performances of a theatrical sort'[56] — almost an echo of Hitchcock's 'photographs of people talking'. Hitchcock's aural experiments in *Blackmail* seem to belong in spirit with the avant garde thinking of the Soviet film makers and the sound statement was, in fact, published in *Close Up* in October 1928, a few months before Hitchcock actually started the production of *Blackmail*. This is not to suggest that Hitchcock read Eisenstein before making the film but that his thinking and the thinking of avant garde intellectuals such as Eisenstein were not so far apart when it came to reflecting on the art of the cinema.

Notes

1. F. Murnau, 'The Ideal Picture Needs No Titles', *Theatre Magazine*, vol. XLVII, no. 322 (1928), quoted in L. Eisner, *The Haunted Screen* (Secker and Warburg, London, 1973), p. 85.

2. G. Mast (ed.), *The Movies in Our Midst* (University of Chicago Press, Chicago, 1982), p. 142.

3. See D. Dusinberre, 'The Avant-Garde Attitude in the Thirties' in D. MacPherson (ed.), *British Cinema Traditions of Independence* (British Film Institute, London, 1980).

4. *The Film Society Programmes* (Arno Press, New York, 1972), p. 4.

5. I. Montagu, 'Interview: Ivor Montagu', *Screen*, vol. 13, no. 2 (1972), p. 72.

6. Ibid., p. 73.

7. I. Montagu, *The Political Censorship of Films* (Gollancz, London, 1929), p. 12.

8. P. Rotha, *The Film Till Now*, 4th edn (Spring Books, London, 1967), p. 416 (Griffith edited and contributed to the second, third and fourth editions of the book).

9. *Close Up*, vol. I, no. 2 (1927), pp. 15-16.

10. *Close Up*, vol. I, no. 1 (1927), p. 7.

11. *Close Up*, vol. III, no. 4 (1928), p. 10.

12. See R. Manvell, *Film* (Penguin, London, 1944); E. Lindgren, *The Art of the Film* (Allen and Unwin, London, 1948).

13. Rotha, *The Film Till Now*, p. 35.

14. Ibid., p. 127.

15. Ibid., p. 129.

16. Ibid., p. 88.

17. Ibid., p. 94.

18. Ibid.
19. Ibid., p. 96.
20. Ibid., pp. 401-2.
21. Ibid.
22. See A. Bazin, 'The Evolution of Film Language' in P. Graham, *The New Wave* (Secker and Warburg, London, 1968), p. 25.
23. R. Low, *The History of the British Film 1918-1929* (Allen and Unwin, London, 1971), p. 130.
24. Ibid., p. 129.
25. See Alan Lovell's essay on Grierson in A. Lovell and J. Hillier, *Studies in Documentary* (Secker and Warburg, London, 1972).
26. S. Hood, 'John Grierson and the Documentary Film Movement', in J. Curran and V. Porter (eds.), *British Cinema History* (Weidenfeld and Nicolson, London, 1983), pp. 99-112.
27. See F. Hardy (ed.), *Grierson on Documentary* (Faber and Faber, London, 1966), Part I.
28. See B. Hogenkamp, 'Film and the Workers' Movement in Britain', *Sight and Sound*, vol. 45, no. 2 (1976) and D. Macpherson, *British Cinema*.
29. Lovell and Hillier, *Studies in Documentary*, p. 35.
30. P. Rotha, *Documentary Film* (Faber and Faber, London, 1936).
31. *Cinema Quarterly*, vol. 1, no. 1 (1932), p. 3.
32. Ibid., vol. 2, no. 4 (1934), p. 205.
33. F.D. Klingender and S. Legg, *Money Behind the Screen* (Lawrence and Wishart, London, 1937).
34. M. Balcon, *A Lifetime in Films* (Hutchinson, London, 1969), p. 51.
35. W. Rothman, *Hitchcock The Murderous Gaze* (Harvard University Press, London, 1982), p. 7.
36. Ibid.
37. *Kine Weekly*, 7 Oct. 1926.
38. F. Truffaut, *Hitchcock* (Panther, London, 1969), p. 49.
39. B. Salt, 'From Caligari to Who?', *Sight and Sound*, vol. 48, no. 2 (1979).
40. B. Salt, *Film Style and Technology: History and Analysis* (Starword, London, 1983), p. 215.
41. See L. Eisner, *The Haunted Screen* (Secker and Warburg, London, 1969), pp. 119-27.
42. R. Durgnat, *The Strange Case of Alfred Hitchcock* (Faber and Faber, London, 1974), p. 77.
43. Ibid.
44. Bazin, 'Evolution', p. 27.
45. Salt, *Film Style*, p. 217.
46. Hitchcock may have become familiar with Pudovkin's editing theory through his links with Ivor Montagu who translated Pudovkin into English in the late 1920s.
47. Truffaut, *Hitchcock*, p. 67.
48. Hardy, *Grierson*, p. 74.
49. L. Anderson, 'Alfred Hitchcock', *Sequence*, no. 9 (1949), p. 115.
50. Durgnat, *The Strange Case*, pp. 29-30.
51. *Close Up*, vol. V, no. 2 (1929), p. 135.
52. *Close Up*, vol. V, no. 4 (1929), pp. 257-63.
53. *Close Up*, vol. III,no. 4 (1928), p. 10.
54. S.M. Eisenstein, *Film Form* (Harcourt, Brace and World, New York, 1949), pp. 259-60.
55. Ibid., p. 258.
56. Ibid.

Chapter Three

The British Film Industry in the Interwar Years

Although Hitchcock had some links with the 'artistic' wing of the British cinema during the 1920s, it was in the commercial film industry that he was to forge his career. In Chapter 1, the notions of 'film industry' and 'national cinema' were unpicked into their different strands and shown not to be neat and unified in terms of their empirical reference. Studies of national film industries or national cinemas involve the study of many different kinds of history which may or may not run happily in unison with each other. The British film industry presents a good example of histories yoked together uneasily. During the interwar years, the exhibition sector of the industry had established itself substantially on the basis of screening American films and had generated a large audience whose tastes were attuned to Hollywood. This factor was important in defining certain limits within which the production industry was obliged to work. The work of building up a cinema audience and the work of building up a national production industry and, by extension, a national cinema, can be seen to have been in a state of contradiction. Hollywood provided a strong profile against which a national cinema could be defined and constructed yet, in Britain, it might be suggested that audiences were far too attached to Hollywood pictures to tolerate a cinema that was substantially different. The course of the British production industry during the interwar years can be seen as a struggle with this paradox.

The Social and Economic Context[1]

The interwar period was one of cataclysmic change in British society with key structural shifts in economic patterns having important consequences for the social and cultural life of the nation. The Victorian economy which had sustained British imperial power and prestige throughout the nineteenth century was moving into a period of decline. The major impact of this decline was felt in the oldest industrial regions, in areas such as South Wales and the North of England which depended for their existence upon the great staple industries of the Victorian economy — coal, steel, ship-building and textiles. However, alongside the decline in the older industries must be set the rise of a number of new industries which were also to have a profound effect on the social life of the period. Amongst the most important of these was the electricity supply industry which, in fact, helped to seal the fate of the older power supply industry, coal. The growth of the electricity industry was dramatic and symptomatic. In 1918, electricity consumption per head in Britain lagged behind the other advanced industrial countries whereas by the 1930s its rate of growth exceeded that of the rest of the world, and the national 'grid' system of electricity distribution was without equal anywhere in the world. Its growth paralleled the decline of the older industries and, as Sidney Pollard has suggested, it 'could be taken as a symbol of the new industrial Britain, freeing other industries from dependence on the coalfields of the north and west and setting in motion a vast migration to the midlands and the south-east'.[2] Such developments led to the growth of the electrical engineering industries and the spread of new electric consumer durables such as cookers, radios, refrigerators, vacuum cleaners and so on, which altered standards of living and life styles for those who could afford them during this period. Another industry to rise to prominence during the interwar period was that of the motor car which had an equally profound impact upon social life. As Pollard has put it:

> The motor car changed people's habits of living, shopping, travelling and holidaying; it affected the layout of towns and suburbs; it created the first conveyor belt factories and stimulated innumerable ancillary industries, some of them of major importance in their own right, including oil refining, rubber, electrical goods, glass, metallurgy (both ferrous and non-ferrous) and mechanical engineering.[3]

A whole new constellation of industries was, in fact, in the process of development, a constellation which was related to advances in science and technology and which, in addition to those above, included the aircraft and chemical industries and the development of plastics. Allied to these was a range of consumer goods and services including the fast-developing 'leisure' industries of which the cinema was an important member. Some of the new industries directly replaced the older, e.g. artificial fibres and canned food; some were simply expansions of long-established industries the home market for which was rapidly growing, e.g. building, shoes, hosiery; and some offered new products such as radios and electrical goods. They differed basically from the old staple industries in a number of ways in addition to their shift to the south-east. They were not so dependent upon the export market and many were sheltered from the competition of foreign manufacturers by the costs of transport, tariffs or the nature of their supply. Many of them were state supported and many were dominated by individual firms, or by a small number of firms.

It was this socio-geographical shift of industrial concentration which provided the contrast in fortune between the various sections of the population during this period. On the one hand, $2^3/4$ million people became unemployed through the combined effects of depression and decline in the traditional industrial areas whilst for those that remained in work, particularly in the service and consumer goods industries concentrated in the midlands and the south east, there was a rising standard of living. A.J.P. Taylor has written:

The 1930s have been called the black years, the devil's decade. Its popular image can be expressed in two phrases: mass unemployment and 'appeasement' ... Yet, at the same time, most English people were enjoying a richer life than any previously known in the history of the world: longer holidays, shorter hours, higher real wages. They had motor cars, cinemas, radio sets, electrical appliances. The two sides of life did not join up.[4]

A new Britain, a consumer orientated society with a stress upon home ownership, the motor car, electrical gadgetry and new forms of entertainment was overlaid upon the grimmer, older, declining industrial Britain with its increasing army of unemployed. That the new Britain was in the ascendant is indicated by the fact that following the slump of 1929 and the depression of the early 1930s, the economic recovery of 1934-37 was led by the newer industries especially house-building. Again, Pollard:

The housing boom may have been the most visible and the largest single component of the upswing in economic activity which signalled the end of the slump, but is was by no means the only one. There were also remarkable increases in many service trades, entertainments, and other 'sheltered' industries. They were the kind of goods and services which the bulk of the lower middle classes and skilled workers demanded with their increased real incomes, and the rise in their real wages or salaries, in turn, was achieved, not by rising money payments, but by falling prices, pulled down by the falling price of imports.[5]

As well as these shifts of emphasis in terms of the kinds of industrial and economic activity on which national wealth could be based, there were also changes in the general structure and organisation of the economy. There was a trend towards greater centralisation and greater state intervention in the economy, best symbolised by the introduction of protectionist economic policies in 1931. The notion of a planned economy, anathema to generations of politicians brought up on *laissez-faire* free enterprise policies, began to be woven into serious thinking about the British economy and society. This was partly due to the undoubted impact on many sections of the population of unemployment on such a large scale.

The poverty and suffering that was brought about by the depression was a forcible reminder of the vulnerability of the British economy and, unlike the poverty and suffering of earlier times, was much more visible through the developing means of mass communication especially the popular press. The impact has been summed up by Branson and Heinneman as follows:

> The early thirties ... faced large sections of the British people with a virtual breakdown of the whole economic system under which they lived. One of the richest countries in the world was patently unable to provide great numbers of its people with any way of making a living. Not only the working-class movement, but a growing number of middle-class and professional people suffered from a sense of insecurity.[6]

Eric Hobsbawm has put it more poetically, referring to the 'acrid fog of anxiety' as 'the atmosphere which men and women breathed during a generation'[7] and it was in such an atmosphere that the ideas of a centrally planned economy were able to take root. There were also examples from abroad of state intervention in the economy — from capitalist America with Roosevelt's New Deal introduced to combat a similar depression in the American economy; and from the communist Soviet Union with its Five Year plans. Alongside state intervention there was also the development of the economy from one constituted by 'the small or medium-sized, highly specialised, family-operated and family-financed, and competitive firm'[8] to one dominated by 'giant corporations, oligopolies, trade associations and so forth'.[9] In 1914 the British economy was one of the least concentrated of the major industrial economies in terms of ownership, but by 1939 it had become one of the most concentrated. The British economy had followed the logic of capitalist development and the 1920s and 1930s witnessed 'the growth in scale of productive units and units of ownership, the concentration of a growing share of output, employment and so on in the hands of a declining number of giant firms, the formal and informal restriction of competition'.[10] It was during this period of amalgamation and merger that formidable industrial combines such as ICI, Unilever and Courtaulds emerged.

This redrawing of the industrial map with its population shifts, its profound impact on social habits, has implications for the development of the British cinema during this period. The production industry emerged as a substantial concern based in London and the Home Counties. Although, in the early days of the British cinema, film makers had been based in Brighton, Yorkshire and Lancashire as well as London, regionalised production eventually gave way to an industry based either in London itself — Shepherd's Bush, Islington, Twickenham — or very close to it — Elstree, Denham, Pinewood. The exhibition sector, of course, was nationwide in its coverage and it can be seen as an important part of the massive growth of the entertainment and leisure industries with a rising graph of cinema attendance throughout the interwar years. The cinema-going habit was a central feature of working class life during the 1930s and admission prices were low enough to be within reach of even the unemployed. British films were produced by film makers based in the affluent south-east of the country but viewed by people from all parts of the country and by those who were victims of the broad shifts in economic activity of the time. This is important because the shift to a consumer-oriented society affected cinema in another way. Consumer goods provided a new range of images and symbols for the film makers, a new iconography yet one which was tied very specifically to the life styles enjoyed by certain sections of British society during the period. Thus there was a considerable cleavage between the producers of cinema and sections of the audience which can be expressed in representational terms. The trend towards the state regulation of economic activity and the concentration of ownership, central features of the economic life of Britain during the 1920s and 1930s, are also reflected in the film industry as the rest of this chapter will indicate. Firstly, however, the most important context for the emergence of a national film industry in Britain was the power and influence of the American film industry and that will be considered next.

Hollywood and the British Production Industry

In the years before the First World War, British film making had developed steadily if not spectacularly. By 1914, in the words of a later government report, 'it has been estimated that ... some 25 per cent of the films shown in the cinemas of this country were of British make'.[11] Britain had provided its own candidate for the invention of cinema in William Friese-Greene, and pioneer British film makers such as Cecil Hepworth and the Smith and Williamson team had made important contributions to the early development of film as a narrative art. Yet, by the mid-1920s the production industry was 'well on the way to extinction'[12] with the proportion of its films being shown in British cinemas drastically below the figure of pre-war years. One key factor in the decline, of course, was the war itself which interrrupted production across Europe generally. Yet the war as a sole factor is not sufficient to explain the dramatic decline in British production. The other European countries similarly affected not only recovered their production industries during the 1920s but also went on to produce many films of considerable importance to the history of cinema itself.

The major beneficiary of the war in Europe in terms of economics was the United States which managed during this period to transform itself from a debtor to a creditor nation. As Thomas Guback has put it the 'war redirected the international flow of capital, as surpluses from Europe were shot away at the front and American capital in the form of war loans and goods was sent abroad'.[13] From the beginning of the war to the mid-1920s, American film exports to Europe increased fivefold and, in Britain, the

American share of the market estimated at 30 per cent in 1909, had increased to 60 per cent in 1914, and to an overwhelming 95 per cent in 1926.[14] In terms of Hollywood's overseas markets the British was the most important or, to put it another way, Britain was the market most vulnerable to Hollywood during this period. There are a number of reasons for this, some of which have to do with the position of power that Hollywood was able to establish during the First World War whilst the European countries were preoccupied with matters other than film production but there are also reasons which have to do with the character of the British film industry of the time. It is a combination of reasons that explains why the British film industry failed to recover from the war in the way in which that of other European countries did, and why it was not capable of meeting American competition without legislative protection. The war period was a crucial time for the internal development of the American film industry. Its production base had shifted to Hollywood in the early part of the second decade and the structural transformations that were to lead to the domination of the industry by an oligopoly had begun. Although the sound revolution of the late 1920s was to add to the number of large companies which made up the 'mature oligopoly', the basic pattern of domination was already established by the early 1920s. By this time Hollywood had become a high-capital production industry with orthodox financial backing from Wall Street and had evolved its characteristic product, the lavish feature length narrative film with star performers. Hollywood's basic strength derived from the seemingly ever-increasing demand for film which characterised the silent period and which can be related to such factors as the rapid development of urbanisation in the United States in the early years of the twentieth century. This massive and expanding domestic market enabled American producers to recover all or almost all of their production costs in the home market which meant that revenue derived from exports represented almost all profit. Consequently, American producers were in a position to offer their films to other countries at extremely competitive prices, often undercutting domestic producers. The problems of production in the European countries were the reverse of the American situation; with smaller populations incapable of providing an adequate internal market for high budget volume production, exporting films was a necessity rather than a bonus for countries such as Britain.

The American film industry, already strong in relation to its potential competitors, had also devised a number of trade and business practices that enhanced its grip on the British market and enabled it to control the British film industry without either setting up production units or owning exhibition venues. 'Blind' and 'block' booking of films had been introduced by the large American companies to eliminate competition. Under these arrangements exhibitors were obliged to rent their film programmes well in advance and to take a series of films (blocks) from single companies rather than putting their programmes together by drawing on a variety of companies. Such blocks would include a small number of highly desirable films plus others and could even include films yet to be trade-shown, or yet to be made. By using these practices, the American companies were able to dominate British exhibition simply through their distribution offices in London. Because these companies made the popular films of the day, those with the leading American stars such as Chaplin and Mary Pickford, British exhibitors had little choice but to contract for the blocks of films diminishing the screen time that might have been available to British films. Thus, even when the industry did manage to make the odd British film there was little guarantee that it would reach a British, let alone a foreign, screen. In the calamitous year of 1926 although around 5 per cent of the films shown to the trade were of British origin (in itself an alarmingly low proportion), it has been estimated that the percentage of screen time devoted to British films was 'probably well below 5 per cent owing to the larger percentage of exhibition dates secured by American films through the system of blind and block booking'.[15]

With control established through distribution, the American film industry did not attempt to set up production units in Britain except in a few isolated cases. Famous Players-Lasky, the production arm of Paramount, did establish a studio at Islington in 1920 but withdrew from Britain in 1924 because 'in the opinion of the American company the productions failed to reach a quality comparable to those made in the States'.[16] American companies also showed no interest in acquiring cinema chains for the exhibition of their films. By the early 1920s cinema-going had become a firmly established social habit in Britain with a high and consistent demand for American films from British exhibitors, and minimal competition from the other film-making countries. There was little to be gained from owning large circuits of British cinemas. Indeed, the leading American companies saw it as in their interests not to compete in this area with the already established exhibitor concerns as this might have led to the development of co-operative renter-exhibitor firms as had happened in the United States with companies such as First National. Co-operation rather than competition seemed the judicious course. The problems of the British film industry during the 1920s were problems for the production sector. The exhibition sector was thriving and successful. Although statistics from the period are not very reliable, those that exist indicate that from 1910 to 1925 the number of cinemas more than doubled from 1,600 to 3,878 and by the mid-1930s the figure had reached 4,448.[17] The same period witnessed a rise of annual admissions to the cinema from 346 million in 1910 to 903 million in 1934.[18] It was the one sector of the British film industry that grew as a profitable concern and which had attracted finance from orthodox commercial sources prior to the general expansion of the industry in the late 1920s.

It has been argued that American pre-eminence was not simply a matter of a strong industry with a solid home base and a head start due to the war although clearly these were crucial factors. The state of the British production industry and the attitudes of leading producers in the post-war period have also been singled out as contributory factors to the decline of production through the 1920s. Many of the leading companies such as Hepworth, Gaumont and Welsh-Pearson returned to the post-war industry with pre-war assumptions. They had learnt their trade in times when the American influence had not been so marked and when film was a kind of small scale cottage industry requiring minimal capital investment. The situation in the 1920s had changed dramatically with the transformation of the American industry yet, as Rachael Low has pointed out:

> the older companies ... faced with the difficulties in getting capital or a wide market, ... allowed themselves to think that films financed cheaply on a pre-war scale could survive in the post-war world. The higher cost of films coming over from America meant, in fact, a completely different style of production.[19]

The strength of the American cinema in Britain has clear economic explanations but it might also be argued that the British audience had become attuned to the American film and preferred it to its British counterpart. Indeed, such an argument was used in the course of a debate on the film industry in the House of Lords in 1925 when the government spokesman suggested that 'the public deliberately preferred American films to our own'.[20] Quite apart from their vastly superior production values, their stars and their lavish costumes and sets, the Hollywood films had the advantage of close cultural and historical ties with Britain. The common language, in particular, was to be an important factor after the introduction of the 'talkies' in the late 1920s. Yet, for the 1920s, it may be difficult to talk authoritatively in terms of audience preference as so few British films actually reached the screen to give the public much choice of what they saw.

The Cinematograph Films Act 1927

The domination of the British screen by American films began to cause concern early in the 1920s. An editorial comment in the trade paper, *Kine Weekly*, in 1923 refers to a letter in *The Times* which drew attention to 'the danger arising from the Americanisation of the British Empire from the excessive number of American motion pictures shown'.[21] The discussions which followed ranged over a variety of considerations about the role of a national film industry and the best means to foster one. Some put forward narrow economic arguments, others stressed the ideological and the cultural and some saw that both dimensions could be reflected in a national cinema. The *Kine Weekly* editorial went on to predict that the 'authorities would have to attend to the problem sooner or later' but much of the concern at this time was about the urgent economic need for the British production industry to secure a place in the large American market in order to provide a stable base for the industry. A number of solutions were proposed and the idea of a distribution consortium for British films in America was discussed in the trade press during 1923.[22] One of the problems, however, was the unsuitability of British films for the American market and this would not necessarily be overcome by a distribution network on American soil however efficiently organised. The importing of American stars and technical personnel was seen as important and was pioneered by some of the more adventurous producers. A year or two later a proposal known as 'the Ridgewell plan' recommended that British producers should work very closely with Americans to make films for the American market. As *Kine Weekly* reported:

> It is proposed to make pictures in Great Britain for the big American market from plans and data provided by American producing and distributing organisations. One of the big arguments in its favour is the comparative cheapness of producing in England and, as American players and producers are said to be incapable of acclimatisation to England, British producers would be used. It is estimated that the pictures would cost only about half as much as if made in America ...[23]

There were, however, other arguments which, whilst having a strong foothold in economic terms, nevertheless had a strong dimension of 'national cinema' about them as opposed to the 'Ridgewell plan' of making films in Britain to American blueprints. Sir Stephen Tallents had argued that a national cinema which provided 'a fitting presentation of England on the world's screen'[24] could be of considerable benefit to British trade. Indeed the nineteenth century imperialist notion that 'trade follows the flag' was gradually being replaced by a twentieth century variant which held that 'trade followed the film'. This seemed to be convincingly borne out by the successful penetration of European markets by American consumer goods. Even before the First World War, according to Benjamin Hampton, businessmen in Britain and other European countries began to perceive the links between the increasing popularity of American films and the increasing sales of American consumer goods. As he argued:

> English and German traders noted that American merchandise was beginning to supersede theirs in markets formerly under their control. Investigation proved that American films were responsible for the change in conditions. They began to complain to their governments that audiences saw American sewing-machines, typewriters, furniture, clothing, shoes, steam shovels, saddles, automobiles, and all sorts of things in cinema shows, and soon began to want these things and insist on buying them in preference to similar articles made in England, Germany, France or elsewhere.[25]

Cultural and economic penetration and projection were seen to merge in the novel documentary medium of the cinema. A lucrative by-product of the narrative pleasures offered by Hollywood films was the informal advertising potential mentioned by Hampton. Indeed, the Federation of British Industries' role in the lobbying of the government in the years before the Act of 1927 was probably partly motivated by the hope of similar benefits for British goods that might be available with a flourishing national cinema presenting a British 'iconography of consumerdom'. The commercial aspects of a national cinema are also reflected in the allocation of state responsibility for the film industry to the Board of Trade. Narrow economic arguments for the existence of an indigenous film production industry were not very strong, as the industry in the 1920s was extremely small, composed of a handful of tiny companies. The final collapse of production would have had a marginal effect on the British economy and although a certain number of business interests were at stake, and a number of jobs would have been lost, this would not have been a major problem. Much of the production industry was located in the new industrial areas of London and the Home Counties and not in those areas of declining industry. The workforce displaced by such a collapse would undoubtedly have obtained employment in the new ascendant light industrial world of the south-east. The exhibitors would have been unaffected by the disappearance of British films as their profitability was based upon the popularity of American films. The broader arguments such as those mounted by Tallents, however, although having quite precise economic and commercial implications, mesh in with a wider national debate about British cinema which embraced ideological, cultural and propagandist considerations.

Little of the rhetoric in the columns of the national newspapers or the trade press was concerned with the preservation of Gaumont, Ideal and the medley of small concerns which constituted the British production industry in the early 1920s. Instead there was stress on the loss of 'national prestige that would inevitably result from the loss of a film industry'[26] and the propaganda danger of foreign-dominated cinema screens. An article in *Kine Weekly* posed the following rhetorical question:

> Supposing 95 per cent of our school books were written and published for us in the United States of America, Germany and France. What would be the nature of the outcry raised? And yet the position is not dissimilar.[27]

'The position', of course, referred to the British cinema screen and its predominant diet of American films — a situation of cultural imperialism that the British people had come to accept and, indeed, expect. Demands for a government enquiry were made by a number of distinct interest groups and cultural lobbies. *Kine Weekly*, in fact, had been pressing for a government enquiry for a number of years and the world of arts and letters weighed in with impressive support in a letter to the *Telegraph* signed by, amongst others, Robert Bridges, Edward Elgar and Thomas Hardy. The letter spoke of the plight of the British film as 'humiliating' and argued that the continuation of the film industry was central to the preservation of the national culture. It argued:

> Important as is the commercial aspect of this problem, high national and patriotic interests are involved. No-one who has followed the development of this new form of popular entertainment can be in any doubt as to the immense importance of films as subtle means of propaganda, none the less powerful because it is indirect. Films have an atmosphere of their own. The bulk of films shown in this country have, to say the least of it, a non-British atmosphere. These films are shown in our Dominions, Colonies and Dependencies, and in all the countries of the world outside the British Commonwealth of Nations. Many of them are inferior productions, neither healthy nor patriotic in tone, while the psychological influences which they convey may have far-reaching consequences.[28]

The letter also called for an enquiry at government level and in May 1925 this central demand was incorporated into a question to the government raised in the House of Lords by Lord Newton. The government, in fact, was reluctant to intervene in the industry and, in particular, did not want to get involved in legislation. Legislative protection for manufacturing industry was not popular at the time and, indeed, the Conservative Party had fought the 1923 General Election on a protectionist platform and had been heavily defeated. Viscount Peel, the government spokesman, drew attention to the Federation of British Industry's consultations with the film trade which were going on at the time with the aim of producing a voluntary plan to help film production, and said that the government was reluctant to jeopardise these discussions. The Federation published its findings in August 1925 and these, together with the House of Lords debate, and numerous interventions on the topic in the national and trade press, guaranteed a public airing of the various options open to the industry. The idea of a national film studio was promoted by T. Welsh, a veteran film maker who had set up the British branch of the French Gaumont Company with A.C. Bromhead in 1898. The co-ordination of the activities of the small British production units might have led to economies of scale and a more efficient use of resources but such a proposal was not taken up immediately. It might be argued, however, that something like this did actually happen in the late 1920s with the development of the two large producing combines which, to a certain extent, did draw together the small existing film-making concerns.[29] Other proposals included an attack on the well-established American distribution practices of block and blind booking but the major discussion centred upon the idea of a compulsory quota for British films to be imposed upon distributors and cinema owners. The model for this was Germany with its 'Kontingent' arrangements whereby each imported film had to be matched by a German-produced film. Yet this was probably the least favoured option at the time. *Kine Weekly* suggested that the international financial system would not tolerate trade restrictions between Britain and America. As the paper argued 'both British and American "high finance" have stood for trade moves in Germany which would not have been accepted so quietly in the case of a stabilised country'.[30] Leading figures in the film industry such as C.M. Woolf and Michael Balcon were either downright hostile to the idea of a quota or sceptical about its impact on the quality of production. The exhibition sector, which had little to gain from an increase in the number of British films, was also opposed to a quota system. It had been pointed out in the House of Lords debate that the exhibition sector was doubtful about the appeal of British films and would resent having to construct their programmes in the coercive context of a quota system. Indeed, the exhibitors' view was that 'American films secured their predominant position by public choice, and are maintained in it by public approval'.[31] Any threat to this situation was perceived as a threat to the prosperity of the exhibition sector which had been built up on a steady unrestricted supply of American films. A further airing of the problems of British production was given at the Imperial Conference in 1926 which expressed interest in the idea of a market within the Empire for British films. It was suggested that such a market would put the British production industry on a par with the American by creating a vast 'home' market for British films.

The numerous attempts at voluntary solutions failed, however, and early in 1927 a Bill was introduced by the government. It incorporated a quota provision and was subjected to heavy criticism particularly from the exhibitors. *Kine Weekly*, in one issue, published two full pages of letters from the trade most of which attacked the quota provision. Harry Hopkins, a Leeds exhibitor, suggested that the Bill would 'not succeed in producing good British films (which we all want), but just quantity'.[32] A statement by the board of Provincial Cinematograph Theatres, the leading exhibition chain of the day, whilst supporting some aspects of the Bill also warned that they were 'not satisfied that the quota provisions (would) secure the establishment of a successful British film producing industry'.[33] *Kine Weekly* also printed a lengthy statement by Robert Lieber, President of the American company First National, which predicted the development of the 'quota quickie' — the cheap film made purely to satisfy quota requirements — as a result of the Bill, an opinion based upon the experience of the German 'Kontingent' legislation earlier in the decade. The renter-producer Sir Oswald Stoll declared that 'the bill was not British'[34] but it began to wend its way through Parliament despite the dire predictions about its relevance to British cinema. Nine months passed before it left the House of Commons and after a briefer passage through the Upper Chamber, the Cinematograph Films Bill became law in December 1927.

The Act had a number of provisions. These included requirements that films be registered with the Board of Trade before they could be offered for hire and that films had to be screened for the trade before they could be so registered. It also restricted the advance booking of films to six months. These measures meant that the system of blind and block booking was checked. As these were the particular trade practices which many thought were responsible for the decline of the British film, their removal was welcomed as a stimulus to domestic production. The Act also provided for the much-resisted compulsory quota of British films for distributors and exhibitors. Distributors were obliged to ensure that at least $7^1/_2$ per cent of their annual offering was of British origin whilst exhibitors were required to ensure that at least 5 per cent of their annual programme consisted of British films. Both quotas were to be increased by stages to 20 per cent by 1936. The quota provision, as we have seen, was the least popular of the measures introduced and the low starting figure together with the built-in gradualism undoubtedly reflected the efforts of the anti-quota lobby. The terms of the Act also specified that for a film to be registered as British for quota purposes 'the author of the scenario had to be a British subject, the studio scenes had to be filmed in a studio in the British Empire, and at least 70 per cent of the labour costs of the film had to be paid to British subjects'.[35]

A New British Film Industry

The Act required the rapid development of a British cinema yet the production infrastructure of the 1920s with its small concerns and its pre-war attitudes was not capable of meeting the new and increased demand for British films. A new infrastructure was necessary to meet the demands of the quota system, a production system capable of providing a regular output of British films on a volume basis. In 1926, as has been noted, British producers failed to provide even 5 per cent of the total of films released and the Act required an immediate increase on that figure to $7^1/_2$ per cent with further increases to come. The industrial configuration that emerged to meet the demands of the Act resembled the developing American film industry in which a small number of firms combining interests in all three branches of the industry — film production, distribution and exhibition — eventually came to dominate the industry. Concerns such as Paramount/Famous Players and Loews/MGM were already fully integrated giants by the mid-1920s and they set the pattern for the development of the other large American companies such as Fox, Warner Brothers and RKO. Such developments combined a number of ingredients necessary for the successful operation of a film company involved in the mass production of films on a regular basis. The key element was theatre holdings, cinema circuits which provided the production wing with a guaranteed outlet for its films. More importantly, perhaps, theatre holdings meant property and this provided collateral for the raising of finance for production and further theatre acquisition. Film production by itself was a risky business but a company with extensive property holdings in the form of cinema and studio sites could be considered less of a risk by banks and finance companies. In the context of a guaranteed market for British films it is perhaps not surprising that the late 1920s saw the development of vertically integrated companies with substantial backing from orthodox capital sources and a redrawing of the structure of the British film industry along American lines. Two large companies emerged out of a mixture of new companies and existing concerns and these were to dominate the British film industry during the ten-year life of the 1927 Act until the rise of the Rank Organisation brought about a new pattern of ownership and control which was to dominate the British cinema in the following decade.

The first of the two new companies was the Gaumont British Picture Corporation which was registered as a public company in March, 1927. Gaumont British merged a number of operations from all branches of the industry into a substantial single concern. The name itself was taken from the Gaumont company, a long established firm dating back to 1898 when it was set up to distribute films made by the French parent company. At the time of the merger, Gaumont was the fourth-largest distributor in the country and, in addition, had long-standing interests in production including studios at Shepherd's Bush which had recently been modernised and improved. Two further distribution companies, Ideal Films and W & F Film Service, were also part of the merger and together these three constituted the largest distribution concern in the country. In 1926 the three companies between them had offered 112 films for hire compared to the 64 films offered by the leading distributor of the year, the Famous-Lasky wing of Paramount Pictures.[36] The exhibition part of the company consisted of the Biocolour and Davis Pavilion circuits although the company rapidly expanded its exhibition interests in the late 1920s, obtaining control of the Provincial Cinematograph Theatres company, the largest of the British circuits, in 1929. The Gaumont production concern was augmented in 1928 when Michael Balcon's Gainsborough Pictures was put on a public footing and drawn into the combine. This gave the company a production capacity of around 18 films per year and laid the base for their ambitious production policies of the 1930s. The financial anchorage for this group of companies was a city finance group which included the merchant banking house of the Ostrer Brothers. The Ostrer Brothers had been involved in the film industry since the early 1920s when they acquired the Gaumont Company in alliance with A.C. Bromhead who was the British manager of the company. It was this finance group which then bought the Biocolour circuit and amalgamated it with the production and distribution concerns of Gaumont to produce the first vertically integrated film company in the history of the British film industry.

The second combine to emerge in the wake of the Quota Act was British International Pictures (later to become the Associated British Picture Corporation in 1933). Its origins were in a company called British National which was set up in 1926 by an American, J.D. Williams in association with a Scottish solicitor named John Maxwell. Williams had co-founded the important First National Exhibitors' circuit in America and had come to Britain intent upon rationalising the fragmented British production industry by creating a large-scale concern. His plans had some affinities with the plans for a national studio put forward by T. Welsh and others. The outcome of his activities was the setting up of British National which involved a lavish plan to construct an expensive modern studio complex at Elstree which would be a British equivalent of Hollywood. Williams quarrelled with his backers and was ousted from British National in 1927 and Maxwell, who had started his own small production concern, took over British National and brought the second large integrated combine into being. An article in the trade press in April 1927 announced the plans and ambitions of the new company including an expanded production programme that would rise to twenty features per year, plans for improving the Elstree studio site, and the signing up of several prominent film makers and players including Sydney Chaplin, brother of Charles and a popular star in America in the 1920s.[37] The British National company had already signed up the young Alfred Hitchcock and he too became part of the production plans of the new company. Maxwell's company together with the Gaumont British combine were to dominate British production for the next ten years or so and their development, which echoed the American pattern, can also be seen as part of the general tendency towards the formation of large corporations in the economy as a whole.

Despite their size, however, the combined production capacity of the two companies would not have been sufficient to meet the needs of an expanding British cinema particularly in the 1930s when the quota was designed to reach 20 per cent. A variety of other companies organised on a more modest scale moved into the space left by the 'majors' and although some of these came and went rather quickly, a number are worth mentioning as important contributors to the kind of cinema that the Quota Act produced. Whilst some of the new companies that emerged in the late 1920s and early 1930s were ambitious, a number were rather more opportunistic and sought simply to exploit the assurance of a British market by producing low budget 'quota quickies' for American companies to distribute as their quota requirement. Some of the American majors such as Warner Brothers and Fox did set up production companies in Britain to produce their quota pictures but the others were content to use the films made by the numerous small British companies which came and went during the period, or to use the services of the more prestigious British companies such as British International which also offered 'quota quickies'.

Three of the smaller concerns stand out as making a significant contribution to the profile of the British cinema in the 1930s. London Film Productions, the British and Dominions Film Corporation and Associated Talking Pictures, whilst lacking the overall resources of the giant concerns nevertheless made their mark on the film world of the 1930s. In terms of impact, the most important of the three was undoubtedly London Film

47

Productions which was run by the Hungarian-born film maker Alexander Korda, later to be knighted for his contribution to British cinema. Korda, indeed, is frequently regarded as the most important influence in the British cinema of the 1930s, shaping its character and determining the extent of its ambition. The penetration of the American market was seen as necessary for the British film industry from the early 1920s onwards but it was not until Korda's film *The Private Life of Henry VIII* (1933) that this seemed possible. The film was a considerable success both in Britain and America and the lesson derived from this was that British films, if ambitiously conceived and lavishly financed, could conquer the all-important American market. It has been suggested that the film changed the course of the British cinema and opened the door to large scale British production of quality feature films as opposed to the quota production of the preceding years.

Korda had worked as a director and producer in his native Hungary before joining the European exodus to Hollywood in the 1920s. He was not a great success in Hollywood, however, and he came to Britain in 1931 to direct quota pictures for Paramount. His ambitions outstripped such a menial function, and with *The Private Life of Henry VIII* he embarked upon a programme of big budget 'prestige' films aimed at the American market. The film had a declared production expenditure of £60,000 although it has been suggested that the actual figure was higher when salary deferments and participating interests were taken into account.[38] The film grossed half a million pounds on its first release and its success, as well as providing an example for other film makers, enabled Korda to attract financial backing from the Prudential Assurance Company. The result of this was a new complex of well-equipped studios at Denham. The film was the initial impetus for a sustained period of production by the Korda company either on its own or in alliance with other British companies. During the period under consideration Korda's company produced in excess of forty films many of which were directed by important foreign film makers such as René Clair and Jacques Feyder.

The second significant 'independent' company of the interwar period was the British and Dominions Film Corporation set up by the producer/director Herbert Wilcox. Wilcox was briefly associated with J.D. Williams, the American producer, and his 'British Hollywood' plans in the 1920s, and although the liason was ill-fated it does indicate the kind of ambition that marked Wilcox out from the old-fashioned producers of the time. Wilcox had made a film, *Nell Gwyn* (1926) which featured the American star Dorothy Gish, and on the strength of this had been signed by Williams to direct three more pictures with the star. Williams, who had formed his company, British National, to 'secure the advantages of large-scale operation for British production'[39] also planned to construct a 'British Hollywood' at Elstree and Wilcox was also closely involved in this ambitious attempt to provide British film makers with a range of studio facilities comparable to those in America. In addition to this, Wilcox also claims that he was involved in signing Alfred Hitchcock, the most promising young director in the country, for British National.[40] Wilcox left the company in 1927 as it became absorbed into the growing British International Pictures combine, and it was then that he set up his own British and Dominions Film Corporation together with his brother and the actor Nelson Keys. During the 1930s the company was closely associated with Paramount Pictures and almost half their annual output of films was designed to fulfil the quota requirements of the American major. Apart from quota production, British and Dominions produced a number of 'quality' pictures including many which starred Anna Neagle, usually directed by Wilcox himself, and a number of the screen versions of the popular Whitehall farces starring the comedian Tom Walls. Wilcox left the company in the mid-1930s. It was taken over by C.M. Woolf who had left Gaumont British in 1935, and subsequently it became part of the embryonic Rank empire.

The third company worth noting was Associated Talking Pictures which was formed in 1929 by the theatre impresario Basil Dean and the actor Gerald du Maurier. The company was very much a product of the newly developed sound picture and its basic intention at its studios in Ealing was to make transcriptions of worthwhile theatrical productions and literary works in the new medium. These lofty ambitions were fulfilled in some of the company's productions such as *Escape* (Dean, 1930) based on the John Galsworthy play, and films such as *Lorna Doone* (Dean, 1935) and *Three Men in a Boat* (Cutts, 1933) suggest the middlebrow literary and artistic aspirations of the studio. However, the realities of the company's main activity were somewhat more prosaic and down to earth. Like many British companies, they were involved in quota production and had a link up with one of the American majors, RKO. The major distinction of the studio and its greatest success, however, was in the production of 'low' comedies with a series of films based upon music-hall stars such as Gracie Fields and George Formby. It was, in fact, the great success and profitability of stars such as these that kept the company afloat during the 1930s. Dean left the company in 1938 and was replaced by Michael Balcon who steered the company into a new and very successful phase of its history when as Ealing Studios it became an important component of the British cinema of the 1940s and 1950s.

The British production industry of the 1930s was made up of the two majors, a trio of significant smaller companies, quota companies set up by American companies such as Fox and Warners, together with numerous little companies some of which had brief existences whilst some such as British Lion, Twickenham and Butchers had longer and more productive lives. However, this apparent diversity is undermined by the fact that most of the companies were either linked in one way or another to one of the two major combines, or to the large American companies. Even significant minor companies such as London Films and British and Dominions were linked to the British subsidiary of United Artists. The question of ownership and control of the British film industry is important in respect of the type of cinema produced and during the period under examination it is clear that orthodox capital from city finance houses and insurance companies was a crucial factor in the production boom of the mid-1930s. Although most discussions of the cinema of the period revolve around the leading producers such as Balcon, Korda, Maxwell and so on, it is important to note that their efforts were based upon the financial backing of the city or on the resources of the large American firms. Prior to the rapid expansion of the production industry in the late 1920s, the industry was characterised by small scale entrepreneurial activity in which there was little need to attract large amounts of capital. There were few large cinema circuits, the majority of exhibitor concerns being one or two theatre companies, and distribution did not really require large-scale financial backing. There is a parallel here between the film industry and British industry in general which before the First World War 'succeeded in financing its own expansion by ploughing back profits or tapping local resources'.[41] The 1920s saw an increase in the supply of finance for British industry from companies established specially for that purpose such as investment trusts or from the expanding funds of the building societies and the insurance companies. These latter institutions were the beneficiaries of the rising disposable incomes of middle class people during the interwar period and the increased popularity of saving. The film industry with its increased need for capital investment after the 1927 Act benefited from the increase in investment funds available especially during the mid-1930s and the production boom which occurred in the wake of the success of *The Private Life of Henry VIII*.

The American involvement with the British film industry was not confined to the wholly-owned subsidiaries producing quota pictures or the United Artists' links with Korda and others. Gaumont British was controlled by the Metropolis and Bradford Trust company, a private firm owned partly by the Ostrer Brothers and partly by the American major, the Twentieth Century-Fox Corporation. In the late 1920s William Fox, who had built the foundations of the company, had acquired shares in the controlling trust as part of his plan to dominate the film industries of both America and Britain. Although Fox lost control of his company after the Wall Street crash of 1929, the American connection remained as a forcible reminder that Hollywood was closely involved in the British film industry not only through its strong distribution position, as had been the case in the 1920s, but also through part ownership of what were ostensibly British concerns and not American subsidiaries. The visible tokens of this American influence were the presence on the Gaumont British board of Sidney Kent, chairman of Twentieth Century-Fox, together with representatives from the American company's British bankers. By comparison, the other British major does not seem to have fallen under American influence in quite the same way. The largest single block of ordinary shares in British International Pictures was owned by John Maxwell and his associates, yet in other ways the company reflected American influence and tailored its production policies to the requirements of the powerful American distributors. Despite the massive injection of capital into production in the late 1920s, and despite the importation of foreign talent and the presence at the studio of important British film makers such as Hitchcock, the company gradually based its output on the 'quota quickie' and the low budget production. Such a policy offered the guarantee of a steady income compared with the risks involved in quality production aimed at competition with the American companies. Gaumont British, under the production supervision of Michael Balcon, had opted for quality production whilst Maxwell's company — 'the businessman's studio' — chose to specialise in the safer, more predictable area of low and modest budget films. In strictly business terms, it can be suggested that Maxwell's course was the correct one. Gaumont British paid an annual dividend to ordinary shareholders of around 6 per cent during the early 1930s compared to the 10 and 12 per cent paid by the then renamed Associated British Picture Corporation in 1935 and 1936 respectively. In fact, in 1936 Gaumont British ran into severe financial problems, and their failure to declare an ordinary dividend led to a revolt of the shareholders. The company was revealed to have an unsound liquid position with assets of £921,755 (excluding the value of films in the process of production) to set against liabilities to creditors and bank overdrafts of £2,626,189.[42]

The Course of Production

The 1927 Act was designed to provide a stimulus to British production and to lay the foundations of a domestic film industry which would eventually function successfully without the need for legislative protection. In terms of stimulating indigenous production, the Act was a success and the catastrophic production statistics of 1926 when a mere 34 British films were screened to the trade were soon consigned to memory. Volume production of British films can be said to have been well established by 1930 when over 100 British films were trade shown and the middle years of the decade saw the boom in production following the international success of the Korda pictures. The early years of the Quota Act coincided with the arrival of the sound picture and the various companies that had been formed to take advantage of the quota provisions found themselves confronted with a dual task. They were faced with the problems of gearing up to volume production and all that was involved in the way of acquiring creative and technical personnel, studio space, equipment and so on, and at the same time, they were faced with the novel demands of sound technology and aesthetics. This imposed a considerable burden on the nascent industry but by 1930 it had settled into a pattern of production which was to increase dramatically as the decade progressed. The 1927 Act had provided for a quota of 20 per cent British feature films to be achieved by the mid-1930s but this figure was actually reached in 1932. In fact, by 1936, almost 30 per cent of the feature films registered for quota purposes were of British origin and the 218 features produced that year indicate quite dramatically the progress that the industry had made since the dismal years of the mid-1920s. The value of production in 1937 was in excess of £7 million compared to the modest figure of £500,000 in 1928. The Klingender and Legg analysis of the industry demonstrated the extent to which the money moving into the film industry increased during the 1930s. In 1931, 201 new companies were registered with a total nominal capital of £972,600 but in 1936, 395 companies were registered with a total nominal capital of nearly £16 million.[43] The advances made by the industry can also be charted by the developments in studio building during the decade. The engine room of the production surge in the mid-1930s was located in the studios of the powerful combines. The Associated British Picture Corporation (BIP) was based at Elstree in the 'embryonic Hollywood' established by J.D. Williams and Gaumont was based at Shepherd's Bush, which was modernised in 1931, and Islington. These were supplemented in the 1930s by Korda's elaborate studio complex at Denham and by the building of Pinewood Studios by Rank in 1936. In terms of production capacity the development was dramatic. In 1928 there were 19 stages in British studios with a total area of 105,200 square feet but after the studio-building activity of 1935-37 this had increased to 70 sound stages and 777,650 square feet, a fourfold increase in the number of stages and a sevenfold increase in floor space.[44]

So far, the discussion of British films of the period has been confined to the statistical indications of health such as are contained in the increase in the number of films produced, the finance flowing into the industry and the expansion of studio provision. Although the character of the cinema produced by these striking statistics is the subject of a later chapter, some general comments on the kind of cinema produced are relevant here and contribute towards an understanding of the crisis that overtook the industry from 1936 onwards. In particular, attention needs to be paid to the notorious 'quota quickie' that many commentators on the period have seen as the most unfortunate effect of the protective legislation. This is made clear in the following passage from the report of the Moyne Committee set up by the government in 1936 to examine the operation of the Act and its effects on the British film industry:

> It was admitted, however, even by the renters themselves, that in recent years the spirit of the Act has not, speaking generally, been given effect. In order to satisfy the renters' quota, the majority of foreign controlled renters appear to have made arrangements for the production of British films at the minimum of expense regardless of quality. Such films were not in a position to attract exhibitors, save in so far as they needed films to satisfy their quota, and indeed they were not, in the main, worthy of exhibition.[45]

The expansion of British production had been achieved, but at the expense of quality, for the powerful American distributors had simply commissioned cheaply made pictures from the numerous small companies which had sprung up in response to the Act, or from directly controlled subsidiaries. The quota requirements were simply expressed in terms of footage with no reference to the quality of the product and there were many companies that were willing to supply 'quota quickies' including Maxwell's Associated British Picture Corporation.

The situation in Britain during the early 1930s had something in common with that in Hollywood during the same period. The rise of the double feature programme in American cinemas led to the formation of a number of small independent companies which were neither owned nor directly controlled by the majors. Companies such as Monogram, Republic, Majestic and Tiffany managed through the 1930s to establish concerns which had some degree of financial viability on the basis of supplying a steady flow of cheaply produced B pictures to fill the lower half of the double bill programme. There was a degree of financial stability about specialising in low budget production because unlike the A picture which was on a percentage of the box-office receipts 'the bottom half picture played for a flat (fixed) rental. Since the rental wasn't based on attendance or popularity, the producer could predict with great accuracy how much he would take in on each B picture'.[46] However, the major difference between the American B picture industry and the British 'quota quickie' industry was that the prestige and influence of British cinema depended upon the quality of such production whereas Hollywood's B films were a marginal form of production. The equivalent of the Hollywood A picture in Britain was confined to a small number of films produced by the larger well resourced companies prior to the 'Korda revolution' in 1933. After this many producers reorientated their production policies towards the international prestige production aimed principally at the American market. The PEP report on the industry referred to 1933 as 'the cross-roads for the British industry' and went on to suggest:

> It could stick to 'quota quickies' and have a reasonable chance of finding enough money for a continuity of employment on a restrained scale; or else it could try to make films for a world market, in which case it would become dependent on the confidence of the financial world. Theoretically there might be a third path. The industry might be able to make 'quality' films which were not so expensive as to demand high overseas earnings.[47]

The success of *The Private Life of Henry VIII* was taken as the example by the industry and a wave of prestige production was embarked upon. The vogue for 'big pictures' swept through the industry and even the practical and cautious Associated British Picture Corporation expressed an interest in this change of direction. Writing in 1935 in *Kine Weekly*, Arthur Dent, managing director of the company's distribution arm, commented that 'the future of the business lies in big pictures produced on a lavish scale, with outstanding casts and exploitation possibilities'.[48] Gaumont British had already set out on the 'internationalist' path and had established a strategy of using American stars as selling points for the films in the American market. The success of the Korda film had opened the way for a massive increase in the flow of orthodox financial capital to the film industry but the precarious nature of the expansion in production and the fragility of the assumptions on which it was built led to the crisis of 1937. Although some British firms did good business in America, the majority did not and the British domestic market, although guaranteed, was too small to provide an adequate return on the capital invested in the production boom. The expansion was primarily loan-financed by investment trusts and insurance companies with inflated expectations of profit. As Klingender and Legg pointed out, the underwriting of the production boom by the investment and insurance companies deviated from normal commercial practice. They commented:

> expansion has with few outstanding exceptions been financed not by increases in the companies' own working capital, but by a spectacular increase in *loans* (whereas in 'normal booms' the actual increase in business usually enables the expanding enterprises largely to liquidate existing loan obligations).[49]

This somewhat slapdash approach to film finance during the period was interpreted in sardonic terms by the PEP report which commented that it 'so happened that during this period the marine market became slack and the underwriters turned their attention to film production which seemed to have proved itself to be a "good risk"'.[50] Such casual involvement with the industry by the insurance brokers was isolated by Sidney Bernstein in his memorandum written in 1939 which reflected on the various reasons for the critical state of the British film industry by the late 1930s. He argued that 'finance for production has usually been found by insurance brokers and financial people without any knowledge of the film industry'.[51] Bernstein went on to cite further reasons such as general incompetence and inflated costs of production and distribution, and the general picture of the industry which emerges from the boom years of the mid-1930s is one of ill-considered opportunism and a failure to understand the power of the American film industry to withstand competition. The 'crash' began in 1937 with the Twickenham Studios, a small but well established company, going into receivership and, shortly after this, Gaumont British announced the closure of its Shepherd's Bush studios as part of a reduced production programme. Other companies also betrayed signs of the crisis but perhaps the most dramatic signal was that the total number of productions for 1938 was less than half the total number of films released in the previous year.[52] Whatever the variety of reasons that may be cited for the failure of the 1927 Act to achieve its objective of establishing a vital and robust British production industry, one clear mistake was the attempt to base the industry on the assumption of access to the international and, particularly, the vast American market. C.M. Woolf, who had left Gaumont British in 1935 to found a new distribution company (General Film Distributors), admitted the failure of the internationalist policies of the mid-1930s, suggesting that 'not only was it a risk to make films for world markets, but an actual liability'.[53] He also pointed out that the British production industry would never get more than a few films into the American market however lavish the production values and however talented the film makers who worked on them.

The crisis in the production industry coincided with the expiry of the 1927 Act which had been intended to establish the industry as a viable concern which would not require continued legislative protection. An editorial in *Kine Weekly* which reflected upon the 'Lessons of the Quota Act' indicates that the problems of the industry were clearly perceptible:

... in this year of Our Lord 1937, what do we see — prosperity on every hand? No. The new era opens up with an inquest. Lord Moyne, chairman of the government commission set up to determine whether or not the Quota Act should be repealed or extended, or the quota percentage increased, finds himself in the unenviable position of coroner, and the chief mourners are the big insurance companies, who have never been called upon to pay out on so many corpses, represented by the failure of well-meaning as well as mushroom, production companies.[54]

The Moyne Committee had been set up in 1936 to examine the workings of the Quota Act and it concluded that protection of the industry was necessary for the continued existence of British film production. It recommended the introduction of quotas for short films after lobbying by Grierson and the documentarists and, in an attempt to eradicate the 'quota quickie' which had brought the British cinema into critical disrepute, it recommended the introduction of some form of quality provision in the new legislation. Its other substantial recommendation was the setting up of a body to provide finance for the production industry on a more sensible basis than that of the production boom years of the mid-1930s. After some discussion with the film industry, the government conceded the need for continued legislative protection of production and introduced a new act in 1938 which incorporated some of the recommendations of the Moyne Committee and, in particular, those which related to short films and to the quality of production.

The Cinematograph Films Act of 1927 had certainly established a British film production industry but one which had not found a clear identity for itself. The alternatives which presented themselves to film makers of the period ranged from the cheap quota picture through the modestly budgeted programme picture up to the ambitious and lavishly financed

55

prestige picture aimed at the international film market. Low budget films invited critical contempt whilst the internationalist prestige policy led to an over-reaching by an industry which could never hope to compete systematically with the might and power of Hollywood which based its strength on a home market some four times the size of the British. The third path, mentioned in the PEP report, in which modestly budgeted 'quality' production would cover its costs in the domestic market whilst attracting an international audience did not seem to be available at the time. This latter path concerns an 'art' cinema in which the particularities of indigenous production are exploited in terms of an international conception of 'art' which provides cinema with a specific international target audience. This modest though financially viable path was to provide many European cinemas with an international market during the 1950s and 1960s although in conditions which were rather different from those obtaining in the 1930s. The failure to find such a solution to the problems of the British cinema in the 1930s may be linked to the sociological pattern of British film making of the time in which the 'artistic' aspirations of many of the new recruits to the medium tended to find an outlet in the non-commercial documentary cinema headed by John Grierson. Yet, for all the problems outlined in this account of the troubled years of the 1930s, a cinema of sorts did emerge and its character is examined in the next chapter.

Notes

1. This section draws on a number of standard texts on the interwar period such as E. Hobsbawm, *Industry and Empire* (Penguin Books, Harmondsworth, 1969); S. Pollard, *The Development of the British Economy 1914-1950* 2nd edn (Edward Arnold, London, 1969); A.J.P. Taylor, *English History 1914-1945* (Penguin Books, Harmondsworth, 1970).

2. Pollard, *British Economy*, p. 99.

3. Ibid., p. 101-2.

4. Taylor, *English History*, p. 396.

5. Pollard, *British Economy*, p. 240.

6. N. Branson and M. Heinemann, *Britain in the Nineteen Thirties* (Panther, St. Albans, 1973), pp. 15-16.

7. Hobsbawm, *Industry*, p. 208.

8. Ibid., p. 214.

9. Ibid., p. 217.

10. Ibid., p. 214.

11. *Cinematograph Films Act, 1927 — The Moyne Report* (HMSO, London, 1936), p. 5.

12. Political and Economic Planning (PEP), *The British Film Industry* (PEP, London, 1952), p. 41.

13. T. Guback, 'Hollywood's International Market' in T. Balio (ed.), *The American Film Industry* (University of Wisconsin Press, Wisconsin, 1976), p. 388.

14. See M. Chanan, 'The Emergence of an Industry' in J. Curran and V. Porter (eds), *British Cinema History* (Weidenfeld and Nicolson, London, 1983), p. 49; and *PEP Report*, p. 41.

15. *PEP Report*, p. 41.

16. *The Bioscope*, 7 Feb. 1924, p. 29.

17. Curran and Porter, *British Cinema*, p. 375.

18. Ibid., p. 30.
19. R. Low, *The History of the British Film 1918-1929* (Allen and Unwin, London, 1971), p. 108.
20. *PEP Report*, p. 32.
21. *Kine Weekly*, 16 Aug. 1923, p. 1.
22. Ibid., 5 Jul. 1923, p. 41.
23. Ibid., 15 Jan. 1925, p. 38.
24. S. Tallents, *The Projection of England* (Faber and Faber, London, 1932), p. 39.
25. B. Hampton, *History of the American Film Industry* (Dover, New York, 1970), p. 351.
26. *PEP Report*, p. 43.
27. *Kine Weekly*, 9 Jul. 1925, p. 69.
28. Ibid., 25 Jun. 1925, p. 40.
29. Ibid., 25 Jul. 1925, p. 40.
30. Ibid., 10 Sept. 1925, p. 54.
31. Ibid., 12 Mar. 1925, p. 47.
32. Ibid., 17 Mar. 1927, p. 5.
33. Ibid., 31 Mar. 1927, p. 41.
34. Ibid., 7 Apr. 1927, p. 25.
35. S. Hartog, 'State Protection of a Beleaguered Industry' in Curran and Porter, *British Cinema*, p. 74.
36. *PEP Report*, p. 41.
37. *Kine Weekly*, 14 Apr. 1927, p. 27.
38. *PEP Report*, pp. 68-9.
39. Low, *British Film*, p. 176.
40. H. Wilcox, *Twenty-five Thousand Sunsets* (The Bodley Head, London, 1967), p. 71.
41. Pollard, *British Economy*, p. 232.
42. F. Klingender and S. Legg, *Money Behind the Screen* (Lawrence and Wishart, London, 1937), p. 29.
43. Ibid., p. 53.
44. *PEP Report*, p. 67.
45. *The Moyne Report*, p. 5.
46. T. McCarthy and C. Flynn, *Kings of the Bs* (Dutton, New York, 1975), p. 17.
47. *PEP Report*, p. 69.
48. *Kine Weekly*, 10 Jan. 1935, p. 70.
49. Klingender and Legg, *Money behind the Screen*, p. 54 (emphasis in original).
50. *PEP Report*, p. 69.
51. Ibid., p. 75.
52. Ibid., p. 70.
53. *Kine Weekly*, 7 Jan. 1937, p. 20.
54. Ibid., 14 Jan. 1937, p. 4.

Chapter Four

A British Cinema?
The British Entertainment
Film of the 1930s

The passage of the Cinematograph Films Act of 1927 led to the creation of an industrial and commercial infrastructure for a national cinema in Britain. The quota system and the guaranteed share of the British market for indigenous producers halted the dramatic decline in production which had reached a trough in the mid-1920s. By the mid-1930s Britain had become 'the most important centre of European film production'[1] and, according to Thorold Dickinson, was able to claim 'the second highest national output in the world'.[2] During the ten years that the Act was to be in force, more than 1,600 British films were produced and British directors, players and technicians enjoyed a period of continuous employment. Yet, during the period and subsequently, a substantial consensus has been highly critical of the kind of cinema that actually emerged. The critical dismissal of the British entertainment film of the 1930s has been formulated in a number of ways. It is suggested that the majority of British films produced were of little artistic value and, indeed, many fell into the category of the notorious 'quota quickie'. Even where production was undertaken with loftier and more serious intentions, it was argued that the films produced lacked authentically British qualities and they failed to add up to a distinctively national cinema compared, say, with their French or American counterparts. In addition to this absence of character, many writers and critics have pointed out that British films of the period tended to have little or no contact with the social and political realities of the time either in national or international terms.

The period under scrutiny was a crucial one for the British cinema. The various forces which had lobbied for protection through the quota system, whether motivated by trading and commercial concerns or by matters of art and culture, had a common concern that the British cinema should develop an authentically national identity. But, what actually constitutes 'national cinematic identity'? We have seen, in Chapter 2, that this was a pressing question for the European film producing countries during the 1920s and that film makers in Germany, France and the Soviet Union frequently interpreted identity in terms of artistic divergence from the classical model of narrative cinema which was being defined by the American film. Identity was constructed in relation to the increasingly powerful economic and artistic hegemony of Hollywood and this led to the emergence of the various different European 'art' cinemas of the mature silent period. Such attempts at artistic differentiation were also accompanied, particularly in the Soviet cinema, by constructing national cinemas which concentrated on the representation of national life and ideology and, indeed, it is in this area that the failure of the British cinema of the 1930s has often been located. In the early 1930s, Norman Marshall writing in *The Bookman*, suggested that 'film is a form of art which is fundamentally unsuited to the expression of the English character and temperament'.[3] Now this rather bleak judgement which calls into question the very possibility of a national cinema in Britain has found many an echo in the critical literature of British cinema. Perhaps the most notorious and the most frequently quoted reprise of such a view is to be found in Francois Truffaut's interviews with Hitchcock where he suggests that there is 'a certain incompatibility between the terms "cinema"; and "Britain"'.[4] Dilys Powell, writing about the state of the British cinema at the beginning of the Second World War, took a less extreme view but still suggested that:

there was no tradition of British films as there was a tradition of French ironic drama or a tradition of American fast comedy. The national characteristics of the British, whether good or bad, had not been infused into a national cinema.[5]

It was not a question of the fundamental impossibility of a British cinema of national identity but it had not happened in the prolific production years of the 1930s. Other writers, however, suggested that certain national characteristics had been 'infused' into certain British films but what had emerged was a highly selective and distorted representation of British life which ignored vast areas of the national experience. As an editorial in *World Film News* put it:

The English film, when it can drag itself away from Plymouth Hoe and Hampton Court and Malplaquet, and when it can forget 1588 and 1815, things to come, and all that, totters only so far as Piccadilly or St. James's, or country houses with forty bedrooms situated in what always looks like Hampshire.[6]

Russell Ferguson, writing in the same journal, continued the same point somewhat satirically when he suggested that the films which came out of Shepherd's Bush, Elstree and Denham presented Britain in the 1930s as 'a nation of retired businessmen, mill owners, radio singers, actors, detectives, newspapermen, leading ladies, soldiers, secret servicemen, crooks, smugglers and international jewel thieves'.[7] According to the British cinema of the period the British people did not 'work in coal pits or fishing boats or shops or shipyards or iron foundries'[8] nor were they 'bothered with unemployment, malnutrition, distressed areas, disease or poverty'.[9] The quest for a national cinematic identity failed because the films that were made during the years of mass production offered a highly restricted iconography of British life that ignored the lives of the ordinary working people who, of course, constituted the bulk of the audience for the cinema during the 1930s. Walter Allen, in a later survey of mass entertainment during the 1930s, suggested that the cinema was 'trivial' in that it avoided the representation of ordinary social reality. As he put it:

> What was wrong with British films of the time? The short answer seems to be the triviality that one is tempted to think the besetting sin of the British industry from its earliest days to the present, the triviality that comes from the failure to mirror the observed facts of English life.[10]

'Triviality' and the 'escapism' implied in many of the comments on British 1930s cinema, are familiar criticisms of entertainment in general and entertainment cinemas in particular. Such criticisms were also levelled at the American cinema of the time yet many critics saw in the Hollywood film, or in some of them at any rate, a greater authenticity and a closer contact with ordinary life, when set against their British counterparts. The *World Film News* editorial previously quoted began with the claim that the American cinema 'has evolved a whole class of films which has no parallel in England — films which tell stories, plain or coloured, of ordinary working people'.[11] Even John Grierson, from the serious, somewhat moralistic, perspective of the documentary movement, drew attention to the 'powerful contact with American life which gives the American cinema its character, its vitality and its capacity to travel'.[12] He went on to lament that 'British films have not reflected the British life to anything like the same extent. Even the occasional choice of patriotic themes has not disguised a lack of really intimate contact with the national idiom.'[13] The British cinema had failed to establish a specific identity which would differentiate its films from those of the American cinema in formal and stylistic terms. British films had not developed along the lines of the major European 'art' cinemas, although it has been argued that such developments did take place in the documentary movement which produced a British 'art' cinema.[14] Its popular entertainment cinema was modelled on Hollywood lines yet it failed to establish that 'contact with the national idiom' which might have provided British films with an alternative identity.

Foreign Influences

The international dimensions of the British film industry have a history almost as long as the history of British film itself. The Gaumont Company which was later to become part of the Gaumont British integrated combine, was originally set up in 1898 as a branch of the French parent company by A.C. Bromhead and T. Welsh to sell French films and equipment. The subsequent history of foreign involvement with the British film industry at the institutional level, however, is concerned with the American film industry although account must be taken of the many continental European film makers, producers, players and technical personnel who began to work in the British cinema especially from the late 1920s onwards. The influence of the American cinema can be thought of in two ways. Firstly, even during the heyday of British production in the mid-1930s, Hollywood provided the vast majority of films that appeared in British cinemas, some 70 per cent of the total. The public image of cinema was formed primarily on the basis of American films in the absence of strong and substantial traditions in the British film. Secondly, through the establishment of production companies in Britain, through financial investment in major British companies and through a variety of co-production and distribution deals, the American film industry was quite explicitly involved with the course of the British cinema during the crucial formative years of the 1930s.

During the 1920s, as we have seen[15], the American giant Paramount had established a production company with studios at Islington. Although they were to pull out after a year or two, they had established production facilities based on American experience and knowledge and using the latest American cinema technology and equipment. This provided a number of British film workers with the opportunity to learn from American methods of production and one of these was, of course, Alfred Hitchcock, who had joined the company as a title illustrator in 1920. This American designed production base subsequently wove itself into the history of British production in a quite substantial manner. The studio was sold in 1924 to Michael Balcon and his associates and an indigenous company thus acquired an up-to-date studio facility equipped with the latest American cameras and lighting equipment. This was significant in the context of the rather out-of-date attitudes which prevailed amongst many of the pre-war figures still active in the British film industry and working on the basis of antiquated pre-war assumptions about production values. Studios were to be re-equipped and refurbished and purpose-built from scratch later in the decade but Balcon's Gainsborough company had acquired a head start in the industry through its acquisition of Islington and it played an increasingly important role in the development of the British cinema over the following 20 years or so. Balcon, himself, from the start of his career as an entertainment film producer, had indicated an ambition to make films for an international and particularly an American audience. His first feature film, *Woman to Woman* (Cutts, 1923), featured an American star actress, Betty Compson, who had been imported from Hollywood at great expense to play the lead character. Indeed, many of Balcon's early films featured American players because Balcon realised that well known names were a vital element in the commercial success of a picture and were important in terms of the international circulation of films. There was a strong economic impetus to Balcon's internationalist perspective and it was seen as a solution to the problem of obtaining film finance during the problem years of the British film industry during the pre-quota act period.

Balcon's internationalist policies were not confined to involvement with Hollywood, however, and towards the middle of the 1920s he developed strong links with the increasingly important German film industry. There was a precedent for Anglo-German co-operation in the Herbert Wilcox film version of *Chu Chin Chow*, the enormously successful stage play. Wilcox had secured a deal which enabled him to produce the film at the UFA studios in Berlin and, as part of the deal, his company had agreed to handle the British distribution of the Fritz Lang film, *Die Nibelungen* (1924). Following Wilcox's example, Balcon set up a number of co-production deals with UFA, the leading German company of the time, drawing into the arrangement W & F Film Service, a prominent British distribution company. The German company was to provide the finance and studio facilities for each production whilst Balcon's Gainsborough Company was responsible for providing the production personnel with the W & F concern handling distribution in the English speaking market. It was in the course of this particular arrangement that Hitchcock was to make his directorial debut working on *The Pleasure Garden* and *The Mountain Eagle* in the UFA studios at Munich. Later, when the Gainsborough company became part of the Gaumont British combine in the late 1920s, Balcon was again to involve himself in co-production arrangements in both Europe and Hollywood. The arrival of sound had led to many joint arrangements to facilitate the production of films in different language versions and this led Balcon into further agreements with UFA in particular. Under such agreements films were to be produced in two or even three different language versions utilising the same scenario, technical staff and studio facilities but changing the players and, if necessary, the director for each different version. This meant that British players and technical personnel gained experience of working in continental studios in addition to coming into contact with foreign personnel in Britain itself. Also, during the 1930s, Balcon was to arrange co-production deals with the minor American company, Tiffany, and out of this came films such as a second version of *Woman to Woman* (Saville, 1929) and *Journey's End* (Whale, 1930) adapted from the successful West End play. Balcon's experience in dealing with companies on an international basis undoubtedly contributed to his appointment as head of production for the MGM British company which was set up in 1936 to make MGM films in Britain. However, this venture was not a success from Balcon's point of view and he left the company after the production of its first film *A Yank at Oxford* (Conway, 1938). Many other producers including Herbert Wilcox and Victor Saville and companies such as British International Pictures also worked under international co-production arrangements during the 1930s.

Although the Quota Act was designed to ensure that the British cinema was, in the words of a contemporary commentator, 'under the creative control of British people'[16], a 'British film' was defined by the 1927 legislation in such a way as to allow a certain percentage of the labour costs on a film to be spent on foreign personnel. Most significantly, from the point of view of the shape and character of a film, the legislation permitted the salary costs of one player or the producer to be excluded from the budget which determined whether a film was British or not. This meant that a substantial sum could be spent on hiring an important star or producer from overseas and although such a person might have played a significant role in determining the identity of the film, it would still count as 'British' for quota purposes. Arrangements such as this were possibly necessary loopholes in the Act because of the parlous state of the British production industry in the 1920s. There was a severe shortage of indigenous production personnel at every level yet the Act required the British film industry to expand its production from the low levels of the mid-1920s to the sustained consistency of a volume production industry. Such an expansion of the industry was not possible without the participation of film makers and technical personnel drawn from the better developed film industries of Europe and America.

In fact, the major American film companies, all of whom had distribution agencies in Britain, were obliged by the Act to offer a percentage of 'British' films for rent in addition to the Hollywood-made films that were their primary reason for being in Britain. This meant that much of the expansion of the British production industry was intimately connected to the American film industry. Some of the American majors followed in the footsteps of Paramount in the early twenties and set up production companies managed largely by American personnel. Warner Brothers established a studio at Teddington in the early thirties and Twentieth Century-Fox set up a production base at Wembley, and Paramount itself renewed its British connection and once again set up a British production base. Other American companies did not set up production companies in Britain but chose to commission their quota requirements from the major British producers or from the numerous small companies which sprang up during the years following the Quota Act. Most of the films made by the American companies or by British companies on behalf of the Americans, fell into the 'quota quickie' category yet the enterprise did, at least, provide an opportunity for aspirant British film makers to learn their craft from experienced American film makers in quite exacting conditions. As director Adrian Brunel has pointed out, it was in the much despised sphere of 'quota quickie' production that 'many technicians and artists got continuity of employment for the first time and became expert performers in their various fields, a number of them graduating to big production'.[17] Indeed, such significant contributors to the subsequent development of the British cinema as Alexander Korda, Michael Powell and Sidney Gilliat worked in this heavily criticised area of film production during the 1930s.

It was not just in the context of low budget production that the foreign influence made itself felt in the British film industry. Alexander Korda, the Hungarian director-producer, although initially working as a 'quota quickie' producer for Paramount, soon moved into the sphere of prestige production with the setting up of London Films. He was able to attract many distinguished foreign film makers to his studio including major directors such as René Clair, Jacques Feyder, Robert Flaherty and Josef Von Sternberg, the producer Erich Pommer, cinematographers such as Charles Rosher, Harry Stradling and James Wong Howe, and stars such as Marlene Dietrich. Such figures constituted a formidable array of international talent and experience, a pool of sophisticated expertise from which British film makers could learn. They were also an important means of access to the international, particularly American film market, the conquest of which was an important ambition of the British film industry during this period. Korda's London Films was an extremely cosmopolitan studio which built its production around the importation of internationally known and recognised directors, technicians and stars but the policy of using international talent was not confined to his company. British International Pictures during its expansionary phase in the late 1920s also avidly pursued a similar policy and recruited directors such as E.A. Dupont and Arthur Robison who had made important contributions to the prestigious German cinema of the 1920s. When Michael Balcon assumed control of production at Gaumont British, he too pursued an internationalist policy, using American stars and directors to provide his films with an appeal for the American audience. However, it has been argued that neither of the two large combines really succeeded with such a policy of utilising international talent. BIP gradually abandoned its prestige production and drifted into a policy of modest to 'quota quickie' level budgeting in order to concentrate on programme films for the domestic market. In itself, such a policy shift may well be a reflection of the failure of its 'international big name' approach of the late twenties. Rachael Low has argued that the foreign film makers who arrived at Elstree in the late 1920s included some film makers who were 'already past their peak' or those who were 'unable to do their best work after transplantation'.[18]

The policy fared equally badly at Gaumont British although Balcon had a somewhat clearer focus on the reasons for using Americans, which had to do with getting British films into the American market. As Balcon himself has written:

> We had brought over Richard Dix, Edmund Lowe, Constance Bennett, Sylvia Sidney, George Arliss, Paul Robeson, Madge Evans, Robert Young — all good 'names' at the time — and we had employed American directors — Raoul Walsh, Chuck Reisner and William Beaudine. I am sure that these were mistaken decisions artistically, and financially they were unrewarding.[19]

Again, as with BIP, the problem seemed to lie in 'transplantation' with players and directors of proven worth in the context of Hollywood being unable to function successfully at Shepherd's Bush and Islington. P.L. Mannock, the studio correspondent of *Kine Weekly*, wrote that it was 'a disconcerting fact that, as a whole, the work of Hollywood directors and stars in this country has been markedly inferior to their work in California'.[20] Although it was not the case that a director such as Raoul Walsh was past his peak when working for Gaumont British, it has been suggested that many of the technical staff imported from the American cinema were, in fact, 'second-graders, men who weren't good enough for Hollywood itself'.[21] The influx of foreigners during the decade was considerable enough to occasion a variety of somewhat xenophobic articles in the trade press towards the end of the decade. An article in *World Film News* of September 1937 sketched the contours of the British cinema in terms of the numerous people from overseas who occupied key positions in many of the leading British film companies. It concluded that 'our British cinema, at the outset of its second decade of life, will be dependent for its prestige upon a large number of foreign gentlemen'.[22] The article cited a lengthy list of international figures including Douglas Fairbanks Jr, the Kordas, Joe Schenck and even Herbert Wilcox who was, in fact, an Irishman, and it ended with the following somewhat ironical statement:

> On these gentlemen and their creative attitude to our English industries, our countryside, our people ... we depend for the projection of our national life. On their deep, inborn sense of our history, our heritage and our customs we depend for the dramatisation of our English traditions as well as for the more mundane business of fulfilling our British quota.[23]

An anonymous technician writing in the same journal was rather more forthright and he condemned 'the easy, weak policy of looking abroad for established talent'[24] which, the writer suggested, inflicted a double blow to the British cinema:

> One of the worst aspects of the policy of trying to break into the world market before conquering your own is that the preponderance of aliens in key positions in the industry not only tends to produce a product lacking national character, but also develops an unhealthy inferiority complex in the rest of the technical staff who are of local growth.[25]

The failure of the British cinema of the thirties to achieve an authentically national status and identity can be linked to the presence of so many foreigners working in a cinema which either addressed itself to an international audience or was concerned with turning films out on a low budget assembly line basis to meet the quota requirements of the big American companies. Yet Hollywood, during the same period, also saw an influx of foreign directors, stars and technicians with rather different results.

Indeed, it has to be argued that such an influx contributed positively to the creative diversity of the American cinema and that certain key Hollywood genres owe a lot to the presence of the emigrés. Examples of the beneficial effects of the European transplantation would include Ernst Lubitsch and the sophisticated comedy, and the numerous German directors and technicians who contributed to the horror film in the 1930s and the *film noir* genre in the 1940s. Hollywood succeeded in harnessing international talent to produce a distinctively national cinema whereas Britain did not. P.L. Mannock suggested that the problems lay with the structure and organisation of the British film industry. There were talented directors and stars available to British film makers in the thirties but 'good films are made by the careful planning of competent, experienced organisations, and not by directors or stars'.[26] Mannock's view was that the British cinema failed through managerial inability and inexperience.

Theatre and Cinema

In one sense the most dramatic interrelationship between the cinema and the theatre during the interwar period concerns the conquest of the older respectable cultural form by the new technological medium. The cinema had moved into a dominant position in the field of entertainment and leisure and the theatres of both the middle and working classes fell before it. As historian A.J.P. Taylor put it:

> The music halls were worst hit. Outside London, nearly all closed their doors ... Provincial theatres vanished almost as fast. They survived only in a few great cities, and even here presented only London successes or pre-London rehearsals. In the 1920s there were still touring companies: two in Shakespeare, two (one conducted by the last great actor-manager, Martin Harvey) in romantic plays. These all expired. Shakespeare dwindled to the London Old Vic and the Memorial Theatre at Stratford upon Avon, which was sustained mainly by American tourists and parties of schoolchildren.[27]

Yet it can be argued that the theatre fought back by providing film makers with a ready supply of raw material — plays — on which films could be based and from which films could be adapted. It was, however, a very special form of theatre which embraced at one social extreme the drawing room comedy and, at another, the music hall act. Absent in the spectrum of theatre's influence on cinema was the kind of experimental theatre which had exercised key influences on the important silent cinemas of Germany and the Soviet Union. The experimental work of Piscator, Meyerhold and Brecht, the expressionist theatre of Max Reinhardt were confined to highly specialised audiences in Britain and they did not make their presence felt in the cinema as they had in the other European countries. Apart from the particular case of the music hall act, the kind of theatre which fed into the British cinema of the period was middlebrow in character and was addressed to a middle-class audience. Its centre was the London West End stage:

> In the West End theatre, Shaftesbury Avenue french-window drama still predominated. It portrayed Kensington or country-house life for the benefit of a largely suburban audience, or (more rarely) suburban life for an audience like the characters in the play ... The West End successes of the early thirties were light romantic or comic plays ... society comedies ... and competent historical plays.[28]

The cinema of the interwar period cannibalised this theatre for its films but, if the production schedules of the different studios are examined, it can be shown that the influence was uneven and that certain studios depended more heavily on dramatic sources than others. For example, during the years that Hitchcock worked at BIP, the company relied very heavily on adaptations from the stage as opposed to adaptations from other sources such as literature, or screenplays prepared specifically for the screen. In 1930, out of the 24 features produced by the company, ten were adapted from plays, and this proportion was to increase in the following two years. In 1931 there were 19 play adaptations out of 27 films and in 1932 the figure was 15 out of 23. By contrast, during the same period at Gaumont British, the number of plays adapted for the screen constituted about half the total films for each year. During the expansionist years of the mid-1930s, when Hitchcock had moved to Gaumont British, the company's reliance on the theatre diminished so that in 1934 only eight of the 19 features produced were dependent upon theatrical sources, whilst in 1935 and 1936 the figures were five out of 19 and seven out of 20 respectively.[29]

One point to note in the context of such statistics is that the high ratio of play adaptations to films based on other sources for BIP might be linked to the arrival of the sound film which had effectively superseded the silent film by 1930. In 1929 about a quarter of all features released in Britain were sound pictures but by 1930 the proportion had risen to about 70 per cent. The key element introduced into the cinema in the late 1920s was dialogue. Other kinds of sound, music and even sound effects, had been part of the cinematic experience for many years but it was not until the late 1920s that 'talking and singing' films were to become an economic and technological proposition. Theatre, as an art form based upon speech and dialogue, provided an obvious source for the newly developed 'talkie' and this certainly proved to be the case in Hollywood as Lewis Jacobs has pointed out:

> Movie art was forgotten as studio doors were flung open to stage

directors, Broadway playwrights, vaudeville singers, and song-and-dance teams. Voice, sound, noise, were all that now mattered.[30]

The situation in Britain, however, was somewhat different and it can be argued that the British cinema had already succumbed to the influence of the West End theatre by the time that the sound picture arrived in 1929. In his reflections on the British cinema during the silent period, Michael Balcon wrote:

> We were mentally 'stagebound'. We looked to the theatre for much of our screen material and our early films would certainly be called 'stagey'. It was no doubt wrong of us to seek to bask in the reflected glory of people like Noel Coward; we followed trends and did not try to make them. It was doubly a mistake to lean on stage plays because we were making *silent* films, so the plays were deprived of their very essence, the words.[31]

Although the American cinema was subjected to a considerable influence from the Broadway stage at the advent of the sound picture, during the silent era it had established a strong and vigorous tradition of essentially visual genres such as slapstick comedy, the melodrama, the Western and the costume epic, and these survived into the sound period albeit often in modified forms. In the British cinema the arrival of the sound track, and particularly the dimension of dialogue, simply accentuated the well established dependence of the British cinema upon the forms and values of the West End play. Part of this influence manifested itself in styles of acting and vocal delivery and the developing British sound film was to adopt the vocal conventions of 'stage' English as the norm. Michael Balcon again, reflecting further on the influence of the theatre, regretted that 'accents, dialect, regional or "class" intonations meant that you were restricted to character parts. The lamentable preference was for English of the drama schools and South Kensington.'[32] Alternatively, if regional accents were featured on the screen, these were the Northern accents of players from another kind of live theatre, the music hall. Gracie Fields and George Formby both became top box office stars during the 1930s, Lancashire accents and all, although their films, regional in their origins, remained regional in their appeal. As Basil Dean, producer of many of the music-hall-based films, remarked of George Formby, 'none of his films did worthwhile business in the West End of London, but elsewhere it was a case of "all seats sold" most of the time'.[33] The highly restricted iconography of the British cinema of the 1930s, mentioned earlier in this chapter, can be related to the narrow theatrical sources frequently drawn upon by British film makers from the days of the silent cinema onwards.

Censorship

Nicholas Pronay, writing in 1982, pointed out that the topic of film censorship had not 'excited much discussion amongst historians of Britain in the twentieth century' and had also been neglected by 'the specialist literature of "film history" of recent years'.[34] His remarks, pertinent at the time, have been rapidly superseded by a flood of publications on film censorship in Britain written since 1982. The work of Pronay himself, Jeffrey Richards, Anthony Aldgate and others, has provided a very detailed account of the development of film censorship in Britain together with many analyses of its operation particularly in the interwar period. A very full background analysis of film censorship is now available for the specialist in film history who wants to understand the relationship between that institution and the kind of cinema that has emerged in Britain.[35] It has been argued that the thematic emphases of the British cinema, its subject matter and iconography, have been determined in part by the structure of censorship. Pronay has suggested that censorship in the interwar period closely controlled the range of representations which appeared in the British film. As he argues:

the first element of reality in feature film in Britain during the interwar period is the reality of censorship: it controlled absolutely, at least where it actually mattered, the relationship between external reality and filmic reality. It defined what aspects of contemporary reality could form the subject of a film at all. It defined what stereotypes about the political system might or might not be put on the screen in great detail. It determined the degree of verisimilitude the film makers could employ about contemporary reality in finely calculated measures.[36]

The consensus amongst historians seems to be that censorship functioned as a 'coherently organised form of social control'[37] as far as the British cinema of the 1930s was concerned.

The British Board of Film Censors, although established and financed by the film industry and independent of both state and government in a formal sense, nevertheless reflected the considerable concern displayed by the social and political establishment, the ruling class, about the subversive potential of such a popular entertainment medium. It did so in a number of ways. The President of the Board was appointed in close consultation with the Home Office which meant, according to one writer, that 'the President and through him the Secretary of the British Board of Film Censors were in practice appointees of the Home Secretary'.[38] There was a further element of informal control embodied in 'the regular contact between the Board and government departments whenever films were submitted which "touch racial or national interests, the history and personalities of great historical events"'.[39] The Board did not possess the power to enforce its censorship decisions and it functioned as an advisory body for local authorities who had the ultimate responsibility for deciding whether a film could be shown in a particular locality. The Home Office played an important role in this process, however, through its system of circulars to the authorities which recommended acceptance of the Board's decisions. The industry itself through its trade associations made sure that the rulings of the Board were adhered to by its members in the exhibition and distribution sectors.

The system of censorship that evolved in Britain represented an interlocking of state and government, industry and local authority, film maker and moral guardian, at a level that was difficult to formalise in any precise manner. Local authorities could, and did, reject the decisions of the Board from time to time, but the system of rules governing permissible subject matter for British film makers in the interwar period was sufficiently powerful to dictate the production policies of the major film companies. The Board had been set up in 1912 and its earliest activities were concerned with the policing of the moral tone of the films screened in British cinemas. Its basic orientation was codified in 1917 in a set of rules which were concerned primarily with morality and which effectively proscribed 'the depiction of prostitution, premarital and extramarital sex, sexual perversion, incest, seduction, nudity, venereal disease, orgies, swearing, abortion, brothels, white slavery and so forth'.[40] Problem areas were termed 'exceptions'[41] and lists of these were published as appendices to the annual reports of the Board. In addition, the Board did publish more general documents relating to its policies as in the case of the 1928 booklet, *Censorship in Britain*.[42] The history of the Board's activities reflects the shifting concerns with attitudes towards personal and public morality. Jeffrey Richards has pointed out that during the 1930s the concerns of the Board moved from the sordid material of 'backstage dramas', through the concentration on sex and nudity in films of the early thirties to the upsurge in horror films towards the middle of the decade.[43] Yet, accompanying such concerns was a set of attitudes and principles which had more to do with explicit political censorship than with personal and sexual morality. In 1931, the Board had published a list of 'political subjects ... which the Board would not permit to be *either* the principal subject of the story of a film, *or* shown in any incidental form within a film.'[44] The list was extensive and detailed and included the unfavourable representation of British forces, misleading themes concerning the British Empire, lampoons on the monarchy, the treatment of relations between labour and capital, industrial unrest and film themes which 'conveyed a false impression of the police ... or involved reflections upon the administration of British justice or upon judges and other responsible officials of the law or public institutions, or upon public characters'.[45] Such a body of rules which forbade cinematic comment upon matters of political and social controversy have led many historians to conclude that the 'escapist' and 'trivial' character of the British cinema of the 1930s was a product of a clear and well organised system of political censorship. The government and the state were able to control screen subject matter and to exclude from public view debate and argument about key institutions and events of contemporary public life as far as the entertainment cinema was concerned. This certainly fits in with the common view of the cinema of the period and is reflected in Michael Balcon's often quoted remark that 'hardly a single film of the period reflects the agony of the times'.[46] The censorship system was designed precisely to keep 'the agony of the times' off the screen because the official attitude towards the mass of the British people who went to the cinema was extremely paternalistic. As the pamphlet *Censorship in Britain* put it, 'nothing will be passed which is calculated to demoralise the public'[47] and this entailed an avoidance of areas of human experience too close to the lives of ordinary people in Britain during the interwar period.

A Cinema of Genres

The mass production of films which characterises the British film industry after the 1927 Act required the development of a system of genres by which production could be organised in a rational manner from the perspective of economics and business. As Stephen Heath has suggested, 'genres are ... necessities of the industry, the optimal exploitation of the production apparatus requiring the containment of creative work within established frameworks'.[48] The standardisation of the genre system permitted some degree of managerial control over resources, it promoted planning and allowed maximum exploitation of important assets such as standing sets, actors whose identities were bound up with particular roles, and the specialist skills of writers, directors and other creative and technical staff. By the 1930s, the American cinema — the model for all commercial cinemas — had developed a clear generic profile based on its massive production capacity of some 500 films per year. Individual studios with their outputs of between 30 and 50 films per year were able to specialise in particular genres and a familiar example of this is the Warner Brothers gangster film of the 1930s. Although all of the leading studios made gangster films and stars such as Gary Cooper and Spencer Tracy played gangster leads, it was Warner Brothers with stars such as Edward G. Robinson and James Cagney that came to specialise in the genre and dominate it. Of course, the British production industry emerged in somewhat different circumstances from its Hollywood counterpart and although the perspective of genre is pertinent in both contexts, certain differences should be acknowledged. The stunted development of the British production industry in the 1920s meant that the cinema which emerged in the 1930s did not have a strong tradition of genres on which to build. Also, although production developed rapidly, making Britain a prominent volume producer of films in the mid-1930s, the rate of production still fell far short of that of Hollywood. There were also fewer large companies in the British industry and these factors militated against the development of a sharply defined and varied generic profile of the kind that developed in Hollywood during this period. What the British film industry did produce given its different conditions was a small number of broadly defined genres with a certain degree of internal diversity. In terms of sheer quantity, there were three genres — the crime film, the comedy and the musical — that dominated the British cinema of the 1930s. The crime picture became a staple of British production soon after the Quota Act, so much so that in 1929 almost 40 per cent of the films registered for quota purposes fell into the crime category. Although this high proportion was to fall in subsequent years with the development of other genres, the crime film sustains a significant presence throughout the period. In 1934, 42 of the 141 films produced were crime pictures and in 1938 the figure was 38 out of 136. These figures indicate the consistency of the genre as a significant aspect of British production in the 1930s. The other prominent genres, the comedy and the musical, were rather more dependent upon the introduction of sound for their presence in the production profile. For example, in 1929, nine comedies were made but only one musical. However, by 1931 when sound had become securely established, 42 out of the 93 films registered for the quota were comedies and the figure for musicals had increased to ten. In 1934, during the boom production years, around 170 films were produced and of these, 56 were comedies and 35 were musicals. If the 42 crime films for the year are added to those figures, the extent of the domination of British cinema by the three genres is clearly indicated. Indeed, only 40 of the total of films made in Britain and released in 1934 fell into other generic categories such as drama, romance and the historical picture.[49]

We have already noted the extent to which the theatre played an influential role in the British cinema even during the silent period. Sound accentuated this dependence and, in particular, the theatre was to be an important source of material for the expanding comedy genre which in fact became the dominant film type in quantitative terms during the period of the first quota act. The West End theatre was, of course, a predictable source although, as Jeffrey Richards has pointed out, 'it was not sophisticated comedy such as that of Noel Coward ... but the less demanding farce which dominated'.[50] In particular, the farces produced by Tom Walls at the Aldwych Theatre made an especially successful transition to the cinema screen and Walls — who also directed the films — and Ralph Lynn became top box office stars of the 1930s. Films such as *Rookery Nook* (Walls, Haskin, 1930) and *Plunder* (Walls, 1931) based upon plays by Ben Travers were amongst the earliest of the Aldwych adaptations and they established the Walls/Lynn team as producers of the most successful comedies in the early 1930s. The middle class orientation of the West End generated comedies was counterbalanced during the period by the regional comedy films based upon music hall performers such as Gracie Fields, George Formby and Will Hay. These films represent a key trend in the

British comic picture and one which also has its origins in a particular kind of theatre. As George Perry has pointed out:

> During this period of the thirties another fruitful and sometimes over-looked genre of British film began to appear in increasing numbers, the broad comedy pictures which featured comedians who had made reputations for hilarious and earthy working class humour in the music halls.[51]

This was a repeat of what had happened much earlier in the American cinema when comedians such as Charles Chaplin and Stan Laurel who had begun their careers in the English music hall embarked upon successful careers in the American silent cinema, along with numerous American comics such as Oliver Hardy and Buster Keaton, who came from the vaudeville theatre, the American equivalent of music hall. Some music hall performers, in fact, had appeared in British films during the twenties, most notably Lupino Lane who made a number of comedy two-reelers whilst Harry Lauder and George Robey both appeared in silent features. The advent of sound in the late twenties gave fresh opportunities for the exploitation of the music hall act and many performers including Flanagan and Allen, Sandy Powell and Tommy Handley appeared in brief sketch films of one or two reels in length from 1930 onwards. Gracie Fields made her screen debut in the full length film *Sally in Our Alley* (Elvey, 1931) and she was followed through the decade by a variety of music hall artists who appeared in feature films which were constructed around their personalities and performance characteristics. George Formby made his first appearance on the screen in 1934 in a film called *Boots! Boots!* (Tracy, 1934) which was not just regional in terms of setting and subject matter but was actually made by a small regional company, Blakeley's Productions, which was based in Manchester. Also, in the same year, Will Hay made his feature film debut in *Those Were the Days* (Bentley, 1934) at British International Pictures. Comedy teams such as The Crazy Gang which included Flanagan and Allen, the Arthur Lucan and Kitty McShane team who brought 'Old Mother Riley' to the screen and many others, also contributed to this formidable array of music hall talent which crystallised into a distinctive category of British film production during the 1930s. It is, however, somewhat ironic that although this was a genuinely British form of comedy drawing upon the long traditions of music hall, two of the directors most closely associated with the genre were foreigners. Marcel Varnel who worked on a number of the Will Hay films was a Frenchman and Monty Banks who made many of the Gracie Fields pictures was Italian.

The influence of the theatre was also marked in the development of the musical genre of the time. As in Hollywood, where the advent of sound had turned the American cinema towards the Broadway musical show for its source material, so the British cinema from 1930 onwards looked to the traditions of the British musical comedy and the revue. Leading performers from the stage such as Jack Buchanan, Cicely Courtneidge, Sonny Hale and Bobby Howes moved to the cinema screen during the thirties and appeared in a variety of musical films, but the leading performer and the most important musical star of the 1930s was undoubtedly Jessie Matthews. She had been an enormously successful revue star in the twenties and, indeed, had attracted the attention of several Hollywood companies in 1929 whilst she was appearing on the New York stage. She returned to England and, after a screen debut which she herself refers to as a 'disaster'[52], signed a contract with Michael Balcon and Gaumont British. She went on to become a top British screen star and, as Balcon records in his autobiography, Jessie Matthews' musicals became one of the categories around which Gaumont British production was organised in the 1930s.[53] Her talents were exploited in a variety of genres but it was in musicals such as *Evergreen* (Saville, 1934) that her performances were singled out for critical acclaim. Jessie Matthews was one of the few British stars of the 1930s who possessed international appeal but, despite several attempts by the large American companies to star her in a Hollywood feature, her screen appearances in the 1930s were confined to Britain. There were even plans to team her with Fred Astaire, the dominant figure in the Hollywood musical of the thirties, and although these came to nothing, they do indicate the status of her appeal and her high standing in the British film community of the period.

Russell Ferguson, in his *World Film News* article quoted earlier[54], had attacked the British cinema for its concentration upon the adventures of assassins, international jewel thieves, crooks and detectives, yet the genre which furnished a home for this assortment of characters merits specific attention as a significant genre in the British cinema of the period. The crime/thriller genre flourished during the period for several reasons. In strict economic terms such pictures were relatively inexpensive to make as they required minimal expenditure on sets and costumes when compared with other genres such as the musical and the historical picture. But economics apart, the genre possesses important cultural roots and it can be related to the interest in the activities of criminals and detectives, in murder and mystery, which gave rise to a significant and distinctive current within literature dating back to the nineteenth century. The novels of Charles Dickens and Wilkie Collins, of writers such as Conan Doyle, 'Sapper', John Buchan and Agatha Christie constitute an important background for the crime picture of the 1930s, a powerful tradition of criminal and espionage fiction. Although the American gangster films which were extremely popular in the early 1930s may have provided a crucial impetus for the genre, it can be argued that the British crime film, like the music-hall-based pictures, drew its strength from an important tradition of British popular culture. In particular, the genre should be related to that strain of the indigenous popular culture which Alan Lovell has referred to as a '*News of the World* culture' whose primary characteristic is an interest in murder with sexual undertones. Such a cultural strand is reflected in 'pulp' literature and in the popular Sunday newspapers — hence the name — but it has also found an outlet in the cinema. Peter John Dyer, in a perceptive article in *Sight and Sound*, has suggested that the genre which emerged from such a tradition was genuinely 'British' especially in the context of the imitative international prestige cinema of Britain in the 1930s. As he suggests:

> The Thirties' British cinema had always been at home with melodrama; unsubtle, somehow innocent melodrama at that, of an oddly national variety, reflecting the carving up of chorus girls by blonde and blue-eyed ex-officers in seaside hotels, the doping of racehorses, and the coffee growing cold over the *News of the World*. This was the world the British cinema understood best: which produced in Alfred Hitchcock, its one true 'critics' director', and in Walter Forde, Carol Reed, George King, Arthur Woods and David MacDonald some half-dozen adept disciples.[55]

Such films, which provided something like one-quarter of all the films made in Britain during the lifetime of the 1927 Quota Act, varied considerably in terms of artistry and ambition. Many were made purely for quota purposes and, as we have noted, were ideal in such a context because of their cheapness. Many, however, including the films of Hitchcock, deserve close attention as distinctively indigenous films although they were never accorded the prestige of the more grandiose and ambitious historical pictures and musicals which were made with the international market in mind.

Comedies, musicals, crime pictures and thrillers dominate the profile of the British cinema of the 1930s with other genres such as romantic dramas and adventure films playing a minor role in quantitative terms. There is, however, one further genre which merits attention because of its overall impact and influence despite the numerical predominance of the other genres. The historical costume picture 'built around the work of Sir Alexander Korda'[56] is frequently credited with starting the British production boom of the mid-1930s. More specifically, it was the success in America of Korda's film, *The Private Life of Henry VIII* (1933), that sparked off a cycle of films based upon historical subject matter with relatively lavish budgets, well known players, and elaborate costumes and settings which were intended to capitalise on the supposed international appeal of such elements. Korda followed his initial success with *The Private Life of Don Juan* (Korda, 1934), *Catherine the Great* (Czinner, 1934), *Rembrandt* (Korda, 1936) and *Lady Hamilton* (Korda, 1941) which offered the spectator 'a "key-hole" view of history' as one film historian has put it.[57] Korda had anticipated his later specialisation in the genre whilst in Hollywood in the late 1920s with *The Private Life of Helen of Troy* (Korda, 1927) but the shift of attention to the British monarchy clearly signalled the possibility of the genre as a component of a specifically British national cinema. The historical picture was not confined to Korda's London Films, however, and following the success of *The Private Life of Henry VIII*, Herbert Wilcox produced *Nell Gwyn* (1934), a remake of his silent version, with Charles II providing the monarchical element. Wilcox went on to make two films based upon the life of Queen Victoria — *Victoria the Great* (1937) and *Sixty Glorious Years* (1938) — which moved the genre away from Korda's blend of sex and history towards respectful biography. The Gaumont British company also contributed to the genre with *Tudor Rose* (Stevenson, 1936) which, like the Wilcox pictures, moved away from raciness and bawdiness with a 'lucid and forceful exposition of the political complexities of the reign of King Edward VI'[58], and pictures such as *The Iron Duke* (Saville, 1934) and *Me and Marlborough* (Saville, 1935). It is also possible to relate the 'Imperial epic' genre of the 1930s to the historical picture and Korda's company was also involved in this cinematic genre which was also based on history. *Sanders of the River* (Z. Korda, 1935) was the first of a number of films which dealt with British colonial life, particularly in Africa. Korda followed this with *Elephant Boy* (Flaherty, 1936), *The Drum* (Z. Korda, 1938) and *The Four Feathers* (Z. Korda, 1939) and Korda's films were paralleled at Gaumont British with films such as *Rhodes of Africa* (Viertel, 1936), *The Great Barrier* (Rosmer, Barkas, 1937) and *King Solomon's Mines* (Stevenson, 1937).

A British Cinema?

As has been mentioned in the introduction to this chapter, the British cinema of the 1930s has frequently been dismissed as a failure. The identification of the reasons for the failure, however, differs from writer to writer. It has been suggested that the films of the period failed to crystallise into a genuinely national cinema and that although numerous films did actually get made in dramatic contrast to the middle of the previous decade, it is not possible to identify specific traditions of British cinema as being established during the period. There was also a problem in terms of the quality of the films produced which failed to match the standards of entertainment provided by their American counterparts and which lacked the artistic distinctiveness of the continental cinemas. It has also been suggested that British films of the period were not popular with British audiences who preferred American films and film stars, gangster films and musicals, James Cagney, Fred Astaire and Ginger Rogers. Perhaps the most consistent attack on the British films of the period is concerned with their lack of evident contact with the social and political realities of the extremely troubled years of the 1930s. Social and political events such as chronic unemployment at home and the rise of Fascism abroad failed to find clear and obvious expression in the crime pictures, the thrillers, the comedies and the musicals which dominated the production schedules of the British studios. The British entertainment cinema was clearly vulnerable to charges of political and social irresponsibility, to the familiar accusation of being simply a 'dream factory' providing an ideological opiate for the masses. At present, such judgements constitute a powerful framework for our thinking about the British cinema and, as part of the conclusion to this chapter, my intention is to unravel them and to indicate some reservations about them.

In one sense, as a riposte to critics such as Dilys Powell who have lamented the failure of the British film industry to produce a genuinely 'national cinema', it could be argued that the industry has simply failed to produce a cinema which fits into dominant conceptions of cinematic excellence and distinction which circulate within the film culture. As a contrast, the British cinema of the 1940s with its 'realist' war pictures and its 'respectable literary adaptations was rather more in accord with the anti-Hollywood film culture of the 1920s and 1930s. The distinctively British films of the 1930s, the crime pictures and thrillers of Hitchcock, Forde and Woods, the music hall comedies of Gracie Fields and George Formby drew heavily on vulgar, popular cultural traditions which were at variance with the 'art' cinema culture of the highbrow critics. Charles Barr has suggested that one characteristic of British cinema is a 'strong under-life — represented most powerfully by the horror film'[59] in which the themes of violence and sexuality — qualities which are often repressed in orthodox British cinema — break to the cinematic surface. This subversive tradition which, Barr suggests, incorporates the Gainsborough melodramas of the 1940s, the films of Michael Powell, the Hammer horror cycle and the *Carry On* films, contrasts strongly with the restrained good taste and serious social commitment of the documentary and 'realist' traditions of cinema validated by orthodox film culture. It is possible to locate some of the British cinema of the 1930s within this tradition. The racy historical pictures look forward to the 'lusty Gainsborough productions of the 'forties',[60] Hitchcock's thrillers and the crime picture in general can be linked to Powell and the horror cycle, and the *Carry On* films might be regarded as descendants of the vulgar music hall comedies. It is thus possible to talk about a cinema of the thirties, or a strand of that cinema, which has some claim to national distinctiveness and which can be regarded as an embodiment of specifically English character traits and preoccupations. The broad vulgar humour of the music hall comedies and the 'keyhole' history films together with the somewhat seedy fascination with violence and sexuality in the crime genre constitute the beginnings of a sub-current in British cinema which finds a more substantial and sustained expression in the genres and film makers cited by Barr.

The notion of a sub-current or an alternative oppositional strand of national cinema is important in the analysis of the idea of national cinema itself. The term 'national cinema' is often locked into a form of essentialism which implies the possibility of a single unitary form of expression which can be designated as representative of a nation. A corollary of this is that there also exists a unitary national culture which can simply be mapped onto a set of cinematic signifiers to constitute the national cinema.

Britain, however, as a political entity has been carved out of a variety of regions and nations, ways of life which can be differentiated from each other, and people who differ from each other in terms of gender, class and race. National cinemas in their overall profile necessarily reflect such differences and, indeed, can be conceptualised as elements of definitional struggle in the broader arena of ideology.[61] Those critics who could not perceive a distinctive British cinema in the production of the thirties may not have been looking at the right genres or with the set of critical presuppositions which enabled later critics to anatomise British cinema into distinctive strands and currents which may be related to each other in terms of conflict and opposition.

The argument against the British cinema of the period in terms of its quality is, perhaps, more difficult to pin down. Historians of film criticism could point to similar judgements about the American cinema prior to the *Cahiers du Cinéma* revaluation of Hollywood during the 1950s. The commercial infrastructure of the American cinema, the factory-like studio system and the organisation of film production around the figure of the star, were seen as compromising factors and Hollywood's films were accordingly downgraded in critical and aesthetic terms. The British cinema had much in common with the American cinema in its organisation and structure during the 1930s and its critical dismissal may also be due in part to the assumptions about commercial cinema which led to the dismissal of American films. The British film industry did however have to contend with the 'quota quickie' problem, a most blatant form of commercial production, which led to Britain's cinematic image being defined and measured by its low budget production especially during the early 1930s. By contrast, America's low budget production sector, the 'B' movie, had a specific minor role to play in the American film industry whose image was defined in terms of its steady output of A grade features.

It has been suggested that a major problem for British film makers was that of cultural and artistic identity. British film makers were torn between the production of 'art' as conventionally understood in Europe and the production of 'entertainment' as understood in Hollywood terms. In Lindsay Anderson's view, the British cinema contrived to fall between the two identities:

> As geographically, Britain is poised between continents, not quite Europe, and very far from America, so from certain points of view the British cinema seems to hover between the opposite poles of France and Hollywood. Our directors never — or rarely — have the courage to tackle, in an adult manner, the completely adult subject; yet, they lack also the flair for popular showmanship that is characteristic of the American cinema.[62]

Hollywood's supremacy in the field of entertainment cinema established during the British cinema's problem period of the twenties may explain the difficulties that British film makers experienced in making entertainment films comparable to those coming from Hollywood but, as social historian Peter Stead has asked, 'Why ... was there no British Eisenstein, no British Renoir?'[63] The answer may be that there were figures comparable to Eisenstein and Renoir, at least in terms of social outlook and artistic ambition, but they gravitated towards the documentary movement rather than the commercial entertainment cinema. A poor quality cinema, then, dominated for parts of the decade by low budget quota production, dependent upon a theatre whose cultural formation was at odds with the context of popular culture in which the entertainment cinema was necessarily set, and dogged by uncertainty about cinematic identity. But was the cinema actually produced so bad? It is worth quoting Roger Manvell's remark that the 'dozen or so good films made each year in British studios by producers of repute were insufficient to stem public reaction against almost all films bearing British credits'.[64] Manvell is writing about the 1930s British cinema as a prelude to the conventional assessment of the 1940s as the 'golden age' of British cinema when the war produced the cinema of national coherence. Yet, to pinpoint 'a dozen or so good films' annually for the 1930s is surely a kind of praise. Would a commercial film industry be likely to produce more than that figure given the exigencies of commercial production and the specific difficulties of the British film industry during the period? Manvell's remark also indicates a public distaste for British films of the 1930s and this is supported by accounts of exhibitors in London's West End cinemas screening British quota films in the mornings whilst the theatres were being cleaned and before audiences started arriving for the first performance of the day.[65] It has also been suggested that audiences of the time would deliberately arrive late for film programmes in order to avoid seeing the British film which was invariably the second feature. Anecdotal evidence such as this, however, has been countered recently by Anthony Aldgate. He mentions the high box-office standing of stars such as Gracie Fields and George Formby and he refers to Simon Rowson's 'Statistical Survey' of the industry published in 1934 which provides 'a clear indication that British films were winning considerable ground and that they were more popular with British audiences than they were given credit for'.[66]

The final criticism of the British entertainment cinema of the 1930s — its failure to confront the urgent social and political issues of the day — can be examined in two ways. Firstly, one can look from the perspective of critical construction in so far as such a judgement derives from a critical position which is bound up with 'realist' aesthetics and the conception of cinema as moralist and propagandist. The cinematic ideal within such a tradition would include the British documentary film of the 1930s with its clear social concern and its presentation of those areas of national life which the entertainment cinema excluded from view. I have already referred to the article by Russell Ferguson in which he suggested that the entertainment cinema implied that the British people did not 'work in coal pits or fishing boats or shops or shipyards or iron foundries'[67] and we may note that his catalogue of exclusion is a virtual catalogue of the concerns of the documentary films of the time. *Drifters* (Grierson, 1929), *Industrial Britain* (Flaherty, 1931-2), *Coal Face* (Cavalcanti, 1935) and many other sponsored documentary films of the 1930s provided images of Britain derived from the ordinary lives of working class people and a form of 'realism' to set against the 'escapism' of the entertainment cinema of the time. Documentary cinema has become lodged within British film culture as an exemplar of cinematic achievement and has had a powerful influence on both the production of British fictional cinema and its critical analysis and evaluation. This narrow focus on certain types of films has been highlighted in a recent editorial in *Screen*:

> One of the problems with the realist aesthetic as it worked itself out in film-making and film reviewing is the assumption that the 'good' and 'worthy' film self-consciously represents the contemporary preoccupations of the conjuncture — and by extension the 'authentic British' film is one which deals with contemporary *British* life. Such preoccupations must constitute the manifest subject matter of the film (as in the social problem picture). The function of *mise en scène* is limited to iconic representation and a deliberate use of metaphor is effectively forbidden.[68]

The privileging of documentary cinema has meant the downgrading of fictional cinema, genre cinema except where that cinema has adopted documentary styles and 'realist' subject matter. Such a critical posture derives from the attitude and opinions of the film intellectuals during the interwar period. The Soviet cinema of the 1920s had exerted a powerful influence on the young, highly educated film intellectuals of the time and they discerned in the sphere of the sponsored documentary the possibility of a similar convergence of art, politics and propaganda for a social purpose. Those film makers and aspirant film makers who had a firm grasp of the various directions that the cinema had taken in the experimental decade of the 1920s, took both their social awareness and their artistic knowledge into the documentary movement rather than into the entertainment cinema. Although it has been said that Britain failed to produce an 'art' cinema along the lines of the other European film making countries during the 1920s, Alan Lovell has suggested that concern with the art of film did find an outlet in Britain through the documentary movement in the 1930s. As he argued:

> The importance of the documentary movement lies, not in the quality of individual films, but in the impact it had in general on the British cinema. Grierson captured the interest in film as an art form that was developing in Britain in the late 1920s for the documentary movement. In effect, this meant that the documentary film became the British art film.[69]

Instead of *The Cabinet of Dr Caligari* (Weine, 1919) and *Un Chien Andalou* (Bunuel/Dali, 1929) the British cinema offered *Song of Ceylon* (Wright, 1934) and *Night Mail* (Watt/Wright, 1936); and instead of the equivalent of Decla Bioscop — the artistic wing of UFA — at Gaumont British the British 'art' cinema had its patterns of circulation separate from those of the entertainment cinema. This meant that there was little contact between the documentarists and the entertainment film makers, in contrast to the position in countries like France and Germany where things were not so strictly compartmentalised. To take some examples, in Germany Fritz Lang made serial thrillers aimed at the popular mass audience during the 1920s as well as making more overtly 'artistic' films such as *Die Nibelungen* (1922-4) and *Metropolis* (1925-6). Similarly, in France René Clair moves from making the dadaist short film *Entr' Acte* (1924) to the direction of comic entertainment films such as *Un Chapeau de paille d'Italie* (1927) and *Le Million* (1931). Something like that fluidity did not emerge in the British cinema until the rather special conditions of the Second World War when the demands of propaganda introduced elements of documentary realism into the entertainment film and brought together film makers from the two sides of the British cinema as it had developed through the 1930s.

The second point to make in relation to the failure of the entertainment cinema to address social and political issues concerns the system of censorship. As we have seen, the censors were guided by an elaborate set of rules and guidelines which proscribed certain themes and topics and particularly those which dealt with matters of controversy. It has been argued that this effectively constructed a cinema which was not permitted to address social and political matters or, at least, was not permitted to present a critical perspective on social and political reality. The 'iconic representation' of social and political life in Britain during the 1930s was steered away from the entertainment cinema by governmental design through the indirect and subtle system of 'arms length' censorship. This meant that 'only films which, in the opinion of a full-time, professional body of long experience, did not carry political messages conflicting with those of the government in any fundamental way could be shown to the "great audience"'.[70]

The various influences on the British cinema during the 1930s have helped to produce different strands of film making and different levels of cinematic ambition. At one end of the spectrum lies the cheaply produced 'quota quickie' whilst at the other end is the historical spectacular with its high production values. Worthy film biographies of Queen Victoria emerged from the same film culture as the knockabout comedies of George Formby. The foreign influence which was reflected at most levels in the industry from producer to directors and stars to technical personnel did not produce the creative diversity that resulted from the foreign influence on the American cinema. The theatre pushed the screen in several different directions and provided models of acting performance which relied heavily on vocal delivery and intonation rather than screen presence. It can be argued that the most vigorous cinematic strands of the period were in those genres which were rooted firmly in British popular culture — the music hall comedy, the crime picture and the thriller — yet critical orthodoxy has often been dismissive of these genres.

Notes

1. S. Hartog, 'State Protection of a Beleaguered Industry' in J. Curran and V. Porter (eds.) *British Cinema History* (Weidenfeld and Nicolson, London, 1983), p. 65.
2. T. Dickinson, *A Discovery of Cinema* (Oxford University Press, London, 1971), p. 66.
3. N. Marshall, 'Reflections on the English Film', *The Bookman*, Oct. 1931, pp. 71-2).
4. F. Truffaut, *Hitchcock* (Panther, London, 1969), p. 140.
5. D. Powell, *Films Since 1939* (Longmans Green, London, 1947), p. 65.
6. *World Film News*, Sept. 1936, p. 4.
7. R. Ferguson, 'Armament Rings and Political Madmen', *World Film News*, Aug. 1937, p. 4.
8. Ibid.
9. Ibid.
10. W. Allen, 'Mass Entertainment' in J. Raymond (ed.), *The Baldwin Age* (Eyre and Spottiswood, London, 1960), p. 225.
11. *World Film News*, Sept. 1936. p. 4.
12. J. Grierson, 'The Fate of British Films', *The Fortnightly*, Jul. 1937, p. 7.
13. Ibid.
14. A. Lovell and J. Hillier, *Studies in Documentary* (Secker and Warburg, London, 1972), p. 35.
15. See Chapter 3, p. 39.
16. *World Film News*, Sept. 1937, p. 18.
17. A. Brunel, *Nice Work* (Forbes Robertson, London, 1949), p. 166.
18. R. Low, *The History of the British Film 1918-1929* (Allen and Unwin, London, 1971), p. 189.
19. M. Balcon, *A Lifetime in Films* (Hutchinson, London, 1969), pp. 95 6.
20. *Kine Weekly*, 11 Jan. 1934, p. 99.
21. M. Chanan, *Labour Power in the British Film Industry* (British Film Institute, London, 1976), p. 27.
22. *World Film News*, Sept. 1937, p. 18.
23. Ibid., p. 19.
24. *World Film News*, Sept. 1937, p. 21.
25. Ibid., p. 20.
26. *Kine Weekly*, 11 Jan. 1934, p. 99.
27. A.J.P. Taylor, *English History 1914-1945* Penguin Books, Harmondsworth, 1970), p. 392.
28. N. Branson and M. Heinemann, *Britain in the Nineteen Thirties* (Panther, St. Albans, 1973), p. 277.
29. These statistics are drawn from D. Gifford, *The British National Film Catalogue 1895-1970* (David and Charles, Newton Abbot, 1973).
30. L. Jacobs, *The Rise of the American Film* (Teachers College Press, New York, 1968), p. 334.
31. Balcon, *Lifetime*, p. 27 (emphasis in original).
32. Ibid., p. 37.
33. B. Dean, *Mind's Eye* (Hutchinson, London, 1973), p. 213.
34. N. Pronay, 'The Political Censorship of Films in Britain between the Wars' in N. Pronay and D.W. Spring (eds.), *Propaganda, Politics and Film* (Macmillan, London, 1982), p. 98.
35. E.g., articles by Aldgate and Pronay and Croft in Curran and Porter (eds.), *British*

Cinema History, and Richards' chapters on censorship in *The Age of the Dream Palace* (Routledge and Kegan Paul, London, 1984).

36. N. Pronay, 'The First Reality: Film Censorship in Liberal England' in K.R.M. Short (ed.), *Feature Films as History* (Croom Helm, London, 1981), p. 134.

37. J. Richards, 'Controlling the Screen: The British Cinema in the 1930s', *History Today*, Mar. 1983, p. 12.

38. Pronay, 'The First Reality', p. 117.

39. Richards, 'Controlling the Screen', p. 12.

40. Richards, *Dream Palace*, p. 93.

41. Pronay, 'The First Reality', p. 118.

42. British Board of Film Censors, *Censorship in Britain* (London, 1928).

43. Richards, *Dream Palace*, p. 93.

44. Pronay, 'The First Reality', p. 119.

45. Ibid., p. 120.

46. Balcon, *Lifetime*, p. 99.

47. Quoted in Richards, *Dream Palace*, p. 90.

48. S. Heath, '*Jaws*, Ideology and Film Theory', *Framework*, no. 4, Summer 1976, p. 27.

49. These statistics are drawn from Gifford, *The British National Film Catalogue*.

50. Richards, *Dream Palace*, p. 254.

51. G. Perry, *The Great British Picture Show* (Paladin, St Albans, 1975), p. 72.

52. In her autobiograhy, quoted in Richards, *Dream Palace*, p. 210.

53. Balcon, *Lifetime*, p. 62.

54. Ferguson, '*Armament Rings*'.

55. P.J. Dyer, 'Young and Innocent', *Sight and Sound*, Spring 1961, p. 80.

56. A. Lovell, 'The British Cinema — The Unknown Cinema', British Film Institute seminar paper (1967), p. 5.

57. R. Armes, *A Critical History of British Cinema* (Secker and Warburg, London, 1978), p. 116.

58. Richards, *Dream Palace*, pp. 262-3.

59. C. Barr, 'A Conundrum for England', *Monthly Film Bulletin*, Aug. 1984, p. 235.

60. C. Barr, *Ealing Studios* (Cameron and Tayleur, London, 1977), p. 57.

61. See A. Higson, 'Critical Theory and British Cinema', *Screen*, Jul.-Oct. 1983, pp. 93-4.

62. L. Anderson, 'Alfred Hitchcock', *Sequence*, no. 9, Autumn 1949, p. 113.

63. P. Stead, 'The People and the Pictures. The British Working Class and Film in the 1930s' in Pronay and Spring, *Propaganda*, p. 86.

64. R. Manvell, *Film*, 3rd edn (Penguin, London, 1950), p. 134.

65. Balcon, *Lifetime*, p. 93.

66. A. Aldgate, 'Comedy, Class and Containment: The British Domestic Cinema of the 1930s' in Curran and Porter (eds.), *British Cinema History*, p. 261.

67. See pp. 60-1.

68. A. Higson and S. Neale, 'Introduction: Components of the National Film Culture', *Screen*, Jan.-Feb. 1985, pp. 6-7 (emphasis in original).

69. Lovell and Hillier, *Studies*, p. 35.

70. Pronay, 'The First Reality', pp. 134-5.

Chapter Five

Hitchcock and the British Cinema

Hitchcock's links with the minority film culture of the interwar period have been analysed and they indicate a director whose work can be discussed in the context of the major artistic trends of silent cinema. However, Hitchcock spent his career in the British cinema as a working professional film maker in the commercial industry and this chapter aims to monitor that career and to explore the development of the image of Hitchcock that accompanied the career. In Chapter 1, reference was made to the notion of 'biographical legend' introduced into critical analysis by the Soviet Formalist critics and revived recently by David Bordwell.[1] Hitchcock's biographical legend, the idea of 'the Hitchcockian' is derived from Hitchcock's films, his public utterances in interviews and press articles, and from the entire output of secondary material which has accompanied his career including press comment, critical analysis and publicity material. Together these elements work towards constructing 'Hitchcock' as a unitary entity, an author of his films. The term 'Hitchcockian' is familiar to contemporary criticism and it possesses a clear range of connotations related to the form and style of his films, and to their subject matter. Yet a cursory examination of Hitchcock's British work reveals a number of films that do not conform to the popular sense of the term, that do not match up to the Hitchcock 'image'. The image is a complex result of the interplay of a number of forces and not a simple extrapolation from the films themselves.

Paramount to Gainsborough 1920-27

Hitchcock's first job in the film industry was as a title illustrator for the British production branch of the most powerful of the American companies — Paramount Pictures.[2] This brought Hitchcock into contact with American film production methods as most of the regular management and production staff were either American or American-trained. Working with directors such as Donald Crisp, George FitzMaurice and Hugh Ford enabled Hitchcock to consolidate and develop his early interest in the

American approach to cinematic narration. Although Paramount soon withdrew from Britain, Hitchcock remained at the studios as an employee of Gainsborough Pictures and his early substantial experience of film production was on a number of films directed by Graham Cutts. On these Hitchcock was to work in a variety of roles including assistant director, screenwriter, art director and editor gaining experience in most aspects of production. The division of labour already established in the American film industry was not part of the regime at Islington in the early 1920s and the rather fluid character of the British film industry of the time enabled Hitchcock to move around the different tasks which constituted the film making process before he specialised in direction. His relationship with Cutts, Balcon's 'house director', was marked by tension and eventually Hitchcock was to usurp the older director to become the central creative force within Gainsborough. Cutts began as an exhibitor but had become a director in the early 1920s, establishing himself as 'the most successful director making films in Britain'.[3] Such an accolade, however, has to be placed in the context of the small indigenous cinema in Britain at the time and the absence of much competition. According to Rachael Low, his films were marked by 'big drama, tricky camerawork and particularly the mobile camera'[4] and he was clearly a vital part of the success of Balcon's early production ventures. Gainsborough Pictures, Balcon's new company, had been formed on the basis of Cutts' directorial prowess and when the Balcon interests were reorganised in 1926 Cutts was given a long-term contract. He left Balcon in 1927 after completing two films under the new contract and went to work for First-National Pathé, an American owned distribution concern that was moving into production in anticipation of the Quota Act. Although he continued working until the 1940s, his career from the mid-1920s onwards can be seen in terms of a decline which is paralleled by the rise of Hitchcock's career. After a few short years as assistant to Cutts, Hitchcock had by-passed him to become Britain's leading film director in his stead.

Hitchcock's relationship with Michael Balcon emerges as the most significant contact that the young film maker was to have during the early 1920s, a relationship that was to 'make' Hitchcock in the silent cinema and to 'remake' his career in the mid-1930s. It was Balcon who gave Hitchcock his first opportunity to make feature films although he claims that he was not especially interested in becoming a director at that particular time (circa 1925). As he said to Peter Bogdanovich:

> I had no intention of becoming a film director, you know. It was quite a surprise to me. Sir Michael Balcon is really the man responsible for Hitchcock. At the time, I had been a scriptwriter, and when I finished that job I became the art director or the production designer. And I did that for several pictures, until one day Balcon said that the director ... didn't want me any more. I don't know what the reason was, some political reason. And it was then that Balcon said, 'How would you like

to become a director?' I had been quite content at the time, writing scripts and designing. I enjoyed it very much.[5]

Cutts understandably resented the threat to his position from Hitchcock's burgeoning talent yet his response rebounded on him by thrusting Hitchcock into the central directorial role in the studio. Hitchcock's first job was in Germany and he soon left Britain for the UFA studios in Munich to direct two pictures as part of a deal between Balcon and the German producer, Erich Pommer. Hitchcock was later to link up with Pommer once again on the production of *Jamaica Inn* (1939) his last film before his departure for Hollywood. He had worked in German studios before as Cutts' assistant on *The Blackguard* (1925) and on that occasion had come into contact with the leading German director F.W. Murnau who was shooting *The Last Laugh* (1924) on an adjacent stage.[6] This experience was to mark the beginning of an important phase of Hitchcock's career, in which he was exposed to the influence of the most powerful and pervasive of the European silent cinemas. As John Russell Taylor has written:

> Professionally, working at Neubabelsburg was an enormously productive experience for Hitch. Up to then he had worked entirely in the one small British studio, making his own mistakes and finding his own way without much reference to the techniques of other film makers. Now suddenly he was dropped in the middle of the most innovative area of film making at that epoch.[7]

Perhaps it would be better to make the point that Hitchcock's early formation as a film maker was under the influence of the American cinema in two ways. Firstly, he clearly had an extensive knowledge of the Hollywood cinema through watching many American pictures and, secondly, as he himself has said, he was more or less trained as an American film maker during his early days at Islington. The Hollywood influence is reflected in the first two films he directed even though they were made in German studios. Of the first, *The Pleasure Garden* (1925), Balcon commented that the 'surprising thing is that technically it doesn't look like a continental picture. It's more like an American film'[8] whilst the second, *The Mountain Eagle* (1926) was even more consciously designed to appeal to an American audience with its Hollywood star, Nita Naldi, in the lead and its American setting. It was his third feature, *The Lodger* (1926), that bore most obviously the mark of the German silent cinema with its unusual camera angles, its dramatic lighting schemes and its macabre theme of violence and sexual murder, although the film was made back in Britain at the Islington studios. Hitchcock was familiar with German cinema even before going to Germany professionally and he mentions to Truffaut seeing Fritz Lang's *Der Müde Tod* (1921) and other Decla-Bioscop pictures in London.[9] He was also able to see German pictures at the Film Society which, indeed, had started its weekly programmes in 1925 with a screening of Paul Leni's

Waxworks (1924) and, according to Ivor Montagu, Hitchcock was a regular attender at the society's meetings.[10] *The Lodger* emerges from this constellation of influences, from Hitchcock's admiration for Hollywood screen techniques with its stress on narrative economy and from his interest in the German cinema with its innovative cinematography and approach to lighting. This represents a confluence of entertainment and art cinema, and Hitchcock, in the mid-1920s, seemed to be straddling the two branches of the film culture, the commercial and the artistic, the world of entertainment and the world of 'film art'. He was not unique in this respect and figures such as Bernstein, Montagu and his fellow director Asquith amongst others also represent a kind of hesitation between the different spheres of cinema. Montagu describes the way in which Hitchcock had some difficulty early in his career with the hard commercial end of the industry when the distributor, C.M. Woolf, rejected *The Lodger* on the grounds that it was 'too "highbrow", too involved with "art"'.[11] Balcon has suggested that the problems may have been bound up with Hitchcock's uneasy relationship with Graham Cutts and that the older director had started a kind of whispering campaign against the film. Cutts was close to Woolf who, according to Montagu, 'felt more comfortable with types like Cutts than with types like Hitch'.[12] Although he does not elaborate on the differences between the two directors it does seem clear that Hitchcock was developing an 'artistic' reputation during this period and an identity as a film maker which was at odds with the expectations of business figures in the industry like Woolf. In some respects, his reputation at this time can be likened to that of a Hollywood figure such as Erich Von Stroheim, an artistic maverick in a commercial jungle, yet a figure like John Ford may be a more apposite comparison. Ford was a director with the ability to turn his hand to the assignments imposed upon him by the studio system but he was also interested in developing his own conception of cinema. With Ford, this meant making studio assignments in order to be allowed the freedom to make the occasional personal project and this model may well fit Hitchcock during his British career. David Bordwell has provided a neat summary of the options available to film directors in the early formative years of the cinema. The most usual path was the contract to a commercial film company and the working to assignments determined by that company and this was the circumstance in which Hitchcock found himself, or, according to his own testimony, chose.[13] Other options available were to contract to the 'artistic' wing of a commercial company as happened in France with Gaumont and Pathé or in Germany with the Decla-Bioscop unit of UFA, or to move outside the commercial industry altogether and make films on a self-financed basis or for groups such as the Surrealists which had access to wealthy patronage. The weak British film industry with its few struggling firms was incapable of sustaining a normal production programme let alone of constructing 'artistic' arms for experimental film and the minority film culture did not seem able to generate the kind of artistic patronage that was available in France. A commercial career was really the only option for a film maker like Hitchcock. Hitchcock and others such as Asquith and Thorold Dickinson who were aware of and interested in the experimental cinemas of Europe were obliged to work out such interests in the context of a narrative cinema necessarily developing along American lines. At the time of the first version of *The Lodger* this meant that Hitchcock was in the business of confronting the industry with his own conceptions of film art and running the risk of rejection by the key middlemen who managed distribution and who staked their reputations on the ability to gauge the tastes of the public accurately. C.M. Woolf and his colleagues were the people who determined which films ended up on British screens and it is clear that this sector of the industry was ambivalent about developments in 'the art of the film' during this period. On the one hand 'art' brought a certain degree of respectability to a medium which still suffered from the social opprobrium of the educated classes, but on the other hand art and experimentation were considered to be at odds with the proven commercially successful patterns of cinema developed by the Hollywood film industry.

Ironically, Hitchcock's problem with *The Lodger* was solved with the help of the central figure in the minority film culture, Ivor Montagu. He was the paradigmatic upper-class university-educated type who began to enter the film world during the twenties. Some, like Montagu, did end up in the commercial industry but many turned towards the documentary movement as we have seen in Chapter 2. Montagu, as well as working for the Film Society, was a member of Adrian Brunel's small film company which specialised in re-editing completed films and in the preparation of foreign films for British screening. It was in their capacity as re-editing experts that they were approached by Balcon to work on *The Lodger* and to make it a commercial proposition. According to Taylor, Montagu was 'completely bowled over by it'[14] and he and Hitchcock worked together on a few changes including a little re-shooting together with more radical alterations to the titles. These were reduced considerably to improve the flow of the film and this was a bold move in a cinema which conventionally employed an abundance of titles. As Montagu himself has said 'long titles especially came as an interruption to the sort of hypnotism of the silent film'[15] and the paring down of these indicates another link between Hitchcock's work and the German cinema of the time. Film makers such as Murnau, for example, were trying to make films which abandoned the use of titles altogether and depended on the visual images to recount the narrative. The stress on the visual aspects of the film implied by the reduction of the titles is credited to Montagu yet Hitchcock himself understood narrative cinema in primarily visual terms and this aesthetic position becomes clearer in his attitude towards the introduction of sound in the late 1920s. One more step credited to Montagu was the commissioning of the American graphic artist E. McKnight Kauffer to design 'art titles' for the film. These illustrated titles had been used in America since 1916 but they were uncommon in the European cinema.[16] After these various alterations and

89

additions, the film was screened to the trade in September, 1926 and was hailed as a significant breakthrough in the history of British cinema with the trade paper, *The Bioscope*, praising it as possibly 'the finest British production ever made'.[17]

With *The Lodger* Hitchcock also had an introduction to one of the key features of commercial film production, the centrality of the star system. The leading player in the film was Ivor Novello who was under contract to Balcon at the time. Novello was a big star on stage and screen in the 1920s, by far the most important in the Gainsborough company, and his star persona was to prove something of an obstacle to Hitchcock's own conception of *The Lodger*. He told Truffaut that his preferred version of the story would have left the identity of the murderer unrevealed thus leaving a cloud of suspicion hanging over the Novello character. The discussion continued:

> *Truffaut:* In actual fact, the hero was innocent. He was not Jack the Ripper.
> *Hitchcock:* That was the difficulty. Ivor Novello, the leading man, was a matinée idol in England. He was a very big name at the time. These are the problems we face with the star system. Very often the story line is jeopardised because the star cannot be a villain.
> *Truffaut:* I gather that you would have preferred the hero to turn out to be Jack the Ripper.
> *Hitchcock:* Not necessarily. But in a story of this kind I might have liked him to go off into the night, so that we could never really know for sure. But with the hero played by a big star, one can't do that. You have to spell it out in big letters: 'He is innocent'.[18]

Hitchcock was to face similar problems early on in his Hollywood career over the casting of Cary Grant as the lead in *Suspicion* (1941). Again, the image of the star nurtured in romantic films and screwball comedies of the 1930s was not felt to be compatible with the playing of a murderer and the Hitchcockian conception of the film had to be modified. Hitchcock's next picture for Balcon, *Downhill* (1927), also starred Novello and was an adaptation of a Novello play. After this Hitchcock was assigned a further stage adaptation, *Easy Virtue* (1927) based upon a Noel Coward play and such films bear testimony to the influence of the theatre on the British silent cinema. It was at this point that Hitchcock was to leave Balcon and to bring to a close what might be regarded as the first phase in his British career.

During this time he had gained experience in many aspects of film production from title designing to art direction, from scenario writing to editing, and eventually as a fully fledged commercial film director. He had nurtured his interest in matters of film art through his contacts with the Film Society, with prominent figures from the minority film culture such as Bernstein and Montagu, and through his professional experience in the

German cinema where the most self-consciously artistic of silent cinemas was being developed. On the other hand, he had been frequently brought up against the tougher, commercial aspects of the entertainment film industry as is indicated by the problems with *The Lodger* and the experience of working with big stars. The major lesson of the period was about the role and function of film critics and their influence over the success or failure of a picture, and the general role of publicity for the film maker. The very favourable notices that *The Lodger* received after its trade showing gave Hitchcock's career a considerable lift and enabled him to overcome the problems with hostile distributors. According to Taylor, he developed the view that a director should make films for critics rather than for distributors or for the public for it was they who determined the destiny of a picture.[19] Hitchcock had realised the role of reviewers in the publicity process and the importance of a public image for a successful film maker. Even before *The Lodger* was taken up by the reviewers, Hitchcock had managed to build up a considerable reputation. *The Pleasure Garden* had received some good reviews after its trade screening in March 1926 and, in the same month *Picturegoer* — a leading fan magazine — carried an article by Cedric Belfrage entitled 'Alfred the Great'. It presented a glowing image of Hitchcock as 'the world's youngest film director' possessing 'a complete grasp of all the different branches of film technique' acquired during his five years of working with Famous Players-Lasky, and Cutts and Balcon.[20] Belfrage, who has been described by Rachael Low as 'one of the better educated and more serious young entrants to the film industry'[21], clearly discerned something in Hitchcock on the basis of his work with Cutts and, one assumes, on the evidence of *The Pleasure Garden*. However, the eulogising tone of the article is quite remarkable as it concerned a film maker whose films had yet to be shown to the public. Perhaps it was the relatively small scale of the industry or the influence of figures like Bernstein and Belfrage who occupied the ground between the 'artistic' wing of the film culture and the entertainment sector, that enabled Hitchcock to acquire such a substantial reputation prior to a test at the box-office. Whatever the reasons, by 1926 Hitchcock had become the most sought-after director in an entertainment industry that was preparing itself for the surge in production that was anticipated with the passage of the Films Bill in 1927. As Ivor Montagu has said:

> The public generally did not know who directed the films they saw, but they had seen Hitchcock's name in the press. The result was that every group that was floating a new company during the Quota Act wanted Hitchcock under contract in order to attract money.[22]

The company that managed to secure Hitchcock's services was British National Pictures which had been set up in 1925 by the American J.D. Williams, as part of his plan to bring Hollywood experience and methods to the British film industry. Hitchcock had signed with the company in May

1926 but by the time he arrived to begin working for them, Williams had been ousted and the company had become part of the Maxwell group. Hitchcock had become a leading director in the British cinema prior to the release of any of the five films he had directed during his years with Michael Balcon. He had managed to secure an identity that included technical expertise, artistic awareness, overall grasp of the medium and, importantly in the context of a British cinema poised to expand rapidly, promise for the future. The artistic persona of 'Hitchcock' so familiar to subsequent filmgoers, although implied in *The Lodger* with its themes of violent crime and 'the proximity of the chaos world'[23] to ordinary everyday life, was more or less absent from the other films of the first 'Balcon phase'.

British International Pictures 1927-32

The next phase of Hitchcock's career was to be spent at British International Pictures and during his five years at Elstree he directed ten feature films, produced a 'quota quickie', contributed to a revue film *Elstree Calling* (1930), and made a one reel comedy sketch film. The circumstances of these years differed dramatically from the years with Gainsborough in a variety of ways. Gainsborough was a modest company with a small annual output operating in the difficult economic conditions before the Quota Act came into force. BIP was to become a large production company, the principal production arm, in fact, of one of the two major film combines that emerged in the late 1920s. The contract that Hitchcock had signed made him the highest paid film director in the country with an annual income of £13,000.[24] Yet, in moving from Gainsborough, where he was undoubtedly the principal asset in terms of creative work, he had become part of a company which was spending considerable amounts of money to attract top talent from home and abroad. The Quota Act meant a vastly increased scale of operation for British companies and considerable expansion was necessary for those firms which wanted to exploit the guaranteed market for home produced films. Although Hitchcock was clearly a very important part of the company's production plans, he was soon to be joined by Balcon's erstwhile colleague, Victor Saville, by leading film makers from Germany such as Arthur Robison and E.A. Dupont, important cinematographers such as Charles Rosher who had worked in Hollywood on *Sunrise* (1927) with Murnau, and an assortment of American stars such as Anna May Wong, Tallulah Bankhead and Lionel Barrymore. The company spent lavishly and attracted a considerable array of talent to the studios at Elstree. Yet, as Rachael Low has commented, the result in terms of films was disappointing and 'although they were of high technical quality and drew on as many English top players, and as much foreign talent as money could buy they were not particularly interesting'.[25] Hitchcock was no longer the leading director in a small company but simply one of a number of film makers including figures like Dupont who had substantial international reputations. In many ways he was deprived of the congenial artistic atmosphere of Balcon's small production set-up which had played a significant role in his early development as a film maker.

Yet he clearly had a high status at BIP and an indication of this is the fact that he was allowed to make his first film for them from an original idea of his own. *The Ring* (1927) was also BIP's inaugural release and it was a great success in critical terms. Superlatives abounded in the press reviews and the film was hailed as 'the greatest production ever made in this country', 'a devastating answer to those who disbelieved in the possibilities of a British film', 'a triumph for the British film industry', and a picture which 'challenges comparison with the best that America can produce'.[26] The newspaper comment was so favourable that as part of the advance publicity for the film *The Bioscope* included a double page spread which simply printed excerpts from 15 newspaper reviews under a banner headline which repeated the *Daily Mail's* judgement of the film as 'the greatest production ever made in this country'.[27] Many interesting critical comments were made on the film. The *Sunday Express* suggested that the 'film is significant mainly because Hitchcock himself is significant' and this centralisation of the director was echoed in many of the reviews. The film was also seen as the spearhead of a renaissance in the British cinema and the *Evening Standard* critic argued, with a sideswipe at protectionism, that 'Mr. Hitchcock has done more for British pictures than a dozen acts of parliament'. In a prescient comment, the reviewer of the *Evening News* suggested that *The Ring* 'succeeds in that very rare accomplishment of being the purest film art and a fine popular entertainment' thus accurately pinpointing Hitchcock's position between art and entertainment at this early point in his career, and anticipating many a later critical comment on the director.[28] *The Bioscope* took a lot of space in its 'Messages from The Bioscope' column to address both Maxwell and Hitchcock and it congratulated the head of BIP for sinking effort and resource in *The Ring*:

> You have set the standard not only for your own company but for every British producer, and if future British films only approach 'The Ring' in quality, we need have no fears for the ultimate success of the entire producing industry in this country.[29]

To Hitchcock were addressed further congratulations along the lines of the newspaper comment but interestingly the article continued with a plea to him 'to continue to make films in this country, because the producing industry — which owes you a debt of gratitude — can ill afford to be without your talent'.[30] Hollywood, of course, was at this time busily recruiting film makers and actors from the European countries and *The Bioscope* correctly anticipated the interest that the international film capital would eventually take in Hitchcock. Hitchcock had achieved considerable success with *The Ring* in terms of its critical reception. It is also one of the few films from the twenties that he remembers with any degree of satisfaction and it provides further evidence for Hitchcock as an experimental director developing new narrative techniques and stylistic variations. In discussion with Truffaut, he discusses the significance of the film in the following comment:

> that was a really interesting movie. You might say that after *The Lodger*, *The Ring* was the next Hitchcock picture. There were all kinds of innovations in it, and I remember that at the premiere an elaborate montage got a round of applause. It was the first time that had ever happened to me.[31]

Despite such a favourable reception and claims in the press that the film would be 'a certain attraction wherever shown'[32], it failed at the box office indicating a considerable distance between the journalist critics' and public taste.

Hitchcock's next project was *The Farmer's Wife* (1928) which, as an adaptation of a successful West End play, returned him to the career trajectory marked out by his last two pictures at Gainsborough. Hitchcock's self-generated project had failed and his subsequent career at BIP was to be dominated by theatrical and literary adaptations of one sort or another, and the great hope of British cinema in the late 1920s marked his departure from the studio in 1932 with the production of a 'quota quickie'! *The Farmer's Wife* was followed by *Champagne* (1928), a film designed as a star vehicle for actress Betty Balfour. In the words of the trade press, it was a 'bright comedy-drama with every opportunity for the star to exploit her talent and personal charm'[33] but for Hitchcock, in words that he was to use more than once about the middle phase of his British career, it 'was probably the lowest ebb in my output'.[34] *Champagne* was a fairly light society comedy and, for his next assignment, Hitchcock was presented with a rather more sombre subject based upon a novel by best selling author Sir Hall Caine. The trade press reception of *The Manxman* (1928) contrasted with the somewhat lukewarm comments upon *Champagne* and Hitchcock's directorial touch was highlighted by *The Bioscope's* reviewer who suggested that only 'a skilful director could have devised from a story of this kind a picture of remarkable power and gripping interest'.[35] The reviewer also drew attention to the 'unflinching realism' of the picture, anticipating subsequent comments on the director's pictures of this period by 'realist' critics such as Anderson and Grierson. Hitchcock himself, however, dismisses the film with the curt judgement that the 'only point of interest about that movie is that it was my last silent one'.[36]

Blackmail (1929), his next picture, is the most famous from the BIP period and it has been celebrated partly for its return to the 'essential Hitchcock' of crime, passion and suspense, a return, that is, to the familiar image of the director from later critical analysis. It was also the first British talking picture and this has given the film a privileged place in most histories of cinema. However a number of other films made in the same year might well have claimed that distinction. About half of BIP's releases for 1929 were sound pictures and, according to Frank Launder, one of these, *Under the Greenwood Tree* (Lachman), 'might have been the first British full-length talking film had Harry Lachman got a move on'.[37] Apart from BIP there were other studios involved in sound production from the start. For example, Victor Saville's *Kitty*, which was first registered as a silent film in January 1929, had dialogue scenes filmed in America during May of the same year. Basil Dean of Associated Talking Pictures claims that his own film adaptation of Galsworthy's play *Escape* more properly enjoys precedence over *Blackmail* because it was actually conceived as a talking picture in contrast to Hitchcock's which began life as a silent film, was subsequently reshot for sound, and indeed was released in both sound and silent versions.[38] However, the position of *Blackmail* as a 'first' is less important than its position in the general history of the sound film. As Rachael Low has said of Hitchcock and *Blackmail*:

> At a time when the whole cinema world was uncertain, most film makers fumbling, the critics theorising and the Soviet film makers as yet lacking the resources to put their ideas into practice, it was this shrewd and practical professional who unhesitatingly showed how sound could be made an integral part of film technique.[39]

So whilst major film makers such as Eisenstein were issuing manifestoes about the way in which the new elements of dialogue, music and sound effects could be incorporated into the medium, Hitchcock was supplying a practical demonstration in *Blackmail*. As we have seen, even the highbrow critical journal *Close Up*, despite its general disdain for mainstream commercial cinema, devoted a relatively large amount of space to the film.[40] The comments in *Close Up* were, in part, grudging and there was a tendency to dismiss the thematic elements of the film, yet writers such as Hugh Castle and Kenneth MacPherson both conceded the innovative use of the sound track especially in the celebrated 'knife' sequence with its expressionist distortion of sound to convey the mental preoccupations of the central character. Their assessment of the significance of the film, in the context of early sound cinema was later to be echoed, albeit with similar reservations, by the film historian Paul Rotha in his comment that *Blackmail* 'may not have been a particularly good film, but it was infinitely better than any American picture of the time'.[41] The trade press also recognised the distinctive quality of the picture and *The Bioscope* hailed it as a breakthrough in the uniting of dialogue with images in the following comment:

> We understand that Mr. Hitchcock began this production as a silent film and was then called upon to adapt his plans to meet the requirements of

dialogue. He has certainly succeeded to admiration, for this is neither the mere adaptation of a stage play to the screen nor a silent film fitted with stage dialogue, and it may well be that Mr. Hitchcock has solved the problem of combining the two and helped towards assigning the true position of the sound film in the ranks of entertainment.[42]

Kine Weekly was less analytical but equally appreciative, referring to the film as 'a splendid example of popular all talkie screen entertainment'.[43] The importance of its appearance is signalled by a mention in *The Bioscope's* 'News in Brief' column which indicates a reception by the film world similar to that given to *The Ring* a few years earlier. 'Last Friday's midnight premiere of "Blackmail", Alfred Hitchcock's first British International "talkie" was', wrote the columnist, 'the scene of tremendous outbursts of enthusiasm'.[44] *The Bioscope's* review also drew attention to the way in which the film utilises typically British settings such as the Lyons Corner House and the British Museum, in which the final chase occurs, thus pinpointing what was to become a specific quality of a Hitchcock picture — the use of familiar locations for the setting of dramatic incident. Again, as with *The Ring*, the film was seen as heralding a boom in British production as the following reviewer suggests:

> By this masterly production Alfred Hitchcock amply fulfils the promise shown in his earlier efforts. He has given us a story of vital interest, played and directed in a manner which is convincing proof that the talking film offers opportunities which cannot be equalled in any other country.[45]

Highbrow analysis and popular commentary were united in their recognition of the distinctive qualities of the picture, and it is not surprising that Hitchcock, with his long-standing interest in the technical aspects of the medium, should produce a film with distinctiveness in its use of the new technological potential.

In interviews, Hitchcock speaks of his interest in the sound track and his recognition that the silent picture would not survive the 'talkie' revolution of the late 1920s. Yet, from the perspective of aesthetic preference, Hitchcock's artistic and cinematic formation in the silent narrative film of the twenties might have led him to a 'purist' attitude towards sound in line with many in the film industry and in the wide circles of the film culture of the time. In some respects Hitchcock does share the highbrow suspicion of sound to be found in the writings of theorists such as Rotha and Rudolf Arnheim, for example, as the following exchange with Truffaut indicates:

> *Truffaut:* Before going on to *Blackmail*, which is your first talking picture, I would like a few words on silent pictures, in general.
> *Hitchcock:* Well, the silent pictures were the purest form of cinema; the only thing they lacked was the sound of people talking and the

noises. But this slight imperfection did not warrant the major changes that sound brought in. In other words, since all that was missing was simply natural sound, there was no need to go to the other extreme and completely abandon the technique of the pure motion picture, the way they did when sound came in.[46]

Hitchcock's concern at this crucial point of technological and aesthetic change was to find an appropriate role for the sound track in the task of cinematic narration which had, by the late 1920s, developed into a highly sophisticated form of visual communication. What is significant about his position is the predisposition towards finding a place for this new element in contrast to the many violent rejections of sound by film makers such as Chaplin, by theorists such as Rotha, and by many in the industry itself including, in fact, Hitchcock's own boss, John Maxwell, who dismissed the sound film as 'a costly fad'.[47] It might be argued that Hitchcock was in the right place at the right time to be the director of the first British 'talkie'. He worked for a highly professionalised business-oriented film company which, despite the individual opinions of its senior figures, would be obliged to conform to the dominant pattern of film production and, more importantly, was in a financial position to so do. The American film industry by 1929 had moved completely over to sound production following the immense success of *The Jazz Singer* (Crosland, 1927), and given the dominant position of the American cinema in international terms, this meant that countries like Britain would have to follow suit. There had been a number of attempts to develop sound pictures in Britain during the 1920s and De Forest Phonofilms had been registered as early as 1923 to make British sound pictures whilst the Gaumont company had actually advertised a sound system in 1926. That it took until 1929 for the first sound pictures to emerge is probably due to the dramatic acceleration of the production industry brought about by the Quota Act of 1927 and the problems of adjusting to large scale production. A certain amount of settling in was necessary before the sound revolution could be accommodated in an industry which really only began to constitute itself in a recognisably modern form in the late twenties.

Despite the structural determinations that were to bring the sound film to the British film industry, it seems clear that a certain amount of manoeuvring by Hitchcock and his production team was necessary to put BIP into the forefront of sound film making in Britain. As we have seen, John Maxwell was not convinced of the future of 'talkies' and *Blackmail* was originally planned as a silent picture though there was a tentative move towards making it as a part-talkie sometime during its production history. From various accounts of its making, notably Hitchcock's own, the film was worked out so that with a little reshooting it could be turned into a fully fledged sound picture. The somewhat devious though astute production strategy adopted by Hitchcock has been substantiated recently in Charles Barr's detailed comparison of the silent and sound versions of the film. This reveals that while shooting the silent version of the film, the official company-endorsed version, Hitchcock was also shooting separate usable takes of each shot in order to prepare a negative for the sound version of the film.[48] With the subsequent change of mind at managerial level, Hitchcock was able to provide a sound version speedily and it was this that was released initially some two months ahead of the silent version. Hitchcock's technical ingenuity was also displayed in other aspects of the production and particularly in the use of process cinematography for the chase sequence towards the end of the film. Owing to problems with the lighting it would not have been possible to shoot in the British Museum itself and Hitchcock had to use the Schufftan cinematographic process to obtain the setting which, as we have seen, so impressed contemporary reviewers. This process, a complicated technique which involved the use of mirrors combined with photographic transparencies or miniaturised sets, was treated with great suspicion by the BIP management and, as with the sound plans, its use required a great deal of ingenuity and subterfuge from the production team. As John Russell Taylor has written:

All this had to be done in great secrecy, because Maxwell was worried about how long the film was taking to shoot and no one in the studio management knew much about the Schufftan process except that they mistrusted it as a new-fangled contraption which might well go wrong. As a cover, Hitch. set up a second camera on the sidelines apparently photographing a letter for an insert. A lookout was posted, and if anybody from the front office was sighted approaching they would all drop what they were doing and suddenly be very intent on the letter until the danger was past.[49]

The Schufftan process, named after its German inventor, was one of the many techniques of process cinematography developed during the silent period. The British rights to the technique had been acquired by British National (BIP's predecessor) in the mid-1920s and it was first used on the production of *Madame Pompadour* which was directed by Herbert Wilcox in 1927. The sophisticated development of such techniques had, in the words of Rachael Low, 'revolutionised and greatly extended film production'.[50] It was no longer necessary to construct elaborate sets or to shoot on location when credible images such as those in the final sequences of *Blackmail* were obtainable through the use of one or other of the process methods. The introduction of the heavy sound cameras in their soundproof booths in 1929 gave further impetus to the adoption of process cinematography as it encouraged or even obliged film makers to work entirely within the confines of the studio. The art direction on *Blackmail* was handled by Wilfred Arnold and Norman Arnold, both of whom had considerable experience of process work. Wilfred Arnold had worked with Hitchcock on *The Ring* and the Schufftan process had been used on that film as well. The account of Hitchcock acting with a certain amount of guile in order to get his British Museum sequences needs to be thought about in the context of an industry in which such techniques were part of the established practices, part of the technological context in which the director worked. Indeed, the role of a figure like Wilfred Arnold in the development of the Hitchcock style may be considered quite significant. Rachael Low makes the point that Arnold's designs for *The Farmer's Wife* included 'a very interesting experiment with a boxed-in set and a long travelling shot'[51] prefiguring what was to become an important part of Hitchcock's film style. Hitchcock was operating in a context of technological possibility which was dependent upon the collaborative activity of a number of film workers and what emerges or what is constructed as 'Hitchcockian' may have much to do with them. Apart from the technical complexities of sound and cinematography, Hitchcock also faced problems with his conception of the plot of the film similar to those he faced with *The Lodger*. He had originally planned a somewhat bleak ending in which the opening of the film, the arrest and imprisonment of the criminal, would have been reprised but this time the heroine would have been in the criminal's position. The producers, however, were unimpressed with the formal elegance of such a suggestion, claiming that it would have been too depressing for audiences, and Hitchcock had to settle for the happy ending in which the heroine goes free.[52]

Blackmail had been adapted from a play by Charles Bennett who was later to play a central role in Hitchcock's career, and this signalled a return to theatrical sources as Hitchcock's next three pictures also drew on the stage for their sources. *Juno and the Paycock* (1930), adapted from the Sean O'Casey play, was a massive critical success although Hitchcock himself attributes this to the 'respectable' literary source rather than to any cinematic distinction that the film might have possessed. The comments in *The Bioscope* endorse this view in so far as their reviewer singled out 'the author's reputation and the success of the play' as the major selling points of the film.[53] Although *Blackmail* had been based on a play, Hitchcock had 'opened out' the film. The sequences of arrest at the beginning of the picture, Alice's dazed walk through London at dawn after the stabbing and the final chase sequences set in the British Museum, had provided Hitchcock with many opportunities to shake off the theatrical origins of the film. He was unable to do this with *Juno and the Paycock* which 'had its own coherence and consistency and would brook very little modification'.[54] Indeed, several problems converged on this particular production. The problem of adapting a very successful play with a well established identity was one which often confronted British film makers of this period. Producers frequently acted on the assumption that success in dramatic or literary form indicated potential success on the screen. There were also the problems of filming with the still novel sound techniques and there was the continuing influence of the aesthetic tradition of the 'cinematic' derived from the recently departed silent era. Raymond Durgnat's comments on the film are illuminating in relation to that particular cluster of factors and he compared Hitchcock to his French contemporary, Jean Renoir, as follows:

> *Juno* seems lacking in dolly-shots, and tends to restrict any depth in groupings to long shot, which suggests problems with sound equipment and shallow-focus lenses analogous to those with which Renoir was grappling. But whereas the French situation gave the director and his creative *équipe* an ascendancy over the technicians, in England the balance between the system and the artist was less favourable to the innovations required to master the new techniques, and for once Hitchcock the redoubtable technical thinker was unable to impose himself.[55]

That conceded, however, we might note the distinctive artistic identities of the two directors as additional factors. Renoir's aesthetic which is based upon the improvised relationship between players and director during the shooting of a film contrasts with that of Hitchcock which is based firmly on the preliminary *découpage* carried out by the director. This latter approach leaves little room for the player/camera interaction that Renoir sought and which encouraged him to confront the problems of staging in depth at this early stage in the history of the sound film. Hitchcock did, in fact, experiment with player improvisation in his next film, *Murder!* (1930) but, as he mentions to Truffaut, the result was not entirely happy:

> I also experimented with improvisation in direct sound. I would explain the meaning of the scene to the actors and suggest that they made up their own dialogue. The result wasn't good; there was too much faltering. They would carefully think over what they were about to say and we didn't get the spontaneity I had hoped for. The timing was wrong and it had no rhythm.[56]

According to Donald Spoto, the move into improvisation which is somewhat 'unHitchcockian' was imposed upon the director because the dialogue adaptation from the play was not finished at the scheduled start of the shooting.[57]

As with *Juno and the Paycock*, the trade press comment highlighted the dramatic origins of the film as an important selling angle although also included in *The Bioscope*'s review was considerable praise for the direction. The review praised Hitchcock's 'striking originality and wonderful technical facility' and suggested, in terms which echo the comment on *Blackmail* a year earlier, that *Murder!* marked a considerable step towards the 'assigning to the talking picture its true position with respect to the silent screen and the legitimate stage'.[58] Hitchcock was indeed becoming familiar with the problems of adapting stage material for the screen and in the following year he completed his fourth play adaptation in a row. Again, the trade press tended to single out the Galsworthy play on which *The Skin*

Game (1931) was based and although in many respects it remains a photo-graphed play, it is less stagebound than *Juno and the Paycock* notably in the filming of the auction room sequence. The *Kine Weekly* review highlighted the use of rapid cutting and a zip-panning camera in this sequence and commented that there 'is an entire avoidance of stage limitations and the camera has been given full scope without destroying or holding up the continuity of the dialogue'.[59] Hitchcock also completed *Rich and Strange* in 1931 and although it is one of the few films from his BIP period that he remembers with any degree of satisfaction, it was both a critical and commercial failure. By that time, he had been assigned a low budget thriller by the studio and *Number Seventeen* which was released in 1932 was the last film Hitchcock directed for the Maxwell combine.

Hitchcock's final year at BIP was affected by the financial problems of the studio and the changes in production policy which kept the company stable during the 1930s. BIP had expanded its production from 14 features in 1928, its first effective full year of releases, to around 30 features in 1931 and 1932. 1933, however, saw a halving of the releases and by this time the company was not only making fewer films but was also making them more cheaply. Hence, the restricted budget for *Number Seventeen* which is indicative of the shift in production policy to the 'quota quickie' end of the market. Hitchcock was to work on one more film for the company, *Lord Camber's Ladies* (B.W. Levy, 1932), a quota picture which he produced. This marked a considerable decline in his prestige and stand-ing for from a position in the 1920s as the director of 'the greatest produc-tion ever made in this country'[60] he had moved to the production of the lowest type of picture in the British cinema — the 'quota quickie' — which had been responsible for giving that cinema such a poor reputation in the early sound period. Part of the explanation for this change in Hitchcock's fortunes may lie in the decision of British International Pictures to settle for making programme pictures (See Chapter 3). Rachael Low has described John Maxwell and his associates as a management team who 'saw themselves as being engaged in big business, not as nourishing and building a team of creative artists in the way that Balcon, Bruce Woolfe and others had tried to do'.[61] Although Hitchcock had been given a certain amount of production freedom for his first BIP film, *The Ring*, its comm-ercial failure rather than its critical success set the future pattern of his career at the studio. The assumption that successful films could be based on proven literary or dramatic sources was particularly marked at BIP and, following the financial failure of *The Ring*, Hitchcock's career is dominated by such material. It might be suggested that this represents a closer super-vision of the director by the management team and a repeat of the suspicion of Hitchcock displayed by the financial figures during his time at Gainsborough. Although the critical reception of Hitchcock's films in the trade press was favourable during this period, his career has to be charted in terms of this decline from prestigious production to 'quota quickie'. Paul Rotha has written scathingly about the press reception of British films in the late 1920s drawing attention to 'a structure of false prestige'[62] which was erected around British films of the time. He wrote of a 'blaze of patriotic glamour' which accompanied British productions and it may be argued that this was the case with, for example, *The Ring*. Its undoubted merits are perhaps disguised by the somewhat exaggerated predictions of its impact upon the British production industry, and its failure to match critical acclaim with financial success might have been instrumental in returning Hitchcock to the pattern of theatrical adaptation that marked his final year at Gainsborough.

Gaumont British and Gainsborough, 1934-38

The next phase of Hitchcock's career really starts in 1934 when he was re-united with Michael Balcon, but in between leaving BIP and joining Gaumont British, Hitchcock almost went to work for Alexander Korda and directed a musical for the independent producer, Tom Arnold. The Korda plan failed to materialise as the producer was unable to put together a package suitable for Hitchcock but he was then signed by Tom Arnold to make a film version of a successful musical play *Waltzes from Vienna* featuring the leading British female star of the day, Jessie Matthews. *Waltzes from Vienna* (1933) marks the most extreme divergence from what was to become established as the Hitchcock image, the director of thrillers, yet it is important to note that during his first seven years or so as a film director, only a handful of pictures actually conform to that image. The critics had noticed his skill and expertise as a director and 'the Hitchcock touch' was frequently noted as a selling point of these films. The trade press comments and those of the more highbrow critics had constructed an image of the director but it was mainly in terms of style and technique rather than theme or genre. John Grierson writing in the early 1930s refers to the 'Hitchcock touch' which gives his films a considerable distinction but goes on to describe him as 'the world's best director of unimportant pictures'.[63] For Grierson it was the absence of serious subject matter that undermined Hitchcock's status as a film maker but the critical writing of the period seems to stress Hitchcock as a stylist turning his hand to a diversity of material much of which was not commensurate with his skill as a director. Hitchcock was characterised as a 'mere' *metteur en scène*, to borrow the later critical vocabulary of *Cahiers du Cinéma*, and his accession to the status of *auteur* might be said to have occurred during his time at Gaumont British.

Waltzes from Vienna, although an independent production, was made at the Shepherd's Bush studio of Gaumont British and it was during the making of this film that Hitchcock was once again to link up with Michael Balcon. It was, of course, Balcon who had started Hitchcock on his directorial career at Gainsborough Pictures in the 1920s and by 1931 Balcon had moved into one of the most commanding positions in the British film industry as head of production at Gaumont British and its associated company, Gainsborough. From 1931 until he left the company in 1936, Balcon supervised an ambitious production programme which saw up to 26 films a year emerging from the company studios at Shepherd's Bush and Islington. Hitchcock was invited by Balcon to return to the more congenial artistic atmosphere that Balcon had established at Gaumont British and his renewed professional relationship with Balcon was to produce the series of thrillers which for most people constitute the 'essential British Hitchcock'. *Waltzes from Vienna* was obviously another 'low ebb' in Hitchcock's career, a point where his control over his career was slipping dangerously and the return to Balcon marked his rehabilitation as a film maker after the years of assignments and indifferent projects. His final year at BIP had seen the critical and commercial failure of films such as *Rich and Strange* and *Number Seventeen* and also the frustration of a number of his own film projects. One of these was a scenario based upon Bulldog Drummond, the character created by H.C. McNeile ('Sapper'), which he had developed with Charles Bennett and D.B. Wyndham-Lewis.[64] It was this project that was to form the basis of his first film for Gaumont British, *The Man Who Knew Too Much* (1934) which at that time became his greatest British success and was the first of a series of spy thrillers which define the popular image of Hitchcock. Accounts of his career at this point invariably move from the crisis of *Waltzes from Vienna* to the creative renewal of *The Man Who Knew Too Much* but it is worth noting that *Kine Weekly* in January 1934 carried a brief story which mentioned that Hitchcock was preparing a film to be called *Road House* which was to be his first picture under his contract to Gaumont British.[65] The film, like its immediate predecessor, *Waltzes from Vienna*, was a musical and it was eventually made by Maurice Elvey and trade shown in the same month as *The Man Who Knew Too Much*. Perhaps the passage from 'low ebb' to creative renewal was not as clear cut as the usual accounts suggest.

The Man Who Knew Too Much was completed towards the end of 1934 and had its trade screening in December. It received a favourable press with *Kine Weekly* describing the film as 'glorious melodrama, an exciting excursion in the realm of artless fiction, staged on a spectacular scale'. The review can be read alongside the various accounts of Hitchcock returning to his essential interest, the thriller genre, and crystallising his public image on the basis of his distinctive versions of the genre. The review went on to argue that Hitchcock had 'obviously learnt by past experience that real money lies only in mass appeal, and with this wise thought in mind he has given us a piece of first class melodrama'. The review also suggests that Hitchcock was catching a changing public mood about the cinematic diet on offer during the period:

> The building up of tension has been cleverly accomplished and herein lies the success of the entertainment. There is no doubt that there is a public reaction against anaemic musicals and frothy drawing room plays

and this welcome return to healthy robust action and punch will, by catching them on the rebound, prove a first class attraction.[66]

Yet, according to many accounts, the picture did not have a smooth journey from production to release because the head of distribution at Gaumont British, C.M. Woolf, held the film up after previewing it, in a replay of his decision over *The Lodger* some eight years or so earlier. Balcon was in America and there was a threat that Woolf might order the picture to be reshot but eventually it was released, though as the lower half of a double bill. This suggests a grudging distribution for the picture yet it was given the normal promotional treatment for an important studio picture including a full page advert in *Kine Weekly* prior to the trade show.[67] Indeed, the facts surrounding the release of the film are not entirely clear. The orthodox account of the talented director clashing with the philistine distributor is given a somewhat different inflection by Balcon's own account of the episode. He actually credits Woolf with securing its release in the face of rejection by the cinema bookers and whereas, for example, Ivor Montagu pinpoints the distributors as the villains of the piece, for Balcon the major problems lay with the attitudes of the cinema operators. As he says in his autobiography:

> Although GB was now a large producer of films, the mental outlook of the theatre companies controlled by the corporation did not easily change, even as far as its own 'dockyard' production was concerned, and many battles were fought to get our own films shown in our own theatres.
> Perhaps the outstanding example of this was when our cinema bookers rejected Hitchcock's *The Man Who Knew Too Much*, now regarded as a classic. It was only after the intervention of C.M. Woolf that they agreed to play the film, and then only at a modest fixed price instead of the standard participation in box-office receipts usually paid for what cinema men thought to be 'good' films.[68]

Although the position for British films had improved during the years of the Quota Act, this episode illustrates that British film makers could still face problems getting their films on to the British screen. American films still constituted the predominant offering on the British screen and it was still in comparison with the popular American cinema that exhibitors judged British films. The problem for British films was even more acute in relation to the lucrative American market which had been the major target of many British companies since the success of *The Private Life of Henry VIII* (1933). Gaumont British, in particular, had pursued a policy of importing American stars, directors and technical staff with a view to breaking into the American market although this was not reflected in Hitchcock's first picture for them. *The Man Who Knew Too Much*, however, was given a release in America and although *Variety* reviewed it in generally supportive terms referring to 'an unusually fine dramatic story ... handled excellently from the production standpoint', the reviewer did enter a number of caveats about the British orientation of the picture.[69] The top billing of Edna Best and Leslie Banks, though reflecting their standing within the British cinema, was seen as a mistake for an American audience to whom they were unknown. The failure to give Peter Lorre a major billing was also seen as a mistake as he was one name in the film that was well known to American audiences partly through his role in Fritz Lang's film *M* (1931) and partly because he was actually in Hollywood under contract to Columbia when the film was released in 1935. The review also complained about the 'dialog' and singled out the use of the term 'point duty' to refer to the work of a 'traffic cop' as not being comprehensible to an American audience. It also suggested that if the 'film had one, or two, American names of fair strength it would romp' and this was taken up by Gaumont British. Hitchcock's subsequent thrillers were to feature British stars such as Madeleine Carroll and Robert Donat who had already worked in America, or the American stars such as Sylvia Sidney and Robert Young whom Balcon had brought over to work in Britain. The failure to exploit Lorre's familiarity suggests that the film was rather poorly marketed for the important American audience.

Hitchcock's standing within the studio was certainly consolidated by the critical success of his first film and the studio's announced production plans for 1935 included *The Thirty-Nine Steps* and two further projects scheduled for the director.[70] Hitchcock had been working on a rather free adaptation of John Buchan's famous novel with scriptwriter Charles Bennett since the completion of *The Man Who Knew Too Much* and although there were some further problems with C.M. Woolf who rejected the script at first, the success of his first film and the return of Balcon from America meant that the production could go ahead. If the distribution of *The Man Who Knew Too Much* had been a little cautious and tentative, the handling of *The Thirty-Nine Steps* indicated a very different attitude towards the director. The film was given major publicity treatment by the studio including a five-page advertising spread in *Kine Weekly*.[71] The film was to amply confirm Balcon's faith in Hitchcock and, according to the *Daily Mirror*, it became 'the most successful British film of the year'.[72] *Kine Weekly* which had enthusiastically applauded Hitchcock's move into the thriller genre with his previous film, was even more enthusiastic about *The Thirty-Nine Steps*. Their reviewer singled out the mixture of elements which marked the film as distinctive. The basic espionage theme of the previous film had been augmented with romance and comedy to produce a formula which Hitchcock was to forsake and then return to in his subsequent British films.[73] He had seen his move to Gaumont British and Balcon in terms of the re-establishment of his creative prestige and the review of his second thriller in the *Sunday Times* certainly indicates that this was achieved. Using a vocabulary remarkably similar to the later *Cahiers du*

Cinéma writing on Hitchcock, the critic singled out his directorial contribution in the following terms:

> Every film of real quality bears the unforgettable stamp of its creator. Individuality is a rare and precious thing. In moving pictures it is exceptionally hard to discover. When it is there, however, it usually assumes a force and a distinction unmistakeably attributable to its director, and its director alone. In *The Thirty Nine Steps*, the identity and mind of Alfred Hitchcock are continuously discernible.[74]

There was some critical dissent from such a judgement and, for example, Alistair Cooke writing in *Sight and Sound* whilst recognising the potential appeal of the counterpointing of suspense and comedy nevertheless found the film 'confused'. He complained that Hitchcock 'seems always distracted to decide the mood of any scene and this indecision passes into the pleasant but teetering performances of Madeleine Carroll and Robert Donat'.[75] Cooke, in fact, expressed a preference for *The Man Who Knew Too Much* — 'an intelligible and even thriller' — to its successor, but this was a minority opinion. The American reception of *The Thirty-Nine Steps* is further evidence of Hitchcock's increasing prestige and the *Variety* reviewer described Hitchcock as 'probably the best native director in England'.[76] Whereas *The Man Who Knew Too Much* suffered because of its lack of star appeal for the American audience, *The Thirty-Nine Steps* featured a hero and heroine who had worked in Hollywood. Madeleine Carroll had appeared in a John Ford film, *The World Moves On* (1934), whilst Robert Donat had appeared in Rowland V. Lee's *The Count of Monte Cristo* (1934) as well as having a part in Korda's *The Private Life of Henry VIII*. In addition to the 'strong cast' *Variety* also pointed to the success of the Buchan novel and to Hitchcock's adaptation which their critic found 'more original than the book from which it was derived', as key elements which would guarantee the success of the picture at the box-office. The reviewer also indicated the American attitude towards British films in general during this period when he suggested that *The Thirty-Nine Steps* proved that 'they can make pictures in England'. The film was very favourably received by the American audience and a report in the *Daily Telegraph* refers to a successful run of the film at the Roxy Theatre in New York, one of the most important of American first-run theatres.[77]

The appeal of the formula which blended suspense, romance and comedy was clearly established by the domestic and international success of *The Thirty-Nine Steps* yet the two films which succeed it whilst remaining within the confines of the espionage genre nevertheless differ considerably in tone and mood. In particular, the comedy elements from *The Thirty-Nine Steps* are virtually absent although the romantic elements are preserved especially in *Secret Agent* (1936). Both *Secret Agent* and *Sabotage* (1936) are based on what might be referred to as 'respectable' literary sources. The previous films based on 'Sapper' and John Buchan drew on traditions of popular culture whereas Somerset Maugham and Joseph Conrad, the literary sources of *Secret Agent* and *Sabotage* respectively, occupy different literary spheres. Both films represent a shift in tone and mood from the lighter qualities of *The Thirty-Nine Steps* towards a darker, perhaps more serious, meditation on the implications of the genre. Rohmer and Chabrol, in their pioneering study of Hitchcock, suggest a certain degree of calculation on Hitchcock's behalf, arguing that these films represent a bid for international prestige as well as international popular success.[78] *Kine Weekly* reflected on the shift in emphasis detectable in *Secret Agent* in the following terms:

> Although conventional in its fundamentals, this espionage drama differs vastly from the orthodox in treatment. Instead of unfolding the tale with the directness usually associated with entertainment of this type, the producer reflects the story in the psychological reactions of the leading characters.[79]

The reviewer praised the picture and described it as 'exciting entertainment of impeccable quality' yet the thematic shift to psychological analysis which betrayed the intellectual ambition of the project was seen as a possible obstacle to the popular appeal of the film in what were quaintly referred to as 'industrial situations, where sustained action means everything'.[80] Graham Greene, who might be regarded as the critical representative of the middle class audience to whom *Secret Agent* was addressed, was unimpressed by the film complaining about 'Mr. Hitchcock's inadequate sense of reality' and dismissing the film for its 'inconsistencies, loose ends, psychological absurdities'.[81]

Sabotage intensified Hitchcock's quest for prestige and ambition, for a more serious artistic profile, and produced what Rohmer and Chabrol somewhat reproachfully refer to as a 'quality' film which was 'too polished to be honest'.[82] They point to the fact that the film was based upon a prestigious literary work that was adapted with 'sufficient fidelity to prevent charges of betrayal, but with sufficient freedom so that it would at all times be possible to see that Hitchcock had remained faithful to his own temperament'.[83] *Kine Weekly* seemed intent on supporting Hitchcock in terms which derived from his image as a director of comedy thrillers with romantic appeal and their review does not really reflect the gloomy quality of the film. Their view anticipates Rohmer and Chabrol to the extent that it claims that the 'picture definitely has class' although it goes on to suggest that this quality is 'wedded to hearty melodrama of universal appeal'.[84] Graham Greene was more impressed with *Sabotage* than with its predecessor, judging that the film was 'convincingly realistic, perhaps because Mr. Hitchcock has left the screenplay to other hands'.[85] Greene drew attention to the weakness of casting John Loder in the role of the detective, a judgement echoed later by Hitchcock in the following comments to Truffaut:

Robert Donat was supposed to play the detective, but Alexander Korda refused to release him. The actor we got wasn't suitable, and I was forced to rewrite the dialogue during the shooting.[86]

Indeed, Hitchcock's general comments on both films suggest a certain regret for including what might be regarded as the troublesome and difficult elements of both narratives. Both films contain episodes in which innocent people are killed and Hitchcock sees such elements as difficult for the public to accept. This was particularly acute in the case of *Sabotage* in which a young boy is killed whilst unwittingly transporting the saboteur's bomb. *Variety* was lukewarm about the film and its criticism was in terms of the move towards psychology noted by British reviewers. The film was described as 'an intimate character study of a thick-skulled brutal criminal' and the reviewer went on to describe that quality as 'a weakness, because average American audiences expect Scotland Yard sleuthing to develop. When it doesn't, the film disappoints'.[87] The success of *The Thirty-Nine Steps* was not repeated by *Secret Agent* and *Sabotage* but Hitchcock's position as the foremost British director was left relatively unscathed. The Gaumont British production programme for 1937 included three films to be directed by Hitchcock although the confidence of the press announcement masked the problems that the company was to encounter during this fraught period in the industry.[88] The company was beset with problems in two different ways. Firstly, there were a number of boardroom changes including the resignation of C.M. Woolf and the company was subjected to takeover bids from the American company, Twentieth Century-Fox, which already had a substantial interest, and from the company's major British rival, John Maxwell. The second problem was the production crisis which hit the industry in 1937 following the overextension of the production boom in the mid-1930s. The boom had meant a dramatic increase in the volume of films emerging from British companies but the anticipated returns were not forthcoming mainly because the expected overseas earnings failed to materialise. A brake was applied to production in 1937 and the Gaumont British studios at Shepherd's Bush were closed down. The company announced that a limited number of films would be made at the Islington studios and it was back at the home of Gainsborough and at the studio where he had started his career in the film industry in 1920, that Hitchcock was to complete the 'classic thriller sextet' for Gaumont British.

The production plans of the company had included a Hitchcock picture starring Nova Pilbeam and this was made during 1937 and shown to the trade late in the year. Nova Pilbeam had appeared in *The Man Who Knew Too Much* playing the kidnapped child but in *Young and Innocent* (1937) she played her first romantic lead at the age of seventeen. As Hitchcock has said it was 'an attempt to do a chase story with very young people involved'[89] and this meant a less explicit approach to sexual encounters than had been the case in, for example, *The Thirty-Nine Steps* which the film resembles very much in other respects. In the fan magazine *Picturegoer* it was said that because of Nova Pilbeam's youth 'Hitchcock ... will put the soft pedal on the sex stuff, and will concentrate on the thrills'.[90] *Kine Weekly* picked out her performance as one of the outstanding features of the film praising the way in which 'she imparts sincerity to every gesture, and, at the same time, invests the stormy love interest with adolescent charm'.[91] *Variety* also drew attention to her 'charming portrayal of innocent girlhood' but were less enthusiastic about the general appeal of the picture which their reviewer found 'slow in patches' and containing 'extraneous over-prolonged shots', a reference perhaps to the celebrated lengthy travelling shot which ends on a close-up of the murderer's twitching eyes and which many later critics have isolated as a highpoint in the film.[92] *Kine Weekly* continued their support of Hitchcock suggesting that the film was 'an artistic and commercial triumph which was fit 'to rank with "The Thirty-Nine Steps", "The Man Who Knew Too Much" and other Hitchcock masterpieces'.[93] A more recent view of the film is less complimentary and according to Raymond Durgnat it is evidence of 'slackening creative tensions'[94] which may be due to the fact that the team which had worked on the previous thrillers was in the process of breaking up. Balcon had left the Gaumont British group in 1936 to become head of production at the newly formed MGM-British and Ivor Montagu had abandoned feature film production in favour of more explicitly political activities. Charles Bennett did work for a brief time on the script of *Young and Innocent* but he was soon to depart to Hollywood with a contract as a scriptwriter at Universal Studios. The production was somewhat interrupted when the production halt at Gaumont British meant that the film had to be moved from the studios at Shepherd's Bush to the recently opened Pinewood complex but it was in the context of J. Arthur Rank's lavishly equipped studios that Hitchcock was able to achieve the famous virtuoso camera movement referred to earlier.

The last film of the thriller sextet was made back at the Islington studios where Hitchcock had begun his film career in 1920. *The Lady Vanishes* (1938) was a great success both in Britain and America where it won Hitchcock the 'Best Direction' section of the New York Critics Awards for 1938. With *Young and Innocent* Hitchcock had steered clear of the darker side of his concerns which had emerged in *Secret Agent* and *Sabotage* and the lighter qualities were to be continued in *The Lady Vanishes*. The picture blended suspense, humour and romance in similar proportions to *The Thirty-Nine Steps* with a similar degree of success. *Kine Weekly* responded with its usual paean to the director in the following comment:

> The direction of this film amounts to genius inasmuch as a wildly improbable plot is converted into gripping entertainment of grand adventure and compelling sportsmanship. The circumstances in which the heroine is in danger of being labelled temporarily unhinged are engineered with a masterly grasp of theatre and, at the same time,

provide a marvellous prologue to the recital of spectacular espionage fare.[95]

Variety also commented upon Hitchcock's directorial contribution and, in fact, suggested that *The Lady Vanishes* 'minus the deft and artistic handling of the director, despite its cast and photography, would not stand up for Grade A candidacy'.[96] The production circumstances of the film were rather different from Hitchcock's usual working methods in which he was involved in projects from the script stage onwards. The script for *The Lady Vanishes* was developed from a novel in 1936 by Frank Launder and Sidney Gilliat to be directed for the screen by the American, Roy William Neill. Although the production did begin with Neill as director it ran into problems during location work in Yugoslavia and the film was abandoned. Hitchcock became interested in the script and it was decided to revive the project with him as director. Although Hitchcock began working in his normal way on the script with the writers, few alterations were actually made and the film was substantially based on Launder and Gilliat's original treatment. Indeed, according to Gilliat, this episode was the 'only case of Hitchcock taking over a script completed for another director'.[97]

The Lady Vanishes was Hitchcock's final film for the Gaumont combine but he had signed a contract with Mayflower Productions, a company jointly owned by Charles Laughton and Erich Pommer, the German producer that Hitchcock had previously linked up with during the 1920s. The result was Hitchcock's second costume picture, *Jamaica Inn* (1939), a tale of eighteenth-century smugglers in Cornwall adapted from a novel by Daphne du Maurier. Although the ever-loyal *Kine Weekly* predictably referred to the picture as a 'box-office miracle'[98] and *Variety* called it excellent entertainment, *Jamaica Inn* represents a radical departure from the thriller cycle which had rebuilt Hitchcock's waning career during the mid-1930s. The *Variety* review described the film as 'a typical Alfred Hitchcock direction job'[99] but Graham Greene was, perhaps, more percipient in his *Spectator* review when he questioned the director's involvement in the film. After praising Charles Laughton's 'superb performance', Greene went on to write 'it is more difficult to know why Mr Hitchcock embarked on this bogus costume piece and submitted himself to a producer. There is only one Hitchcock incident here in embryo'.[100] Despite the box-office success of the film, Hitchcock himself expressed regret at his involvement describing it as 'an absurd thing to undertake'.[101] Hitchcock's involvement with the Pommer/Laughton company had been mooted originally in 1936 and the contract negotiated during 1937, which was a year of considerable uncertainty for the British film industry in general and for Hitchcock's career in particular. It was during this period that Hitchcock was also negotiating the contract with the American independent producer David Selznick which would eventually take him to Hollywood. By the time that *Jamaica Inn* went into production late in 1938, Hitchcock had signed a contract with Selznick thus clearing up the uncertainties about his future and the direction of the film was undertaken in a somewhat reluctant frame of mind. After the film was completed, Hitchcock finally departed for Hollywood and although he did return intermittently to Britain to make films or to shoot locations, his subsequent career belongs to the history of the American cinema.

Notes

1. D. Bordwell, *The Films of Carl-Theodor Dreyer* (University of California Press, California, 1981), p. 4.
2. See Chapter 4, p. 62.
3. J.R. Taylor, *Hitch* (Faber and Faber, London, 1978), p. 51.
4. R. Low, *The History of the British Film 1918-1929* (Allen and Unwin, London, 1971), p. 168.
5. P. Bogdanovich, *The Cinema of Alfred Hitchcock* (Museum of Modern Art, New York, 1963), p. 10.
6. Taylor, *Hitch*, p. 56.
7. Ibid.
8. F. Truffaut, *Hitchcock* (Panther, London, 1969), p. 46.
9. Ibid., p. 30.
10. See 'Interview: Ivor Montagu', *Screen*, vol. 13, no. 3 (1972), p. 76, and Taylor, *Hitch*, p. 72.
11. 'Interview: Ivor Montagu', pp. 76-7.
12. Ibid., p. 76. See also, M. Balcon, *A Lifetime in Films* (Hutchinson, London, 1969), p. 26.
13. Bordwell, *Dreyer*, pp. 10-11.
14. Taylor, *Hitch*, p. 74.
15. 'Interview: Ivor Montagu', p. 77.
16. B. Salt, *Film Style and Technology: History and Analysis* (Starword, London, 1983), p. 161.
17. *The Bioscope*, 6 July. 1926, quoted in Low, *British Film*, p. 168.
18. Truffaut, *Hitchcock*, p. 48.
19. Taylor, *Hitch*, p. 82.
20. *Picturegoer*, Mar. 1926, p. 60.
21. Low, *British Film*, p. 165.
22. 'Interview: Ivor Montagu', p. 80.
23. P. Wollen, 'Hitchcock's Vision', *Cinema* (UK), no. 3 (1969), p. 4.
24. Low, *British Film*, p. 177.
25. Ibid., p. 188.
26. Remarks drawn from the *Daily Mail, Daily News, Daily Sketch* and *Daily Herald* respectively and incorporated in the advertisement in *The Bioscope*, 6 Oct. 1927.
27. Ibid.
28. Ibid.
29. *The Bioscope*, 6 Oct. 1927, p. 27.
30. Ibid.
31. Truffaut, *Hitchcock*, p. 59.
32. *The Bioscope*, 6 Oct. 1927.
33. *The Bioscope*, 22 Aug. 1928, p. 39.
34. Truffaut, *Hitchcock*, p. 63.
35. *The Bioscope*, 23 Jan. 1929, p. 38.
36. Truffaut, *Hitchcock*, p. 66.
37. G. Brown, *Launder and Gilliat* (British Film Institute, London, 1977), p. 26.
38. B. Dean, *Mind's Eye* (Hutchinson, London, 1973), p. 122.

39. Low, *British Film*, p. 192.
40. See Chapter 2.
41. P. Rotha, *The Film Till Now*, 4th edn (Spring Books, London, 1977), p. 83.
42. *The Bioscope*, 26 Jun, 1929, p. 31.
43. *Kine Weekly*, 27 Jun. 1929, p. 43.
44. *The Bioscope*, 26 Jun. 1929, p. 17.
45. Ibid., p. 31.
46. Truffaut, *Hitchcock*, p. 66.
47. Low, *British Film*, p. 207.
48. See C. Barr, 'Blackmail: Silent and Sound', *Sight and Sound*, vol. 52, no. 2 (1983), p. 123.
49. Taylor, *Hitch*, p. 101.
50. Low, *British Film*, p. 246.
51. Ibid., p. 247.
52. Truffaut, *Hitchcock*, p. 71.
53. *The Bioscope*, 1 Jan. 1930, p. 74.
54. Taylor, *Hitch*, p. 82.
55. R. Durgnat, *The Strange Case of Alfred Hitchcock* (Faber and Faber, London, 1974), p. 107.
56. Truffaut, *Hitchcock*, p. 82.
57. D. Spoto, *The Life of Alfred Hitchcock*, (Collins, London, 1983), p. 126.
58. *The Bioscope*, 6 Aug. 1930, p. 25.
59. *Kine Weekly*, 5 Mar. 1931, p. 46.
60. *The Bioscope*, 6 Oct. 1927, p. 27.
61. Low, *British Film*, p. 189.
62. Rotha, *The Film Till Now*, p. 313.
63. F. Hardy (ed.), *Grierson on Documentary* (Faber and Faber, London, 1966), p. 72.
64. See Truffaut, *Hitchcock*, p. 92.
65. *Kine Weekly*, 4 Jan. 1934, p. 25.
66. Ibid., 13 Dec. 1934, p. 21.
67. Ibid., 22 Nov. 1934, p. 42.
68. M. Balcon, *A Lifetime in Films* (Hutchinson, London, 1969), p. 62.
69. *Variety*, 3 Apr. 1935.
70. See *Kine Weekly*, 3 Jan. 1935, p. 33.
71. Ibid., 6 Jun. 1935.
72. *Daily Mirror*, 9 Sept. 1935.
73. *Kine Weekly*, 13 Jun. 1935, p. 29.
74. *Sunday Times*, 9 Jun. 1935.
75. *Sight and Sound*, Summer 1935, p. 72.
76. *Variety*, 19 Jun. 1935.
77. *Daily Telegraph*, 24 Sept. 1935.
78. E. Rohmer and C. Chabrol, *Hitchcock* (Ungar, New York, 1978), p. 37 ff.
79. *Kine Weekly*, 14 May, 1936, p. 26.
80. Ibid.
81. G. Greene, *The Pleasure Dome* (Secker and Warburg, London, 1972), p. 75.
82. Rohmer and Chabrol, *Hitchcock*, p. 48.
83. Ibid.
84. *Kine Weekly*, 10 Dec. 1936, p. 25.
85. Greene, *Pleasure Dome*, p. 123.
86. Truffaut, *Hitchcock*, p. 118.
87. *Variety*, 3 Mar. 1937.
88. *Kine Weekly*, 24 Jan. 1937, p. 41.
89. Truffaut, *Hitchcock*, p. 127.
90. *Picturegoer*, 3 Jul. 1937.
91. *Kine Weekly*, 25 Nov. 1937, p. 41.
92. *Variety*, 8 Dec. 1937.

93. *Kine Weekly*, 25 Nov. 1937, p. 41.
94. Durgnat, *The Strange Case*, p. 20.
95. *Kine Weekly*, 25 Aug. 1938, p. 17.
96. *Variety*, 31 Aug. 1938.
97. Brown, *Launder and Gilliat*, p. 90.
98. *Kine Weekly*, 11 May, 1939, p. 24.
99. *Variety*, 31 May, 1939.
100. Greene, *Pleasure Dome*, p. 272.
101. Truffaut, *Hitchcock*, p. 138.

Chapter Six

Hitchcock and Genre:
'The Classic Thriller Sextet'

Our perception of British Hitchcock tends to be dominated by films such as *The Thirty-Nine Steps* and *The Lady Vanishes*, the films of the 'classic thriller sextet'.[1] Indeed, *The Thirty-Nine Steps* emerges as a quintessentially Hitchcockian film when related to subsequent American Hitchcock pictures such as *Saboteur* (1942) and *North By Northwest* (1959). By contrast, the run of middlebrow theatrical adaptations that Hitchcock directed for Gainsborough and British International Pictures seem out of character and difficult to relate to the authorial profile of subsequent criticism. Yet it was partly on the basis of such films that Hitchcock acquired his high reputation within the British cinema during the late twenties and early thirties. Rohmer and Chabrol, in their influential study of the director, did suggest that the British International period, in particular, was 'rich in remarkable works'[2] but most critics pass over this phase of the director's career characterising it as one of creative confusion and decline despite intermittent successes such as *Blackmail*. It is a view which Hitchcock himself appeared to endorse when he described the first film in the thriller cycle — *The Man Who Knew Too Much* — as 'the picture that re-established my creative prestige'.[3] Subsequent critical opinion, by and large, was to argue that it was the Gaumont British thrillers that enabled Hitchcock to discover a specific artistic identity after a decade or so of experiment in a variety of film genres and with a variety of film styles. There is, perhaps, a certain irony in this in so far as the truly Hitchcockian is identified in the transindividual context of a film genre. The stress in this chapter is upon the different strands of tradition which feed into the thriller, especially those from literature, together with some comment upon Hitchcock's particular manipulation of the generic elements.

Genre and the Production Base

Certain genres ... have a clear existence; their homogeneity, already felt in the simple viewing of films, is confirmed by historical facts: we know that, in the cinema of Hollywood in its 'golden era' genres were in some sort institutions ... Each genre had its regular scriptwriters, sometimes on a yearly contract, its directors, its craftsmen, its studios ... .[4]

Christian Metz's comment upon the generic character of Hollywood film production during the thirties and forties can be applied to the British cinema during the same period if it is accepted that a structure of genres is an inevitable artistic corollary of a mass-production cinema based upon the studio system. The managerial oversight of annual multi-film production schedules, the economic logic of standardisation, the efficient utilisation of previously demonstrated talent and expertise and the repetition of popular success were among the factors from the production sector of the film business which tended to structure the making of films along generic lines. It has already been mentioned that the critical consensus on Hitchcock's artistic progress from the 1920s to the 1930s tends to use the rhetoric of self-discovery. Despite intermittent excursions into what might now be regarded as typical Hitchcock territory (*The Lodger, Blackmail, Murder!, Number Seventeen*) it was not until 1934 that the director fully realised that the thriller genre 'was the form ideally suited to his talent and temperament'.[5] But can the pattern of consistency which dominates Hitchcock's career from 1934 until 1938 simply be explained in terms of self-discovery and personal decision? *The Man Who Knew Too Much* (1934), *The Thirty-Nine Steps* (1935), *Secret Agent* (1936), *Sabotage* (1936), *Young and Innocent* (1937) and *The Lady Vanishes* (1938), the six films which constitute the thriller cycle, were all made for the same company, the giant Gaumont British combine. The first four were made at the Gaumont British studios in Shepherd's Bush, *Young and Innocent* was started at Shepherd's Bush then moved to Pinewood and then to the Gainsborough studios at Islington for editing, and *The Lady Vanishes* was made at Islington. A key figure in the context of institutional stability was the production head at Gaumont British, Michael Balcon. Hitchcock, as we have seen, began his directorial career in 1925 at Balcon's Gainsborough company and amongst the five films he directed during this phase of his career was *The Lodger* described by the director himself as the first true 'Hitchcock movie'.[6] It is worth noting, however, that this perception of the 'Hitchcock movie' came with the benefit of hindsight and that the career profile marked out for Hitchcock by Balcon in these early years did not differ significantly from that which he followed at BIP. He was assigned a number of literary and theatrical adaptations which were the stock in trade of the contract film maker in the British film industry at this time. By the mid-1930s, Balcon had established himself as one of the leading producers in the industry, supervising the entire output of the Gaumont British and Gainsborough studios. His regime was relatively liberal and he created an atmosphere in which directorial initiative was encouraged. As Ivor Montagu has said:

Mick would be inclined to make pictures that his contract directors wanted to make. They would ask to do a thing and he would say no or yes but they would be expected to make suggestions ... Hitch could choose his own picture and we were choosing these sort of pictures to go back to.[7]

Montagu, drafted into work with Hitchcock by Balcon, was assigned the task of Associate Producer on the first four of the thriller sextet and his comment on 'these sort of pictures' refers to the thrillers as opposed to the more 'ambitious', middlebrow theatrical adaptations such as *Easy Virtue* (1927), *Juno and the Paycock* (1930) and *The Skin Game* (1931). Such films, which Hitchcock had made both at Gainsborough and BIP, 'had no Hitchcock' according to Montagu, unlike the thriller cycle which was to revive the quality which had intermittently surfaced in films such as *The Lodger* and *Blackmail*. It may be significant that Montagu himself had worked with Hitchcock during the Gainsborough period most notably on *The Lodger* after it had been shelved by the distributor.

A certain degree of continuity was also maintained amongst the other production personnel on the sextet. In particular, Charles Bennett, whose play *Blackmail* had provided the basis for the Hitchcock film, worked on the scripts of four of the films and provided the original idea for a fifth, *The Man Who Knew Too Much*. Bennett had worked for the British Intelligence Service during the First World War and brought this personal experience of the world of espionage to the making of the spy thrillers. Hitchcock's wife, Alma Reville, received script credit on three of the films and clearly Montagu, Bennett and Mrs Hitchcock constituted an important creative ensemble that provided a substantial degree of stability and continuity, particularly during the production of the first four films of the cycle. The extent to which the films reflect a collaborative approach to film making, however, is difficult to pin down. Montagu's comments on the genesis of *The Man Who Knew Too Much* suggest an author at the creative centre establishing a sounding board pattern of working with the other members of the production team:

> That was really an original of Hitchcock's. You see Charles Bennett had the credit for story-making in that but you see what happened with Hitch's stories was that he would want an amanuensis. He originally used Alma Reville on a lot of things .... He wanted a screenwriter to talk to and the screen writer would get the credit. The screen writer and the associate producer would throw out ideas. Hitch would go around London and he'd see something from a bus, he would go, for example, to the Albert Hall. We would work these into stories. And thats how he would get the atmosphere of local scenes and local sets, and the sets would develop collaboratively like that. The writer would be given the credit because Mick wouldn't allow associate producers to have any credit at all.[8]

This consistent creative context was further augmented by the continuities of the technical personnel on the films. The cinematography on four of the films was supervised by Bernard Knowles, the art direction on three was by Otto Werndorff and Albert Juillon, three were edited by Charles Frend and the musical direction on all six was by Louis Levy.[9] The stable studio context also enabled Hitchcock to work with leading British screen performers of the day such as Robert Donat — 'the British equivalent of a Clark Gable or a Ronald Colman'[10] — and during the course of the production assault on the American market he had access to some of the specially imported American stars. For *Secret Agent* Hitchcock had the services of Robert Young, cast in the role of the attractive villain, whilst the young wife in *Sabotage* was played by Sylvia Sidney. In addition to these film stars proper, Hitchcock was also to work with many of the leading British stage performers of the day including John Gielgud (*Secret Agent*), Peggy Ashcroft (*The Thirty-Nine Steps*) and Michael Redgrave (*The Lady Vanishes*).

The consistencies in the films can be related to the consistencies in the production context from which they emerged. This consistency in turn can be related to the stable period of production that characterised the British film industry during the years from 1934 to 1937 and which offered opportunities for a continuous and sustained output, albeit in a context of underlying precariousness which began to manifest itself in the studio crises of 1937 and onwards. The high critical reputation of the films may also be related to the increasing production values represented especially by Hitchcock's access to important actors and stars through the studio system and through the adoption of American-oriented production policies by Gaumont British. The professional relationship with Michael Balcon was clearly significant to Hitchcock although the success of their thriller cycle was only barely prefigured during their earlier time together with the success of *The Lodger*. As this latter film owed something to the intervention of Ivor Montagu, he too can be seen as an important part of the thriller phase. Balcon's conception of Hitchcock during these years is indicated by his decision to use 'Hitchcock films' as one of the production categories for the Gaumont British output during the 1930s and although other individuals also were important enough to stand as a production category, these tended to be stars like Jessie Matthews and George Arliss rather than directors. Thus Hitchcock was lodged in the studio production schedules as a kind of genre in himself by the mid-1930s, firmly established in terms of directorial identity in contrast to his career at BIP which may fairly be described as meandering.

Moving outside the specific studio context, we can note an increase in the production of espionage-oriented films during this period. During the years from the Quota Act to 1933, spy pictures appeared intermittently in the schedules of a number of British companies but it is between 1934 and 1938 that they begin to appear with any degree of regularity. Whilst only two or three a year were made between 1928 and 1933, the figures increase for subsequent years to, for example, eight in 1936 and twelve in 1937.[11] The sources for these films were rather varied, ranging from actual bio-graphical accounts of espionage such as *I Was a Spy* (Saville, 1933) which was based on a series of newspaper articles written by a Belgian agent, Marthe McKenna, to adaptations of 'Sapper', Dennis Wheatley and plays by Arnold Ridley and Charles Bennett. A number of leading directors were involved in this sub-genre including Victor Saville whose three excursions into the world of espionage make him something of a specialist. In addition to *I Was A Spy*, Saville had also made *The W Plan* (1930) and *Dark Journey* (1937). Other prominent directors to work in the sub-genre were Anthony Asquith, Carol Reed, Arthur Woods and Walter Forde, and one or two imported directors such as Raoul Walsh and Jacques Feyder. Yet, perhaps, too much should not be made of the immediate cinematic generic context as the number of films is low and, judging by the trade paper synopses and source material, they were extremely varied in character.

Hitchcock and Genre

Hitchcock's assiduous cultivation of his 'authorial legend' has, in many ways, masked his status as a director of genre.pictures. The critical power and strength of his authorial profile has discouraged investigation of the affinities between his work and that of other film makers and writers associated with the thriller genre. Yet, as a professional working in a commercial industry, the framework of genre and tradition constituted his working context. The stability provided by the production context at Gaumont British was complemented at the level of artistic structure by a concentration upon films of a particular type, films with interlinked patterns of narrative form, setting, situation and character. During this period, Hitchcock became a specialist thriller director and although, as we have seen, his reputation as a film maker of considerable ability was estab-lished on the basis of a variety of genres, it was the thriller which gave him a particular identity. Alan Levell has written of his consistent adoption of the genre in terms of artistic self-discovery, whilst Rohmer and Chabrol suggest a quite conscious decision on the part of Hitchcock to mix together generic elements from previous films in a blend that would guarantee their appeal to audiences. This latter point raises questions about the nature of the genre in which Hitchcock worked, the exact pattern of narrative form, setting, situation and character which is derivable from the sextet. Answers to those questions may well return us to Hitchcock the author in so far as the category 'Hitchcock thriller' may be the most pertinent generic title to adopt in relation to the sextet.

The overall context for the sextet is the British crime film of the 1930s which, as we have noted, formed an important segment of production during this period. Within that broad category is the thriller and within the thriller genre is the sub-genre of the spy-thriller. The latter is the immediate context for five out of six of the Hitchcock cycle. Before attempting a specification of the Hitchcock variant of the spy-thriller I want to examine the genre, drawing upon the work of both film and literary critics. Indeed, the most extensive writing on the genre is to be found within literary rather than film criticism and although ultimately a critical definition of the genre in cinema terms will be necessary, the particular dependence of the cinematic genre on its literary antecedents more than justifies a literary critical detour. This link between a film genre and a body of literature is not peculiar to the thriller and, indeed, many film genres can be traced to literary sources for their thematic and symbolic elements. For example, many of the iconographical elements of the Western are to be found in the dime novels of the nineteenth century and although there are important transformations to be noted in the film/literature transaction which produces a cinematic genre, the literary context can be an important starting point for definition. To turn specifically to the Hitchcock films, four of the five spy thrillers are based upon literary sources directly whilst the fifth is loosely based on the Bulldog Drummond character from the 'Sapper' novels.

Although espionage as a military-cum-political activity has a long history, its existence as literary subject matter is largely a twentieth century affair.[12] The origins of the genre have been traced to the novels of William Le Queux and Erskine Childers, dating from around the turn of the century, and by the 1930s there had developed a substantial sub-current of popular literature based upon the exploits of secret agents. The spy thriller can be related to the rise of a variety of literary sub-genres in the nineteenth century which include the work of writers such as Edgar Allan Poe, Sir Arthur Conan Doyle and Wilkie Collins particularly in respect of the themes of mystery and violence. The distinct status of the spy thriller is partly a matter of the specific subject matter of espionage and partly a matter of the precise weight allocated to the elements which it shares with adjacent literary currents within the general sphere of crime fiction. For example, the spy story shares elements such as mystery, murder and theft with the detective story. But whereas the detective story concentrates upon the mystery of the criminal act, the theft of the jewellery and so on, and seeks to solve mysteries and to identify thieves, such elements function as background to the exploits of the protagonist in the spy story. Their solution is frequently less important than their presence as triggers for the adventures of the leading characters. In Hitchcockian terms such elements would constitute 'the MacGuffin'.[13]

The most extensive definitions of the thriller genre are to be found in literary criticism and, in particular, in the work of Jerry Palmer.[14] Palmer suggests that the key thematic elements of the literary thriller are twofold. Firstly, there is the hero, the central character who is distinguished by an instinctive competitive personality. Secondly, that hero is invariably confronted with a conspiracy which is intrinsically mysterious and which constitutes a threat to the general set of values or social ideology which the hero stands for and defends. Palmer goes on to define the thriller situation as one in which the hero as representative of competitive values is opposed to the collective conspiratorial forces which threaten the character of his world.[15] The element of conspiracy is defined as central to the thriller, distinguishing the genre from its literary neighbours such as the classical detective story. The world of the thriller is a paranoid one in which the major problem confronting the protagonist is the pervasive surrounding threat, the abiding context of menace. The thriller then pits a hero against a shadowy conspiracy, a basic oppositional structure which lends itself to a variety of permutations and transformations. As Palmer says:

> This pair — conspiracy and hero — constitute the most fundamental layer of the thriller. The plot — the story — is the process by which the hero averts the conspiracy and this process is what provides the thrills that the reader seeks.[16]

In referring to 'process' i.e. the operation of reading in relation to the thriller, Palmer introduces an essential formal component of the genre, its dependence for generic identity on the creation of suspense for the reader. The genre can be defined partially in thematic terms — the 'fundamental layer' of conspiracy and hero — but it also requires definition in terms of its mode of address to the reader, the manner in which the reader is positioned by a thriller text. It is this quality which is of supreme importance to the genre in the cinema, as Steve Neale has pointed out:

> Whatever the structure, whatever the specificity of the diegesis in any particular thriller, the genre as a whole, unlike that of the gangster or the detective story, is specified in the first instance by its address, by the fact that it always, though in different ways, must have the generation of suspense as its core activity.[17]

The hero versus the conspiracy, the suspense generated by struggle, these are the bare bones of the genre as outlined by Palmer and from such a basis we can begin to construct the genre in more detail.

The characteristic hero of spy literature is, of course, often the professional secret agent, the spy. This is not an invariable feature of the genre, however, and John Buchan's hero — Richard Hannay — although functioning as the central character in his novels, is not a professional agent. Yet the literary genre is dominated by professional agent figures such as Somerset Maugham's Ashenden, Cyril McNeile's (Sapper) Bulldog Drummond and Ian Fleming's James Bond to bring the genre up to date. In addition to this central figure, there is the benevolent institution for whom the agent works, usually represented by an individual figure such as R in the Ashenden stories or Bond's superior — M. In narrative terms, such figures play an important role in setting the tasks for the hero, usually at the beginning of the story when the stock scene in the office of 'central control' takes place. The orders are delivered to the hero in broad terms, the assassination of an enemy agent, the stealing of enemy plans and so on and although the task is usually defined for the hero, the exact trajectory of the narrative is normally left unspecified. Indeed, the series of adventures which invariably ensue in the course of a thriller are, perhaps, less tied to formulae than those in other genres such as the Western. The motivation for the adventures is simply the testing of the hero in a series of novel ways so that he can demonstrate his ingenuity in coping with whatever is thrown at him. One feature of the genre which does impose a certain direction on the narrative, however, is the travel motif. The work of the secret agent is frequently international and the global odyssey of many thriller heroes is an important component of the genre. This does give rise to a certain number of conventionalised situations such as the denouement at the border crossing, the problems of disguise in unfamiliar environments and cultures, communication problems, liaison with undercover agents, the difficulties of remaining in touch with central control and so on. Ian Fleming's James Bond novels present the international flavour of the genre most emphatically but this feature is to be found in many examples of the spy story including those that provide the immediate context for the Hitchcock cycle such as Maugham and Buchan. The international travel motif is closely related to the flight and pursuit structure which plays a role in numerous spy novels and films and is often a central mechanism in the Hitchcock thriller. The other central thematic element in the genre — the conspiracy — frequently remains shadowy and ill-defined except in terms of its threat to the social and political stability represented by the institution for whom the hero works.

Our discussion thus far has been rooted in the literary thriller or spy thriller and has concerned itself mainly with theme and narrative pattern. I want now to move these concerns towards cinema which involves considering the visual and aural specificity of film and incorporating into a definition of the film thriller, material drawn from genre film criticism. Traditional genre criticism has defined individual film genres in terms of narrative structure and thematic material — elements which are often literary in their origin — together with a distinctive visual surface or iconography. Individual critics have often given differing weights and emphases to the different elements in their definitions of particular genres. Robert Warshow, for example, in his discussion of the gangster picture stresses the specific narrative trajectory which traces the rise to power of the central gangster figure, a kind of anti-hero, and his inevitable downfall and death. Colin McArthur, on the other hand, starts his definition of the gangster genre from its visual distinctiveness, its patterns of recurrent imagery or iconography which embrace the use of leading players such as James Cagney and Edward G. Robinson with their particular performance styles and modes of dress; the urban setting of the genre, the seedy hotel, the speakeasy, the dark back alleys in which the doomed odyssey of the gangster takes place; and the technological accoutrements such as guns, cars and telephones. Such elements collectively constitute a body of distinctive visual signals which mark the genre off from other genres and which facilitate swift communication of mood and incident, character and situation to an audience. The iconographic ensemble generates a specific system of audience expectation for the genre.[18] To mention one well documented example, the inevitable death of the gangster hero at the end of the film was established as a firm generic convention in the very early days of the genre with films such as *Little Caesar* (Leroy, 1930), *Public Enemy* (Wellman, 1931) and *Scarface* (Hawks, 1932). The longevity of such a convention can be seen in a slightly different form in the ending of *The Godfather Part Two* (Coppola, 1974). Although the central figure of Michael Corleone (Al Pacino) does not actually die, the film concludes with a medley of gangster deaths which dispose of three of the subsidiary characters and a striking close-up of Michael, sitting alone and left in a world of spiritual death. The tone of the ending is totally in keeping with the spirit of the convention although amended for a contemporary audience attuned to the more open endings of a post-classical cinema.

Steve Neale has approached genre definition in rather broader terms, attempting to position genre cinema within the overall category of mainstream classical cinema. He suggests that genres are modes of the classical narrative system which 'function simultaneously to exploit and contain the diversity of mainstream cinema'.[19] Different genres represent a different balancing of the general categories of discourse to be found in the classical cinema such as those of violence, law and order, morality, emotions, social institutions — the broad range of themes to be found in a cinema such as that produced by Hollywood. Also, different genres represent the different formal and stylistic possibilities of cinema with each genre possessing its own characteristic articulation of *mise en scène*, cinematography, montage and sound. The French critic, Marc Vernet, has made the same point in the following terms:

Each genre ... requires an ensemble of cinematic codes which are specific to it. These codes proper to the genre are both distinct from general cinematic codes (valid for all films) and joined to them insofar as the general cinematic codes are equally present in a genre film. There is, for example, a particular lighting code for the classical detective film which produces a very strong contrast between zones which are lighted and those that are less so, and a parcelling out of space that can no longer be apprehended in a single glance (which augments the suspense) ...[20]

Thematic specificity, visual distinctiveness in terms of conventionalised motifs and the registers of film form and style, construct for each genre a particular fictional world, a precise ensemble of character, situation and setting with sufficient stability to satisfy the expectations of an audience but with the possibility of sufficient variation to preserve audience interest.

Let us return then to the definition of the spy thriller in the cinema and its specificity as a genre. What are its central thematic concerns, its distinctive visual qualities, motifs and stylistic conventions? What is the nature of the fictional world marked out by such a title? We have started to provide an answer in the discussion of the literary genre and I want now to attempt an integration of these insights with the specific cinematic properties of the genre. The world of the spy thriller centres on the perceptions of the central figure, the hero, and this usually means a world perceived as mysterious, conspiratorial, potentially evil and paranoia-inducing. Appearances, the focal point of cinematic attention, are deceptive for both hero and spectator. The world of paranoia occupied in a fictional sense by the hero figure is also occupied in an experiential sense by the spectator watching a spy thriller. The source of thrill and suspense lies in the construction of images and sequences of ambiguity. In one sense, this means that the spy thriller cannot have the clearly defined iconography of character types that less ambiguous genres such as the Western or the gangster film depend upon. For example, villainy in the Western has an accumulated visual definition in terms of the many actors who have been cast in such a role over a period of many years. Figures such as Arthur Kennedy, Jack Palance, Jack Elam, Lee Marvin and Lee Van Cleef have an appearance which swiftly and economically defines their position in the clearly articulated moral spectrum of the genre. The spy thriller requires a more circumspect iconography and one which allows for the suspension of the audience in a position of hesitation concerning the identity and position of many of the figures in the generic world of espionage and, in particular, the important figure of the double agent. These ambiguities of presentation, of course, cannot extend to the central figure of the hero who functions as the reference point for such ambiguity and the primary identification figure for the spectator. The opaque characterisations are normally complemented by an opacity in the situational structures of the genre. This opacity, however, is often delayed until the narrative gets under way and the hero has been assigned his specific task. Thus the spy thriller often begins with the unambiguous sequence in which the hero meets the spymaster. Good examples of this convention occur in the Bond pictures with their invariable early sequence of M's interview with Bond. The convention derives from the literary genre so that in the Maugham *Ashenden* stories the first few pages of the story are usually taken up with Ashenden receiving his instructions from R. The specific details of the spying mission are rarely important except in so far as they provide the hero with specific objectives in relation to the larger, more significant, battle against the conspiratorial forces which threaten the social and political order of which he is a representative. Hitchcock's MacGuffin, of course, represents the most extreme expression of the relative unimportance of the details of espionage for the thriller genre which usually disposes of them in these early scenes so that the hero can soon be plunged into the nightmarish world of disorder and deception to begin his task of ordering and clarifying. The elements of mystery which are an important component of the detective or crime picture are less important in the spy thriller where they simply function as a background for the expression of individual competitiveness necessary to defeat the forces of conspiratorial evil. Equivocal identity, ambiguity and the other qualities which provide the genre with its specific character, can be analysed in thematic terms using conventional notions of character. But, more importantly, they can be seen as key elements in the viewing experience in which the diegetic character position of the hero with its ambiguities and uncertainties is aligned with the position of the spectator thus generating the core of suspense — the definitional heart of the genre.

The Hitchcock Thriller

Eric Rohmer and Claude Chabrol, in their study of Hitchcock, see the classic thriller sextet as a powerful and appealing crystallisation of elements drawn from earlier Hitchcock pictures which constitute a new cinematic genre. This new genre — 'le feuilleton d'espionage intelligent' — yokes together the somewhat austere moral universe of *Murder!* (1930) with the twists and turns of action in *Number Seventeen* (1932) to produce a type of film characterisable in terms of an abundance of action, chases and journeys, a variety of locales, gloomy and macabre plots and, significantly for their subsequent analyses of Hitchcock's American films, moments of unexpected profundity.[21] For Rohmer and Charbrol, the two strands of Hitchcock's work — the serious moral dimension and the side of popular entertainment — are combined in different proportions in the films of the sextet with greater or lesser degrees of success. The balance, they argue, is most perfectly achieved in *The Thirty-Nine Steps* in which Hitchcock whilst preserving 'the appearance and form of a perfect espionage thriller ... manages to express a certain number of ideas which are dear to him'.[22] Although Rohmer and Chabrol use the term 'genre', they confine their contextualisation of the thriller sextet to its Hitchcockian antecedents and this is understandable as the book was written during the French period of 'high auteurism' in the 1950s. It is, however, the transindividual connotations of the term 'genre' that have provided the critical focus for later writers. Although the relation between Hitchcock and the thriller is frequently discussed in ways which gravitate towards making the two synonymous, I want to spend some time on the broader generic context of the sextet if only to make for a more precise understanding of the Hitchcock variant of the genre. As mentioned previously, the spy thriller was not a substantial context for the Hitchcock films in cinematic terms although the broader crime genre was a significant and well established part of the British cinema of the period. Cinematic antecedents, however, can be found in the Gaumont British production schedules with the Walter Forde film, *Rome Express* (1932) and *I Was a Spy* (1933) directed by Victor Saville. The latter film provides the espionage theme whilst the former film with its 'train' setting foreshadows Hitchcock's use of this motif in *The Thirty-Nine Steps*, *Secret Agent* and, most notably, *The Lady Vanishes*. Few cinematic genres, though, are wholly internal to the medium and just as American film genres such as the Western, the *film noir* and the horror film have their literary antecedents so the spy thriller associated with Hitchcock can be traced to a variety of literary sources. The central figure is popular novelist John Buchan whom Hitchcock cites as 'a strong influence a long time before ... *The Thirty-Nine Steps*'[23] and whose spy stories dating from the First World War period provide various sources for the Hitchcock canon. The general quality of adventure, the themes of fear and guilt, the narrative patterns of flight and pursuit, the climactic combat, the theme of the 'thin protection of civilisation' to quote Buchan's own words from his novel *The Power House*, the secret assassination gang working against established governments, are all part and parcel of the thriller genre, specific qualities of Buchan's novels, and, indeed, evocative of the familiar 'Hitchcockian universe' in many respects. Another direct source for Hitchcock was the work of Herman Cyril McNeile ('Sapper') author of the Bulldog Drummond stories from which the scenario of *The Man Who Knew Too Much* was derived. Both Buchan and McNeile can, in their turn, be set into the larger literary current of the spy thriller which was a popular form during the interwar period. In fact, a number of films were made from the work of writers in this genre such as E. Phillips Oppenheim, Saxe Rohmer and, particularly, Edgar Wallace, both in Britain and America. John Cawelti has written of this popular genre, drawing attention to its dominant theme of 'racial subversion'. In his own words:

> The British Empire and its white Christian civilisation are constantly in danger of subversion by villains who represent other races or racial mixtures. Saxe Rohmer's Fu Manchu and his hordes of little yellow and brown conspirators against the purity and safety of English society are only an extreme example of the pervasive racial symbolism of this period.[24]

The Bulldog Drummond stories, for example, in the words of Julian Symons, are 'markedly xenophobic' tales in which 'Europeans are rarely referred to except as wogs and dagos'[25] and this anti-foreigner aspect of the genre is marked in a number of the Hitchcock pictures albeit in a lighter and more humorous manner.

The themes of espionage were not confined to the realm of popular literature and neither was Hitchcock's source material confined to writers such as Buchan and McNeile. After *The Man Who Knew Too Much* and *The Thirty-Nine Steps* derived from the popular strand of the genre, Hitchcock based his next two films on the work of Somerset Maugham and Joseph Conrad. *Secret Agent* was based upon a series of short stories by Somerset Maugham which chronicled the adventures of a British Agent during the First World War whilst *Sabotage*, somewhat confusingly, was an adaptation of *The Secret Agent*, the novel by Joseph Conrad. The latter was written in 1907, somewhat earlier than the popular cycle of spy stories which began roughly at the outbreak of the First World War, and is a serious psychological novel concerned with the mentality of the central figure, the saboteur Verloc. Maugham's *Ashenden* stories were written much later, in 1928, and these too can be distinguished from the popular work of Buchan and McNeile particularly in terms of their credibility and 'realism'. As Julian Symons puts it:

> The stories in *Ashenden* (1928) which sprang from Maugham's own experience in the Secret Service, were something new in spy fiction. After the easy absurd assumptions made by Buchan,' 'Sapper' and Oppenheim, the *Ashenden* stories have the reality of a cold bath.[26]

In a preface to the collection, however, Maugham was at pains to point out that despite the origins of the stories in his own personal experience of the world of espionage, they remained works of fiction with the source material of experience made 'coherent, dramatic and probable' through the skill and craft of the author.[27] Nevertheless, distinctions of purpose, tone and flavour can be drawn within the overall body of literature which uses espionage as its subject matter, and if Conrad's novel is something of an oddity in a generic context the Maugham stories have clear relationships with the more popular end of the genre. After four spy thrillers based upon very contrasting sources, Hitchcock's next film — *Young and Innocent* — was a departure from the world of espionage although not from the world of flight and pursuit. The final film in the sextet, *The Lady Vanishes*, sees a return to the spy thriller and also an expansion of the train motif from *The Thirty-Nine Steps* and *Secret Agent*. Set almost entirely on board a trans-European train, it fits into the loose cycle of 'train' films of the 1930s which includes, for example, *Rome Express* (1932) and *Night Train to Munich* (Reed, 1940) from Britain, and *Shanghai Express* (Sternberg, 1932) from Hollywood. Bernard Bergonzi has pointed out that the train was a popular setting for novels of the period and, as examples, he cites Graham Greene's *Stamboul Train* and Agatha Christie's *Murder on the Orient Express* which were published in 1932 and 1933 respectively. The final two pictures in the thriller sextet were also based upon literary sources with *Young and Innocent* deriving from a Josephine Tey detective novel, *A Shilling for Candles*, and *The Lady Vanishes* from *The Wheel Spins* written by Ethel Lina White. Both represent a return to the popular end of the genre after the excursion into the highbrow realm of Conrad.

A specific literary current drawn from a variety of literary types including a major serious contribution to the development of the English novel, a range of popular writers (Buchan referred to his adventure novels as 'shockers'), female detective writers and the comfortable middlebrow appeal of Somerset Maugham, provides a series of influences which are the literary context for the thriller sextet. The sources bar one (*A Shilling for*

Candles), whatever their differences, are linked together through the themes of international espionage. Much of the writing mentioned predates the 1930s, the period of the films, yet it has been suggested that the subject matter had a particular relevance for the time which was, of course, one of developing international turbulence. Bernard Bergonzi has drawn attention to the presence of espionage themes and issues in a range of thirties' literature, both highbrow and popular, in the following terms:

> Frontiers and spies, bombers and the threat of war, were facts of the age, a palpable part of public consciousness, in literature they occurred not only as signifiers of an external reality but also as metaphors and recurring formal constituents.[28]

Such a configuration of features, 'frontiers and spies, bombers and the threat of war', serves very well to sketch the broad outline of the Hitchcock spy pictures and it may be argued that, although drawing upon literature written during a different period in the context of different ideological concerns, the films do reflect the key ideological currents of the international politics of the time, albeit in a highly mediated fashion.

In comparing the films with their literary sources, the differences, particularly in tone and mood, between the films can be explained by reference to their contrasting literary origins. The first two films of the cycle, *The Man Who Knew Too Much* and *The Thirty-Nine Steps*, are basically adventure stories although neither adheres particularly closely to its origins. The 'Sapper' hero, Bulldog Drummond, is 'a sportsman and a gentleman. And the combination of the two is an unbeatable production'.[29] The lead male in *The Man Who Knew Too Much* partly fits this description as he is a 'gentleman'. Bob Lawrence (Leslie Banks) is clearly marked out as a member of the upper middle classes by accent, home (furnishings, maid etc.) and by the fact that he and his family take their holidays in the ski resort of St Moritz. He is not, however, a 'sportsman'. In fact, the sporting prowess is possessed by a woman, his wife Jill (Edna Best), whose skill as an expert markswoman proves crucial in the 'climactic combat' of the film. It is as if Hitchcock had split the masculine Drummond character in two, into gentleman and sportswoman, with the combination remaining equally unbeatable. Although, as many feminist critics have pointed out, there are problems with the ways in which Hitchcock represents women on screen, here at least is a dilution of the chauvinism of the original Drummond character. *The Man Who Knew Too Much* was loosely based on the Drummond character but the next film in the cycle, *The Thirty-Nine Steps*, was based directly on the Buchan novel of the same name. The film follows the novel in so far as the central character, Richard Hannay (Robert Donat), is plunged unwittingly into a series of adventures which transport him from London to the Highlands of Scotland and back again. Yet numerous episodes have been added to the original Buchan story. The film opens and closes in a London music hall, focusing upon a character known as Mr Memory who was based on a real life music hall personality. There is an additional lengthy sequence in a crofter's cottage in the Highlands, and a romantic theme has been added. The episodic structure of the novel is reflected with the hero moving swiftly from music hall to apartment, to the Flying Scotsman, to the Highlands of Scotland, to capture by the foreign spies and back to the music hall for the climax. Indeed, it is the very pace of the film that Hitchcock remembers with some considerable satisfaction as he mentions to Truffaut:

> What I like in *The Thirty-Nine Steps* are the swift transitions .... The rapidity of the transitions heightens the excitement. It takes a lot of work to get that kind of effect, but it's well worth the effort. You use one idea after another and eliminate anything that interferes with the swift pace.[30]

It is the commitment to the helter-skelter of adventure that keeps *The Thirty-Nine Steps* and its predecessor which also skips from adventure to adventure, on a light rather than sombre course although both films do have their dark moments. The crofter's sequence in *The Thirty-Nine Steps*, in particular, introduces a powerful current of sexual repression and cruelty which contrasts somewhat starkly with the tone of the rest of the film. It is in this respect especially that the Hitchcock version of *The Thirty-Nine Steps* marks a profound gap between Hitchcock and Buchan. As Peter Wollen has pointed out in relation to a later American Hitchcock film which closely parallels *The Thirty-Nine Steps*:

> clearly it is only a step from Hannay or Leithen in *The Power House* to Thornhill in *North By Northwest*. Only a step, yet with Hitchcock we are made aware of realms of experience which never existed for Buchan. There is the inflection towards the grotesque — the tradition of Hoffman, Poe, Kafka — and the influence of a spell at the UFA studio, German Expressionism, the affinity with Fritz Lang and, finally, the impact of Freud ...[31]

The impact of Freud, the sexual dimensions of Hitchcock's pictures, takes us into areas proscribed by the puritanical and masculine world of the Buchan hero. Whilst the crofter sequence, previously mentioned, is interesting for its dark underscoring of the situation with the theme of sexual repression, it is later in the film that an explicitly sexual element is introduced. Hannay becomes handcuffed to the reluctant Pamela (Madeleine Carroll) whilst they are being taken off by the enemy agents and although their relationship develops to the traditional romantic conclusion at the end of the film, this is not before a good deal of *risqué* humour is extracted from the situation of enforced intimacy in which the couple are placed. Madeleine Carroll as Pamela fits into the long line of English sexual stereo types that populate Hitchcock's films, both British and American, and characterised by the director in the following terms:

> Sex on the screen should be suspenseful, I feel. If sex is too blatant or obvious, there's no suspense. You know why I favour sophisticated blondes in my films? We're after the drawing room type, the real ladies, who become whores once they're in the bedroom. Poor Marilyn Monroe had sex written all over her face, and Brigitte Bardot isn't very subtle either.[32]

Pamela, the sophisticated blonde, with her combined traits of innocence and knowingness, her coolness and reserve which hide a passion, is placed in an impossible situation with Hannay when the couple are obliged to spend the night handcuffed together in a remote Highland inn masquerading as newlyweds.

The next two pictures, *Secret Agent* and *Sabotage,* represent a development of the dark tone and mood intermittently present in *The Man Who Knew Too Much* and *The Thirty-Nine Steps* and they reflect in a more marked way influences such as Fritz Lang and the traditions of the German silent cinema cited by Peter Wollen. Rohmer and Chabrol refer to a different balancing of the moral elements ('sincerity' to use their own term) and the entertainment elements in favour of seriousness and profundity. Such a rebalancing can be linked quite precisely to the literary sources that Hitchcock went to after the popular works of 'Sapper' and Buchan. We have already noted that Maugham's *Ashenden* stories have been contrasted with 'Sapper' and Buchan in terms of their 'realism' and Hichcock's *Secret Agent* reflects the distinction in a number of ways. Firstly, the central character, Ashenden (John Gielgud), lacks the positive determination, the simple single-mindedness, of heroes such as Bulldog Drummond and Richard Hannay. Indeed, Hitchcock attributes the commercial failure of the film to the lack of positive commitment and purpose in the central character as he makes clear in the following remark to Truffaut:

> There were lots of ideas in the picture, but it didn't really succeed and I think I know why. In an adventure drama your central figure must have a purpose. That's vital for the progression of the film, and it's also a key factor in audience participation. The public must be rooting for the character; they should almost be helping him to achieve his goal. John Gielgud, the hero of *The Secret Agent* (*sic*), has an assignment, but the job is distasteful and he is reluctant to do it.[33]

The Ashenden character whose mission is to eliminate an enemy spy has no taste for the job and this feeling is compounded when an innocent man, Caypor (Percy Marmont), is mistakenly identified as the target and killed by Ashenden's Mexican accomplice (Peter Lorre). Ashenden is also assisted by a woman, Elsa Carrington (Madeleine Carroll), who is posing as his wife. The theme of imposed intimacy from *The Thirty-Nine Steps* is thus reprised in a slightly different form. Elsa Carrington functions as an index of transition from light adventure tale to the gloomy world of espionage. We learn that she had begged her superiors for such an assignment wanting action, shooting and killing, the supposed excitements of spying, but the mistaken slaying of the innocent Caypor provides her with a salutary lesson in the grimmer realities of international espionage. The Mexican, sympathetically portrayed by Peter Lorre, is himself killed just before the end of the film and although this does not constitute the unhappy ending that Truffaut misremembers, it is an event entirely in keeping with the sombre mood of the film.[34] The final image of Ashenden and Elsa Carrington although conventionally romantic in certain respects is nevertheless unsmiling and perhaps to be regarded as a wry comment on the film itself.

Sabotage, however, remains the bleakest film of the cycle and it might be argued that it reflects the project of the Conrad novel on which it was based which was to portray the 'wholly evil nature of revolution, in which spies naturally play their loathsome part'.[35] Certainly, the central character, Verloc (Oscar Homolka), is presented as an evildoer who is responsible for the death of an innocent young boy thus repeating the theme of innocent death from *Secret Agent*. Yet the film is concerned also with the characterisation of Verloc as a man caught within a network of espionage activity over which he has a limited control. Like the Mexican from the previous film, Verloc emerges as a not wholly unsympathetic character despite the terrible nature of his crime. Like Ashenden, he is reluctant to take life, reluctant to press to the limits his function as saboteur. He is eventually stabbed to death by his wife (Sylvia Sidney) in retribution for the killing of her brother, yet, as Truffaut has argued, the treatment of this scene 'almost suggests suicide rather than murder. It's as if Homolka were allowing himself to be killed by Sylvia Sidney'.[36] Hitchcock's reply to Truffaut indicates that the scene was designed to be read as an accident rather than a deliberate killing in order to sustain spectator sympathy for Sylvia Sidney but the momentum of the film does indicate that by this time Verloc was actually at the end of his tether and possibly predisposed towards what might be read as a suicidal gesture. Whatever the reading of this particular episode the overall thrust of the film is on the presentation of character rather than on the helter-skelter of adventure or the mechanics of spying. In that sense we can differentiate *Sabotage* from *The Thirty-Nine Steps* and suggest that Buchan's 'shocker' and Conrad's 'serious' novel have left their substantial traces on the two films and this also holds true for *The Man Who Knew Too Much* and *Secret Agent,* for 'Sapper' and Somerset Maugham.

The remaining two films of the sextet, *Young and Innocent* and *The Lady Vanishes,* reintroduce the lighter tone of the earlier films and, as with those, both are based upon popular thriller sources. *Young and Innocent* also deviates from the espionage genre, being based upon the adventures of a young man (Derrick de Marney) falsely accused of the murder of a woman. He becomes involved with a young woman (Nova Pilbeam) and together they set off on a hunt for a missing clue which may prove his innocence. However, despite the absence of the spy theme, the film does occupy the territory of *The Thirty-Nine Steps* with its thematic constellation of 'fear, guilt, flight', the pursuit and the chase. In addition, the film continues the theme of enforced intimacy between the hero and heroine although the sexual implications of this are not developed as in the earlier film. *The Lady Vanishes*, the last film of the cycle, returns to the world of espionage and, as with *Young and Innocent*, the darker side of Hitchcock's work is subordinated to the comic and romantic elements. Rohmer and Chabrol's notion of the balance of elements which forms the basis of the success of the thriller sextet is a useful one but it should be related explicitly to the literary bases of the cycle. The variations of tone and mood depend to a large extent on the literary origins so that Buchan's popular entertainment yields the dash and verve of *The Thirty-Nine Steps* whilst Conrad's sombre work yields the bleak world of *Sabotage*.

The Sextet and the Spy Thriller

I want now to examine the sextet from the point of view of its relationship to the spy thriller genre as sketched out earlier in this chapter, and in terms of the various interrelationships between the films themselves. Rohmer and Chabrol have suggested that the inaugural film of the cycle, *The Man Who Knew Too Much*, marked a politic return by Hitchcock to the proven successful elements of his earlier films viz. crime, suspense, thrills and so on. They characterise the film as a judicious blend comprising '50 per cent *Murder!*, 50 per cent *Number Seventeen*'[37] and whilst this does indicate much about the film, it does omit one central element, espionage. *The Man Who Knew Too Much* introduces the world of international espionage into the Hitchcockian universe for the first time and the centrality of the medley of themes which relate to spying has been stressed by Peter Wollen in the following terms:

> The centre, the *axis* of Hitchcock's films is the manhunt, the pursuit of the prey by the predator, a pursuit which is reversible, so that roles may be exchanged. Allied to the hunter is the spy, in essence an ambivalent figure — hunter and hunted, policeman and criminal — and therefore the pivot on whom the structure turns. But, for Hitchcock, it is not the problem of loyalty or allegiance which is uppermost, but the mechanisms of spying and pursuit in themselves, mechanisms which have their own psychological significance.[38]

It is as if the genre enabled Hitchcock to release into his cinematic world a number of themes which, whilst not necessarily tied to the espionage genre, nevertheless achieve a concentrated expression within it. Significant aspects of 'spying' are indeed present in *The Lodger* where much of the force of the film turns upon the various 'views' of the lodger available to the other characters. This is particularly true of Mrs Bunting who literally spies on him as he makes one of his midnight forays, stealthily creeping down the staircase.

Five of the six films of the cycle are firmly rooted in the fictional domain of espionage, drawing upon the literature of spydom cited earlier and working the familiar themes and situations through different narrative patterns to produce a series of variations on the thematic and iconographic constituents of the genre. I want to begin by looking at the hero/conspiracy couplet which, it has been suggested, lies at the heart of the thriller genre in general. *The Man Who Knew Too Much*, *The Thirty-Nine Steps*, *Secret Agent* and *The Lady Vanishes* certainly are organised around such a conflictual pattern although the concept of the hero requires a certain degree of elasticity to accommodate the particular definition of the hero function in Hitchcock's films. *Sabotage*, although set in the world of espionage, does not present the conflict between a hero and the conspiracy in such a clear fashion partly because the focus is largely on one of the conspirators. A case might be made for Ted, the detective figure (John Loder), as occupant of the hero position but the weight of the film seems to lie elsewhere than in the conflict between him and the conspiracy. Interestingly enough, Hitchcock attributes the problems with the film to the characterisation of the detective which had to be altered during the production of the film when Hitchcock's first choice for the role — Robert Donat — became unavailable. Whether the hero/conspiracy theme would have been highlighted with a stronger actor in the detective role is, however, open to doubt given the specific orientation of the Conrad novel on which the film is based. The remaining four spy films do offer a more explicit play upon the hero/conspiracy theme although it is possible to draw some distinctions between the different films in terms of the way in which the basic structure is presented and developed. The hero functions in *The Man Who Knew Too Much*, *The Thirty-Nine Steps* and *The Lady Vanishes* are occupied by individuals who are constructed as heroes by accident, by the vagaries of circumstance. By contrast, the central characters in *Secret Agent* and *Sabotage* are professional agents, 'heroes' — if that is the correct designation — by design. In *The Man Who Knew Too Much*, the Lawrence family are holidaying at a ski resort where an assassination gang happen to be gathering before going on a mission. The family befriend a Frenchman called Louis Bernard (Pierre Fresnay) who, in fact, is an agent on the trail of the gang. He is killed by them but just before he dies he manages to pass on a series of vital clues to Bob Lawrence. The gang retaliate by kidnapping the Lawrences' young daughter to prevent them from alerting the authorities and the narrative develops with the Lawrences' pursuit of the gang back to London. Jill Lawrence, in the course of the pursuit, manages to prevent the assassination in the famous Albert Hall sequence, and finally the child is rescued and the family reunited. *The Thirty-Nine Steps* centres on the adventures of Richard Hannay, a Canadian on holiday in London. The film begins in a London music hall where Hannay becomes involved with a mysterious woman who returns with him to his flat. He assumes that she is an 'actress' to use his own euphemism, but she turns out to be a spy working to prevent a conspiracy from smuggling aeronautical secrets out of Britain. She is killed whilst in the flat and Hannay is forced to go on the run from the police, who assume that he is the murderer, in order to unmask the real murderers, the spy network. Although caught in the frequent Hitchcock situation between two sets of pursuers, the police and the conspirators, he eventually succeeds in defeating the spies in the dramatic finale at the London Palladium. *The Lady Vanishes* concerns a woman returning from a holiday in central Europe on board a trans-European express. She befriends a Miss Froy, an elderly governess returning to England after many years working abroad, who disappears mysteriously during the course of the journey. The woman, Iris Henderson, doggedly attempts to unravel the mystery with the eventual assistance of a young man, Gilbert, and we finally learn that Miss Froy is, in fact, a British secret agent whose abduction was carried out by an enemy conspiracy. In all three films, 'ordinary people' — a middle class family on a skiing holiday, a Canadian visitor to London, a young woman returning from holiday in Europe — are plunged into the nightmare world of spies and spying. The protagonists in each film are obliged to occupy the role of heroic agent when the professionals in the films are either eliminated entirely in the early stages as in *The Man Who Knew Too Much* and *The Thirty-Nine Steps*, or are kidnapped and missing for the best part of the film as in *The Lady Vanishes*. It can be argued that the films deal with, a familiar Hitchcock theme which Peter Wollen has called 'the proximity of the chaos world'[39] into which ordinary people may be cast by accident. It is a theme which embraces many of Hitchcock's non-espionage pictures and examples from the British films would include *The Lodger* in which the Bunting family are thrown into a world of fear and anxiety with the arrival of the lodger, *Blackmail* in which Alice White opens up the antiworld of chaos and disorder through her flirtation with the artist, and *Rich and Strange* which differs in so far as the central couple actively seek the world of excitement as a contrast to their suburban dullness and discover that it is a world of chaos and disorder. There is a distinct contrast when the theme of the chaos world is located within the spy genre however. In both *The Lodger* and *Blackmail* the characters who are plunged into 'the chaos world' are helpless and are buffeted by circumstance through the course of the film. In the three spy thrillers, although the central characters are also plunged into 'the chaos world' the circumstances are such that they are set quite precise goals which determine the narrative trajectory of the films. The Lawrences need to rescue their daughter from the assassination gang, Hannay needs to unravel the secret of 'the thirty-nine steps' in order to clear his name, and Iris Henderson needs to find Miss Froy to prove that she is not suffering mental delusions. These celebrated 'MacGuffins', the pretexts for adventure, although unimportant in themselves nevertheless provide the central characters with a measure of control over events and with the means of restoring order to their worlds. It is this latter point which distinguishes say, Hannay or Iris Henderson, from Daisy Bunting or Alice White.

The other two spy thrillers, *Secret Agent* and *Sabotage*, differ in so far as they focus upon espionage from within, with undercover agents as their protagonists. They are peopled by characters for whom 'the chaos world' is the working world, and for whom the dangers and excitements are an essential part of professional existence. In the three spy thrillers discussed before, the defeat of the conspiracy is an incidental result of the activities of the protagonists. Jill Lawrence prevents the assassination in the course of rescuing her daughter, Hannay proves himself innocent of murder by uncovering the plot to smuggle secrets abroad, and Iris Henderson foils the gang who have kidnapped Miss Froy and proves her sanity. The protagonists of *Secret Agent*, by contrast, have a straightforward espionage mission, the identification of an enemy double agent and his elimination, and are professionally assigned to the task. There is a vague sense in which Ashenden and Elsa Carrington are caught up in events. Ashenden is a reluctant agent deflected from his career as a writer into espionage duties whilst Elsa Carrington is a somewhat naïve agent with an 'adventure novel' view of what the work entails. Yet, they are both professionals doing a job rather than ordinary people on holiday who get caught up in the nightmarish world of the spy. *Sabotage* also focuses on a professional, Verloc, a saboteur. Like Ashenden, he is reluctant particularly when it comes to taking life, and the film presents a somewhat sympathetic portrait of an enemy agent who is to a certain extent caught up in the sabotage machine and unable to extricate himself from it. A case might be made for Mrs Verloc as the ordinary person plunged into 'the chaos world' as she is ignorant of her husband's double life. One might also argue that she is structured into the hero role after the death of her brother, when she kills Verloc. Ostensibly, the hero figure is Ted, the detective who has been assigned to uncover Verloc yet his role seems weighted towards the romantic entanglement with Mrs Verloc rather than the uncovering of the sabotage plots. The film moves away from the hero/conspiracy format towards other concerns and it seems less implicated in the spy thriller genre than the other films, less dependent upon the conventions and situations characteristic of the genre. The final film to be considered, *Young and Innocent*, is not a spy thriller yet its structure is almost identical to that of *The Thirty-Nine Steps*. As in that film, a young man is falsely accused of murder, gets caught up in a whirlwind of events, and spends the film searching for a clue that will prove his innocence. As in the previous film, he is accompanied by a young woman who is inadvertently and reluctantly drawn into the nightmare world of fear, pursuit and flight.

The world of the film is close to that of the 'non-professional' spy thrillers and it shares their juxtaposition of the ordinary and the chaos world, and the narrative structure of the hunt.

It has already been suggested that a somewhat 'elastic' notion of the hero is required for the Hitchcock sextet, one which is somewhat more complicated than the simple definitions of Buchan and 'Sapper'. Each film of the cycle centres upon a heterosexual couple in the structural position of hero in some form of conflict with the conspiracy. There are differences in presentation, however, across the films and some attention to these will help in defining the relationship between the thriller genre and the Hitchcock variant. The central role in *The Man Who Knew Too Much* is occupied by a married couple, the Lawrences, who eventually defeat the conspiracy in order to rescue their kidnapped daughter. The couple are present at the outset of the film although there are hints about problems in their relationship before the kidnapping occurs and the adventures begin. The film proceeds to restore the family to a unity encapsulated in the final image of mother, father and daughter together again. *Sabotage* also begins with a married couple. They also have a 'child' in the form of Mrs Verloc's young brother, Stevie, and thus constitute a family unit like the Lawrences. However, the film proceeds to dissolve the relationship of the married couple through the killing of the 'child' and, simultaneously, constructs another heterosexual couple with Mrs Verloc and Ted, the detective. The four remaining films of the cycle also emphasise the construction of the couple by bringing the leading characters together during the course of the adventures. They do this, however, in different ways and with different inflections of the theme. In *The Thirty-Nine Steps*, the initial emphasis is on the male character (Hannay) with the woman (Pamela) a sceptical and unwilling partner in the adventures until the later stages of the film. *The Lady Vanishes* reverses this pattern with the woman (Iris Henderson) in the central position to begin with and the man (Gilbert) playing the sceptical and unwilling partner for part of the film. *Young and Innocent*, as I have suggested, is very similar to *The Thirty-Nine Steps* with its innocent male protagonist (Robert) and its central female character (Erica) becoming accidentally involved in his flight from the law. Like Pamela in the previous film she is unwilling at first but ends up as his accomplice and as part of the couple. *Secret Agent* varies the theme of the couple by throwing Ashenden and Elsa together at the beginning of the film as agents masquerading as a married couple during the course of a mission. The situation of enforced intimacy is similar to that in *The Thirty-Nine Steps* but this time there is a mutual reluctance to be overcome before the ending which transforms the 'artificial' couple into a conventional romantic couple. A married couple in a somewhat strained relationship, a couple pretending to be married as a cover for their spying, and various couples thrown together, provide the central concerns of the thriller sextet with five of the six films also involving the world of espionage. The congruence of *Young and Innocent* with the spy thrillers at the level of romantic theme, however, indicates the specific Hitchcockian inflection of the espionage genre. Michael Renov, in an article devoted to *Notorious* (1946), has referred to the film as a 'romance-thriller'[40] and this is, perhaps, the most pertinent generic title to allocate to the sextet. The primary emphasis of the films is on the romantic encounter and the development of the relationship between the leading characters played, however, through the suspenseful and dangerous diegetic world of the thriller. The adventures are less a test of the resilience and skill of the conventional thriller hero than tests of the relationship between romantic hero and heroine. Jerry Palmer, in his work on the thriller, has argued that the thriller hero although often romantically entangled, remains basically an outsider not capable of establishing a sustained relationship with a woman.[41] Sexual encounters are frequent in the writers to whom Palmer refers — Mickey Spillane and Ian Fleming — but the heroes do not move from such encounters to the kinds of relationships implied for the characters in the Hitchcock films. A good illustration of this occurs in the James Bond film *On Her Majesty's Secret Service*, in which Bond actually gets married but the film concludes with his new wife being assassinated as they drive to their honeymoon. The 'essential isolation' of figures such as Fleming's James Bond and Spillane's Mike Hammer does not allow for the domestic entanglements of the romance genre and this marks out the Hitchcock thriller as a form constituted by conventional thriller elements together with the romantic theme of the couple with the latter in dominance. Hence, Renov's order of words — 'romance' then 'thriller' — importantly highlights the weighting of the generic balance. William Rothman has argued that *The Man Who Knew Too Much* relates to the 'comedy of remarriage' genre which centres on the reconstruction of once romantic couples now broken apart and this may provide another generic dimension for the Hitchcock thriller which again pulls it away from the mainstream of the genre.[42]

The other structural pole of the thriller is the conspiracy and, in the spy thrillers, it is represented in different way. In *The Man Who Knew Too Much, Secret Agent* and *Sabotage* the conspiratorial grouping has a set of clearly defined objectives which the hero/heroine couple have to prevent from being carried out. *The Man Who Knew Too Much* has its assassination gang with its target, *Secret Agent* concerns the interception of plans during wartime and *Sabotage* has the planting of the bomb at Piccadilly Circus. The conspiratorial objectives are not quite so clear in *The Thirty-Nine Steps* and *The Lady Vanishes*. The respective enemy agents do have objectives — the smuggling of aeronautical secrets, the prevention of a message reaching England — yet these are not revealed until the later stages of the films. The origins of the conspiracies, their allegiances and political affiliations, are quite opaque. They clearly exist as evil enterprises dedicated to various forms of destruction and deceit but not clearly on any particular behalf. They remain shadowy in origin — except for *Secret Agent* which has a degree of historical specificity — and this is to be understood in the context of the thriller genre in which the weight of emphasis is on the hero's self validation as a skilled and resourceful opponent of generalised threat. In the Hitchcock variant, the conspiracy poses a challenge to the development of the romantic couple and the validation is couched in terms of the maturing of the relationship between the central characters. The conspiracy, although an integral part of the diegetic world of the thriller, is not required to be precisely defined either in terms of its origins and identity or in terms of its activities. Hitchcock's 'MacGuffin' — the secrets to be stolen, the assassination plot — are motors which drive the fictional machine onwards but they have little real significance in themselves being pretexts for the central concerns of the films, the consolidation of the romantic couple. It is possible, however, to locate the 'shadowy conspiracy' in the context of Europe in the 1930s. The British cinema of this period has often been attacked for its failure to reflect 'the agony of those times',[43] yet it can be argued that the spy thriller genre is an indication of the growing consciousness of the political turbulence in Europe, the rise of Fascism and the troubled international situation which was to erupt into the Second World War. Although the links between the films and contemporary political realities are not over-explicit they are none the less tangible. Political assassination of the kind represented in *The Man Who Knew Too Much* was not unknown in interwar Europe, the leather-coated villains in *The Thirty-Nine Steps* evoke the Nazis whilst the middle European accents of Abbott (*The Man Who Knew Too Much*), Verloc and his spymaster (*Sabotage*), and the assortment of continental voices on the side of villainy in *The Lady Vanishes* provide a distinctive aural token of the European menace from the British point of view.

Hitchcock, Romance and the Thriller

In the literary spy thriller, romance is not centralised and the usually male hero remains alone as the isolated combatant of evil. The hero can be involved in sexual adventures although, for example, Buchan's Hannay is not, but what Jerry Palmer calls 'the warm, erotic companionship of adult love'[44] is normally excluded from the world of the thriller. Yet, it is precisely this form of relationship which is constructed in *The Thirty-Nine Steps*, *Secret Agent* and *The Lady Vanishes*, or, at least, constructed as a strong possibility for the protagonist duo. *The Man Who Knew Too Much* restores a marriage represented as dull and unfulfilling in the early part of the film whilst *Sabotage* presents an embryonic relationship between Mrs Verloc and Ted which will replace the destroyed marriage. *Young and Innocent* does not deal with adult love yet it does construct an adolescent couple out of the 'young and innocent' central couple. The particular blend of elements from Hitchcock's earlier pictures such as *Murder!* and *Number Seventeen* which Rohmer and Chabrol have suggested defines the qualities of the thriller sextet needs to be expanded to accommodate the theme of the couple. The romantic theme has been isolated as a vital component in each of the films though it has a different importance and weighting in the different films. For example, the construction of the couple is a more important part of *The Thirty-Nine Steps* than of *Sabotage*. Although the pre-sextet thrillers undoubtedly contribute to the cycle it is also necessary to consider some of Hitchcock's non-thrillers and especially the relationship between *Rich and Strange* and the sextet. The former focuses on a married couple who set out to revive the dull routine of their life in the suburbs by embarking on a world tour. Their relationship is subjected to a series of tests ranging from infidelity to shipwreck but they survive to return to their suburban anonymity 'remarried', restored as a married couple and grateful for the stability that their conventional life offers. The couple in *Rich and Strange* opted to explore a kind of 'chaos world' whereas the thriller sextet plunges its protagonist into the nightmare world often through accident and coincidence, but the common element is the test of the couple through adventure. It is this blend of flights and pursuits from *Number Seventeen*, murder and mystery from *Murder!* together with romance and the idea of the couple from *Rich and Strange* which specifies the Hitchcock thriller. The films of the sextet can be looked at as tracing 'courtship rituals' between the central characters against the particular background of the espionage story and its nightmarish world of deception and subterfuge, mystery and death. It is a formula which is reflected in some of Hitchcock's American films such as *Notorious* (1946) and *North by Northwest* (1959). One of the disruptive elements in relation to the couple in the two American films is the triangular situation in which the women characters are placed. *Notorious*, in particular, takes the triangular situation to an extreme by having Alicia (Ingrid Bergman) married to one of the conspirators whilst being in love with Devlin (Cary Grant), the 'good' agent. *Secret Agent* and *Sabotage* from the thriller cycle play with such a theme and although this ca be traced back to pre-sextet thrillers such as *The Lodger* and *Blackmail*, the fullest exploration of a triangular romantic situation occurs in *The Manxman*, Hitchcock's last silent film, made in 1929. Rohmer and Chabrol offered a useful way into the successful cycle of thrillers upon which Hitchcock was to rebuild his ailing reputation but the job of tracing the films to their Hitchcockian antecedents needs to take account of the romantic elements in films such as *The Manxman* and *Rich and Strange* which perhaps contain elements which are as Hitchcockian as those to be drawn from the films which square more easily with the director's popular image.

Notes

1. R. Durgnat, *The Strange Case of Alfred Hitchcock* (Faber and Faber, London, 1974), p. 20.
2. E. Rohmer and Claude Chabrol, *Hitchcock* (Ungar, New York, 1978), p. 37.
3. F. Truffaut, *Hitchcock* (Panther, London, 1969), pp. 91-2.
4. C. Metz, *Language and Cinema* (Mouton, The Hague, 1974), p 122.
5. L. Anderson, 'Alfred Hitchcock', *Sequence*, no. 9 (1949), p. 117

6. Truffaut, *Hitchcock*, p. 48.

7. 'Interview: Ivor Montagu', *Screen*, vol. 13, no. 3 (1972), p. 88.

8. Ibid., p. 87.

9. Bernard Knowles (*The Thirty-Nine Steps, Secret Agent, Sabotage, Young and Innocent*); Otto Werndorff and Albert Jullion (*The Thirty-Nine Steps, Secret Agent, Sabotage*); Charles Frend (*Secret Agent, Sabotage, Young and Innocent*).

10. C.A. Lejeune, quoted in D. Shipman, *The Great Movie Stars The Golden Years* (Hamlyn, London, 1970), p. 165.

11. These statistics have been drawn from Denis Gifford's invaluable *The British National Film Catalogue 1895-1970* (David and Charles, Newton Abbot, 1973). I have used his broad generic categories which are based on trade paper descriptions and production company publicity material.

12. For more on the genre see J. Symons, *Bloody Murder* (Penguin, Harmondsworth, 1974).

13. Hitchcock discusses the MacGuffin with Truffaut in the volume of interviews. See Truffaut, *Hitchcock*, Ch. 6.

14. J. Palmer, *Thrillers* (Edward Arnold, London, 1978).

15. I use the word 'his' because the thriller is a male-dominated genre.

16. Palmer, *Thrillers*, p. 53.

17. S. Neale, *Genre* (British Film Institute, London, 1980), p. 29.

18. R. Warshow, *The Immediate Experience* (Atheneum, New York, 1970); C. McArthur, *Underworld USA* (Secker and Warburg, London, 1972).

19. Neale, *Genre*, p. 20.

20. M. Vernet, 'Genre', *Film Reader 3* (1978), p. 15.

21. Rohmer and Chabrol, *Hitchcock*, p. 37 ff.

22. Ibid., p. 43.

23. Truffaut, *Hitchcock*, p. 102.

24. J. Cawelti, *Adventure, Mystery and Romance* (University of Chicago Press, Chicago, 1976), p. 31.

25. Symons, *Bloody Murder*, p. 240.

26. Ibid., p. 241.

27. W. Somerset Maugham, *Collected Short Stories*, vol. 3 (Penguin, Harmondsworth, 1963), p. 7.

28. B. Bergonzi, *Reading the Thirties* (MacMillan, London, 1978), p. 76.

29. 'Sapper', quoted in Symons, *Blood Murder*, p. 240.

30. Truffaut, *Hitchcock*, p. 108.

31. P. Wollen, 'Hitchcock's Vision', *Cinema* (UK) no. 3 (1969), p. 2.

32. Truffaut, *Hitchcock*, pp. 277-8.

33. Ibid., p. 114.

34. Ibid., pp. 114-5.

35. Symons, *Bloody Murder*, p. 239.

36. Truffaut, *Hitchcock*, p. 120.

37. Rohmer and Chabrol, *Hitchcock*, p. 38.

38. Wollen, 'Hitchcock's Vision', p. 2.

39. Ibid., p. 4.

40. M. Renov, 'From Identification to Ideology: the Male System of Hitchcock's *Notorious*', *Wide Angle*, vol. 4, no. 1 (1980), p. 30.

41. Palmer, *Thrillers*, Ch. 3.

42. W. Rothman, *Hitchcock — the Murderous Gaze* (Harvard University Press, Cambridge, Mass., 1982), p. 110. See also S. Cavell, *Pursuits of Happiness* (Harvard University Press, Cambridge, Mass., 1982).

43. M. Balcon, *A Lifetime in Films* (Hutchinson, London, 1969), p. 99.

44. Palmer, *Thrillers*, p. 33.

Chapter Seven

Hitchcock and Classical Cinema

Terms such as 'classical cinema', 'the classic narrative film' and 'the classic realist text' are scattered throughout the literature of contemporary film theory and criticism. In the context of the politics of film such terms often function as polemical counters without precise definition, yet, in the context of critical analysis, the idea of a 'classic cinematic model' defined with some degree of precision has an important role to play. As David Bordwell has suggested, the classical model and its system of narrative and spatial construction 'are meant to have the same explanatory status as the concepts of classicism or baroque in the history of painting and music'.[1] Such a model can establish 'the norms and conventions of dominant stylistic practices of a period'[2] and thereby enable the film critic and historian to specify the particular and distinctive qualities of a film or a body of films with a greater degree of precision and accuracy. As a model, classical cinema is an abstraction, a generalisation, and individual films will correspond more or less to its inventory of features. Also, as a model, it remains subject to change and refinement as new, individual films are examined in terms of their relationship to the established model. The purpose of this chapter is to offer a broad definition of the classical film and to use this definition to examine the particular qualities of Hitchcock's British work. As an English film maker working within a film culture dominated by Hollywood films, Hitchcock was inevitably influenced by the classical model of narrative cinema as it developed during the period from the early 1920s onwards. Hollywood's conquest of the international film market after World War One meant that the American narrative film provided a model for other film-producing nations to emulate or to react against.

The main features of the classical film are detailed in a variety of writings ranging from texts of advanced film theory such as Stephen Heath's 'Narrative Space'[3] to technical production manuals such as *The Technique of Film Editing* by Karel Reisz and Gavin Millar.[4] The conventions of classical cinema embrace characteristic approaches to the structuring of a narrative, to the construction of an image and its relationship to other images in the context of a film, and to the use of dialogue, noise and music on the sound track.[5] At another level, the classical film can be defined in terms of a series of interrelationships between the various constituents of narrative form and style using ideas of repetition and variation, unity and coherence. At yet another level, the classical model can be constructed in terms of thematic concern, meaning and significance as in approaches which stress the individualist quality of Hollywood films in particular. To take another example from the realm of significance, Raymond Bellour has argued that 'the problematic of the formation of the couple' is a central, even constitutive, thematic concern of the classical American cinema as a whole.[6] Hollywood films, he suggests, are 'machines for producing the couple' regardless of generic variations and the variety of thematic traits that they display.[7] Such remarks, though reductive in the extreme, interlock with my comments on the Hitchcock thriller sextet in Chapter 6 and the suggestion that it is the focus on the theme of the couple that distinguishes the Hitchcock thriller from the literary thriller in particular.[8] It may be that the Hitchcock thriller represents a meeting of certain themes drawn from the literature of espionage with the demands of classical cinema for the kind of thematic emphasis to which Bellour draws attention. The model of classical cinema, then, can be defined in a number of ways embracing narrative structure, stylistic tendencies governing the image and the sound track, and the realm of meaning and significance, theme and ideology.

Narrative Structures

The classical cinema is first of all a narrative cinema although its approach to narrative is not exhaustive of the possibilities of the story film. The central characteristic of classical cinema is that narrative concerns dominate the other elements such as style. Decisions about the composition of the image, the angle and movement of the camera, the choice of sounds and their qualities, are governed by the need to tell a story as clearly as possible. Classical narrative structure involves a conventionalised relationship between the story of a film, the 'series of causal events as they occur in chronological order and presumed duration and frequency',[9] and the plot or 'the way in which these events are actually presented in the film'.[10] The variations between story and plot in terms of presentation have to do with the way in which the vast majority of film narratives are involved in the compressing of a number of days, months or years of story time into a plot which unfolds in around two hours. The classical film is an art of ellipsis and compression in which the events of the story have to be rendered down in particular ways, glossed over briefly, repeated or expanded or even omitted, and presented in a particular order which may or may not be the chronological story order. In fact, the typical classical film has a linear narrative structure with the chronology of the story paralleled by the chronology of the plot. Classical Hollywood films begin at the beginning of a story, progress through its middle and terminate at its end. Such a generalisation requires some qualification, however, although it does describe the main tendency in classical narratives. Hollywood has devised ways of presenting story events out of order and in the case of the flashback we have a thoroughly conventionalised disruption of the linear chronology which normally governs narrative development in the classical film. The intermittent flashback has its own system of signals which shift the time structure in a clear fashion through the use of image blurring and particular musical forms accompanied frequently by voice-overs which guide the spectator carefully through the narrative disruption. Hollywood has also developed a specific genre which has as one of its defining characteristics a complicated temporal structure which utilises amplified and extended flashback sequences as the basic narrative pattern. The *film noir* genre of the 1940s and films such as *Double Indemnity* (Wilder, 1944) and *Out of the Past* (Tourneur, 1947) with their relatively complicated temporal structures offer a contrast to the straightforward linear narrative patterns characteristic of the classical cinema.

There are few if any examples from the classical cinema of films in which story duration and plot coincide exactly and a battery of devices have been developed to provide a firm continuity between the few plot events which classical cinema selects from the story events in order to tell the story. These include the characteristic methods of sequence transition such as the fade to black followed by a fade in from black or the mixed shot. Both of these editing devices connote indeterminate, though significant, shifts in story time in the classical film. Other methods of speeding through story time in the classical cinema include the 'montage' sequence in which a series of brief shots depicting, to take the most familiar example, the rise to power of a gangster, are cut together, usually with a unifying musical or voice-over sound track, to represent several years of story time. The most blatant method of ellipsis is the simple title insert which announces the passage of time along the lines of 'ten years later'. In addition to the conventions of inter-sequential ellipsis, the classical film has also developed conventions for the individual sequence itself. The same relationships between story and plot apply and story duration can be expanded or contracted within the boundaries of the individual sequence. The main tendency is towards the close alignment of plot and story time with elisions within the sequence minimised to provide a strong impression of temporal unity and continuity. There are important exceptions to this including what Christian Metz has called 'the episodic sequence'[11] and the possibility of expanding plot time at the level of the sequence is often used in the thriller genre to prolong a moment of suspense.

I have been using the term 'events' to refer to those individual sections or segments of the classical film which are excerpts of the story chosen to constitute the plot of the film. Their relationship to each other within the film is an important factor in determining the character of the film. Thus a film which strings together a series of events which are not tightly related to each other such as *L'Avventura* (Antonioni, 1960) we would describe as episodic or meandering. The classical film, by contrast, tends towards a tight causal relationship obtaining between its series of events. The logic of relationship between events in a film can be emphasised in various ways but perhaps the most common feature of the classical cinematic protagonist is a key factor here. The hero and heroine of the classical film tend to be clearly goal oriented and faced with tasks and problems which both propel the narrative onwards and bind together the events of the film. A final point to make about narrative structure and the classical film has to do with its overall coherence and unity. The elements of the narrative are required to cohere, usually in terms of causality, but they are also required to terminate in a conclusive fashion. The classical film is marked by 'closure', the questions posed in the early stages of the film are answered, the mysteries are solved, the central characters achieve their goal and so on. As one critical text puts it:

> ... most classical films display strong degrees of closure at the end. Leaving no loose ends unresolved, these films seek to cap their causal chains with a final effect. We usually learn the fate of each character, the answer to each mystery, and the outcome of each conflict.[12]

Often this coherence and unity is expressed in terms of a formal symmetry, a circularity in which the ending of the film strongly recalls the beginning, the point of departure, as in the John Ford film *The Searchers* (1956). Raymond Bellour has drawn attention to this feature of the classical film in the following terms:

> The principle of the classical film is well known: the end must reply to the beginning; between one and the other something must be set in order; the last scene frequently recalls the first and constitutes its answer.[13]

Style in the Classical System

In theory, film makers have at their disposal a variety of methods or techniques for constructing a pro-filmic event (*mise en scène*), filming it (cinematography) and relating the resulting image to other film images (editing). In addition, film makers also have another set of materials and techniques in the form of the sound track which provides a variety of recorded sounds including speech, noise and music. Film style refers to the particular choices of techniques and their relationships to one another in specific films. It is not simply concerned with how a particular pro-filmic event is constructed, how the mise en scène is arranged, but also with how the cinematography relates to the mise en scène and to the editing pattern and the sound track. It is the patterning of these relationships in a systematic manner that defines the style of a particular film. The stylistic system of a film can interact with the narrative system of a film in various ways. In the case of classical cinema that interaction subordinates the stylistic system to the demands of narrative clarity with style organised to facilitate an apparently direct access to the fictional world of the narrative. Style is rendered anonymous or 'invisible' and images are composed and photographed so as to register a narrative point with important characters and objects positioned at centre frame and key details enlarged through close ups. Camera movements tend to be dictated by character movements and the editing together of the separate images is subject to a variety of conventions which are designed to sustain spectator orientation. The 180 degree rule, the 30 degree rule, eyeline matching, cutting on action together constitute a set of conventions which work to minimise the potential distractions of editing and ensure that the spectator is always correctly oriented towards the image on the screen and capable of relating it quite precisely to the neighbouring images. The passage from one image to the next is designed to be 'flowing' and 'harmonious' providing a seemingly unbroken and continuous image flow, a unitary and coherent space within which the narrative action takes place. Style and narrative need not cohere so closely, however. Style can interpose itself between spectator and narrative world as in the films of a director such as Max Ophuls whose flowing camera movements often seem distinct from the narrative flow. Critical recognition of such a relationship between style and narrative in his films often gets expressed in terms of decoration or embellishment. Bordwell and Thompson suggest that in certain films style can constitute 'a somewhat independent system'[14] running alongside the narrative system. An example of this would be the cinema of Godard, particularly a film such as *Vivre Sa Vie* (1962) from his early period of reflexive narrative film making. The film has a number of sequences in which the central character, Nana (Anna Karina), is having a conversation with someone or other. The conversations are not constructed in the conventional short/reverse shot style of classical cinema which is the clearest way of presenting the narrative content or meaning of a fictional conversation. One conversation is shot from behind the characters so that we do not see their faces and the camera travels laterally from one to the other during during the course of the scene whilst another is shot so that the camera can move behind one character in order to hide the other from the gaze of the spectator. The experience for the spectator is partly one of attending to the content — we do try to understand the content of the conversations and to grasp their narrative significance — but the means of presentation also impose themselves upon us. We understand these sequences as parts of a discourse on how to film a conversation. The style of *Vivre Sa Vie* means that the film has an oscillating relationship with the classical cinema. At times it provides a sketchy narrative trajectory which permits the spectator identification with the central character which is characteristic of classical cinema yet other elements of the film such as its style and techniques pull the film away from the classical norms and offer a different kind of reading experience to the spectator. The different elements of the picture — the narrative system and the stylistic system — do not co-operate to ensure the unified and coherent experience that the classical film tends to offer; the narrative system does not dominate the stylistic system which breaks through as an independent element of the film at various times.

Hitchcock and the Classical Film

The historical location of the emergence of the classical film style varies from historian to historian and from critic to critic. Janet Staiger has drawn attention to an article on screenwriting in the American trade journal *The Moving Picture World* in 1911 which describes 'many of the characteristics we now associate with classical Hollywood cinema'.[15] She goes on to relate the emergence of the classical film to the development of the American cinema as a mass production industry with the normal characteristics of modern industrial organisation such as managerial control and the division of labour. The standardisation of stylistic techniques is thus given a firm economic explanation. John Ellis writes of 'the classic Hollywood film that dominated world markets from about 1915 to 1955'[16] whilst David Bordwell defines classical Hollywood cinema in terms of a 'model of typical traits of narrative feature filmes between 1920 and 1960'.[17] Noel Burch cites Fritz Lang's *Doctor Mabuse* diptych of 1922 as a cornerstone of cinematic illusionism and an exemplary demonstration of the system of spectator orientation which lies at the centre of the classical system of representation. 'By 1922', Burch suggests, 'every practising filmmaker was more or less familiar with this system of orientation, though few of them so thoroughly as Fritz Lang'.[18] Some critics have defined the classical model in terms of the sound period and André Bazin discusses the classical film as a convergence of some of the different stylistic directions taken by the silent cinema.[19] The advent of sound clearly had an impact on the system of classical continuity which had developed during the silent period and one example would be the shot/reverse shot couplet for the shooting of conversations which becomes a central device for the classical sound picture.

Hitchcock's career as a film maker is roughly coterminous with the history of classical cinema. His early filmgoing was dominated by American films and his interest in classical film style was reinforced at Famous Players' London studios where he worked with experienced American writers and directors learning the principles of classical narrative style. As a film maker in Britain during the twenties and thirties he was subject to the powerful influence of conventional Hollywood cinema especially in the period when the industry was attempting to break into the American market. Yet his films frequently display quite complicated relationships with the norms of classical style. This chapter will examine the ways in

146

which Hitchcock's cinema during the twenties and thirties conformed to the classical model and the ways in which it reflected other conflicting tendencies in film form and style.

Narrative Structure

The ideal classic narrative is totally unified and coherent with each element of the plot, each 'move' or event, clearly relevant to the central thread of the narrative which is normally organised around a goal-oriented character or group of characters. As David Bordwell has written:

> The goal orientation of the Hollywood hero springs from a desire to remake circumstances, and the development of this desire, the move towards the goal, constitutes the primary line of action.[20]

In *The Lodger* the central character is certainly goal oriented in the sense that there is a deliberation about his movements, his excursions into the night, his poring over the map. The narrative, however, plays upon the ambiguity of his goal — is it murder? or what? A web of suspicion is constructed around the central character through a careful restriction of spectator knowledge typical of later Hitchcock pictures and through an exploitation of ambiguity in narrative presentation. For example, the first time that the lodger appears on screen he is dressed in a manner that matches a description of the murderer figure — 'the Avenger' — given earlier in the film. He looms out of the foggy night with his scarf muffled around his mouth and the spectator is invited to confuse compositional motivation — the matching description identifying him as 'the Avenger' — with realistic motivation — the scarf simply protects him from the fog — and the network of suspicion is established. Subsequently, key narrative moves feed such suspicion. The lodger is shown as having an aversion to the paintings of blonde women in his room including the one which depicts a woman tied to a tree, he paces around his room implying anxiety and tension in the famous 'glass floor' shot, and he is shown leaving the house very late at night. The suspicion and fear of his midnight excursion are conveyed to us through Mrs Bunting left alone on that particular night when her husband is working as an extra waiter at a society function. The lodger is certainly involved in the remaking of circumstances but the exact nature of these is withheld from the spectator until the explanatory flashback sequence towards the end of the film. In this, he reveals to Daisy that his sister was the first victim of 'the Avenger' and that he had promised his mother on her deathbed that he would track the killer down and bring him to justice. He is retrospectively revealed as pursuer rather than pursued and the bulk of the film depends upon a confusion of the two roles, which again is a typical Hitchcock trait to be found in films such as *The Thirty-Nine Steps* and *North by Northwest*. Many writers on the classical narrative

147

have identified violence as an important narrative trigger, the first cause which begins the narrative chain and underpins the narrative logic. *The Lodger* begins with a literal sequence of violence including a close-up of a blonde woman screaming and a title which reads 'Tonight Golden Curls', and a subsequent sequence which explains the opening as an 'Avenger' murder. This event, however, does not inaugurate the narrative proper but functions as a kind of surrogate for the flashback which occurs at the end of the film. It forms part of what might be called the film's prologue in which the terrifying event of the murder is represented in an oblique fashion — a screaming close-up and a title — to be taken up in what amounts to a little documentary film on the various ways in which news of the event is transmitted to the community by the press, radio, neon sign, by the modern means of communication. The narrative then shifts to a short sequence in a theatre dressing room where the chorus girls from the revue (*Tonight Golden Curls*) are discussing the murder with some degree of fear and trepidation. It is only then that the main narrative actually begins with a title announcing 'Daisy' and a short scene of her working in the fashion salon as a model. This starts the process of gathering together the major characters of the story so that it may begin. The opening sequences construct a general environment of fear which the narrative is to occupy partly through the 'documentary montage sequences' and partly through fictional sequences which do not involve the main characters in the film. The narrative proper is delayed in order to provide the atmospheric contextualisation and also because the actual beginning of the story (the murder of the Lodger's sister) has to be withheld from the spectator until the end of the narrative and requires a kind of surrogate which is provided by the murder scene. In *Blackmail* there is a similar delay in beginning the narrative proper with the central characters of Alice and Frank introduced after some ten minutes of screen time have elapsed. The opening, as has already been pointed out, presents a kind of dramatised documentary on criminal pursuit and although one of the central characters (Frank) is seen during the course of the opening, he is not identified in any specific way. Like the opening of *The Lodger* there is a mixture of documentary style passages with fictional episodes although in *Blackmail* there is a much more fluent link between the two. As in the *The Lodger* the function of the sequence is scene setting for the narrative as a whole although it does so with less precision. In *The Lodger* the presentation of 'the Avenger's' deeds and the consequent spread of terror is important to the subsequent narrative in quite precise ways whereas the opening sequences of *Blackmail* seem more detachable from the narrative as a whole. It is worth noting, however, that Hitchcock had originally intended to repeat the opening sequences which dealt with arrest, interrogation and imprisonment but this time with Alice in the prisoner's position and this would have given the film the classical circularity mentioned by Bellour and would have endowed the opening sequence with a more precise role in the film. The openings of both *The Lodger* and *Blackmail*, though, share qualities of delay and they might be compared with the opening of *The Man Who Knew Too Much* made a few years after *Blackmail* in which the opening sequences are used not to set the narrative scene but rather to introduce the central characters as swiftly and as economically as possible.

The Man Who Knew Too Much opens during a ski contest in which one of the skiers swerves to avoid a dog and crashes into a group of spectators. As they rise to their feet, some of the central characters are introduced: Louis Bernard, the skier, later to be identified as a secret agent; Bob Lawrence, later to be plunged into the midst of the assassination plot; his daughter, Betty, whose dog has caused the accident and who later will provide the mainspring for the series of adventures when she is kidnapped by the assassination gang; and, lastly, Abbot, leader of the gang of killers whose cool exchange of glances with Louis Bernard hints at the dangers to come. The remaining key characters are introduced in the second sequence which is also set in the course of a contest, a clay pigeon shoot between Ramon Levine, who will later be revealed as kidnapper and assassin, and Jill, Bob Lawrence's wife. In addition to presenting the leading characters in a swift and economic fashion, the opening sequences also prefigure the pattern of conflict in anticipation of later narrative development. For example, the tension between Abbott and Bernard has already been mentioned but the shooting match between Jill Lawrence and Ramon Levine relates quite precisely to the end of the film in which she shoots Levine as he is chasing Betty across the rooftop of the gang's London hideout. In the less menacing atmosphere of the first contest, it is Levine who is victorious, Jill being distracted by Betty just as she is about to have her final shot. Later, in the return 'contest' she proves herself to be an expert shot by shooting Levine whilst Betty is in great danger. This paralleling of events places the film firmly within the classical system from the point of view of narrative structure. I have referred to Raymond Bellour's suggestion that in classical cinema 'the last scene frequently recalls the first and constitutes its answer'[21] and the symmetrical relationship between the two shooting 'contests' of *The Man Who Knew Too Much* is a good example of such a strategy. Gone are the quasi-documentary sequences of the previous films, the sequences which bear on their narratives in a tangential way, and instead we are plunged immediately into the plot with the introduction of the main characters and their placing in relation to each other. Bordwell and Thompson suggest the importance of a film's opening sequences in the following passage:

> The opening provides us with a basis for what is to come; it integrates us into the film. Causes of subsequent narrative events, significant motifs, and important features of the initial plot situation are all laid out in the opening.[22]

The Man Who Knew Too Much conforms to this pattern in its opening sequences whereas *The Lodger* and *Blackmail* do so only in a partial sense.

The openings of the other films of the thriller sextet are also organised to introduce the narrative as quickly as possible with Hannay plunged into the chaos world during the music hall sequence which opens the film, with Ashenden's task revealed in the opening sequences of *Secret Agent* and with Robert in *Young and Innocent* very quickly implicated in the murder of his actress friend. *Sabotage* differs to a certain extent in so far as it opens with a somewhat elliptical sequence dealing with an act of sabotage although it is not long before the unidentified saboteur of the opening sequence is identified as Verloc, one of the central characters in the narrative. *The Lady Vanishes* does, in fact, have a more meandering opening with the narrative trigger — the abduction of Miss Froy — delayed until some way into the film. Yet this may be attributed to the generic context of the journey film to which *The Lady Vanishes* relates. Films of this type such as *Channel Crossing* (Rosmer, 1934) or *Stagecoach* (Ford, 1939) require a somewhat leisurely opening in which a variety of characters, who are to be thrown together in the course of the journey, can be introduced and established.

The opening of *The Man Who Knew Too Much* can be firmly located within the classical paradigm with its clear and simple introduction of character and situation. Its ending is equally conformist with the gang apprehended and the family restored to a unity. The final image is of the three members of the Lawrence family shot from below peering through an opening in the roof of the hideout building, framed within the frame. The loose ends have been tied up, the assassination has been thwarted, the gang captured or killed and the family reunited. It is instructive to compare this ending with that of *Blackmail*. There is a degree of circularity at the formal level in so far as Alice is in the police station waiting for Frank at the beginning of the film and the final sequences also take place at the police station and there are similar scenes of them going off together. Such formal symmetries, however, are not reflected at the level of content and meaning. The ending of the film turns on a false resolution made possible by the death of Tracy, the blackmailer. The police pursue him through the British Museum to the highest point of the building and he loses his footing and plunges to his death in what was to become a familiar situation in the Hitchcock narrative (for example, similar deaths occur in *Jamaica Inn* (1939), *Foreign Correspondent* (1940), *Saboteur* (1942), *Vertigo* (1958) and *North by Northwest* (1959)). Tracy is presumed to be the killer of the artist thus masking Alice's responsibility for the death. The film has a 'troubled' ending in which Alice and Frank are left with a guilty secret at the heart of their restored relationship. *Sabotage* ends in a similar fashion when a fortuitous bomb explodes and apparently kills Verloc. In fact, he is already dead, stabbed by Mrs Verloc but this fact is similarly masked by the explosion and she and Ted are also left with a prospective relationship to be built on the guilty secret. In both films, the women attempt to confess their crimes but in both cases fate intervenes to prevent revelation. In both films something like the normal satisfactions of the 'happy ending' are offered. A relationship threatened is restored in *Blackmail* and a new and preferable relationship for Mrs Verloc is promised in *Sabotage*. Yet, a loose end — the disguised guilt — remains to offset the closure of the classical text. Other Hitchcock pictures from the period end in rather more orthodox fashion with unity restored, with loose ends resolved, with their causal chains terminated by a final effect. *The Lodger* for example, ends with a shot of Daisy and the lodger in the traditional lovers' embrace at his opulent family home. This being said, however, the alert viewer can just discern the 'Tonight Golden Curls' neon message flashing in the background behind them, a window which overlooks the city. A touch of irony, perhaps, which slightly detracts from the closure effect. The endings of *Murder!, Rich and Strange, The Thirty-Nine Steps, Secret Agent* and *The Lady Vanishes* have various versions of the couple united or reunited whilst *Young and Innocent* has a close-up of the 'innocent' heroine reunited with her prospective lover and her father as she gazes from one to the other in a scene which lends itself to an extended Freudian analysis.

The Image (*Mise en Scène*/Cinematography)

In the classical cinema the filmic space created by the arrangement of the mise en scène and the deployment of the camera (cinematography) is governed by the needs of the narrative. The narrative line is the dominant element in classical film and other elements of film art are subordinated to the process of narration. 'Cinematic space', in the words of David Bordwell, 'became a means of manifesting and sustaining narrative'.[23] Space is constructed to offer a setting for narrative action and is filled with objects which function either as guarantors of 'realism' or as elements which are utilised by the narrative. Often elements of the mise en scène can fulfil both functions. The camera is manipulated to present the mise en scène in an undistracting manner, to centre the elements of key narrative importance including the players through careful framing and reframing. Above all, the 'space must not come forward to distract from the narrative'[24] by calling attention to itself as it does in films such as Michael Snow's *Wavelength* (1966) or *Back and Forth* (1968) to take two quite extreme examples of films which deviate radically from the norms of the classical system.

Hitchcock's films provide numerous examples of the use of elements of the mise en scène, such as settings and objects, in order to contribute to the narrative, whilst also functioning as tokens of 'realism'. The 'pastry' sequence in *The Lodger* has already been mentioned as an example of classical structuring of the mise en scène for both 'realist' and narrative reasons.[25] The pastry array on the kitchen table contributes to scenic verisimilitude and Joe's play with the heart-shaped pastry cutter provides a comment on the uneasy relationship between himself and Daisy. The details of the mise en scène are pressed into service in the interests of narrative economy and this was an important consideration in the silent era when narrative points had to be established either through the use of titles which interrupted the visual flow or through the exploitation of visual detail. Film makers developed skills in mobilising elements of the diegetic world of their films in order to further the narrative line rather than relying on titles. The classical system also moved away from the use of the non-diegetic metaphor which was being developed especially in the Soviet cinema of the time. Eisenstein's celebrated contrastive and symbolic montages enabled him to develop quite elaborate points about character and narrative in his films but the classical cinema tended to look for narrative metaphor and symbolism in the surface detail of the fictional world of the film. This can be related to the 'realism' of classical cinema and the double function of the mise en scène mentioned earlier.

Many more examples can be found in Hitchcock's British work from the silent films of the 1920s through to the sound films of the 1930s. In *The Ring* there is much play on 'ring' motifs which embraces the boxing ring itself, which is the centre of the film, and the wedding ring and the bracelet worn by the heroine. In the crucial wedding sequence at the very moment that the hero is putting the wedding ring onto the bride's finger, a bracelet given to her by a rival suitor slips down her arm. Raymond Durgnat has described this part of the film as 'an extremely American scene' because of its specific use of motifs such as the bracelet as 'terse reminders of simple feelings, contrasts and conflicts already stated in the plot'.[26] Early in *Blackmail* during the Lyons Corner House sequence, Alice, the heroine, loses one of her gloves. Frank, her boyfriend, retrieves it and notices the holes in the fingers. Later whilst he is searching the murdered artist's studio for clues, he discovers the glove, catches a glimpse of the artist's face and realises that Alice must be implicated in the crime. *The Man Who Knew Too Much* has a number of examples including the chiming watch that becomes Abbott's calling card and the little brooch that is used as a reminder of Betty's plight during the assassination sequence. In *The Thirty-Nine Steps*, Margaret — the crofter's wife — gives Hannay her husband's topcoat as he is about to flee from the police. Later it saves his life as the crofter's Bible which is in the breast pocket of the coat stops a bullet fired at Hannay by the professor, the leader of the spy ring. Caged birds are used as a reminder of Stevie after he has been killed in *Sabotage* and in *The Lady Vanishes* it is the label from Miss Froy's packet of herbal tea that eventually convinces the sceptical Gilbert that Iris is correct in her suspicions about abduction. Raymond Durgnat has used the term 'narrative marker' to refer to such uses of elements of the mise en scène in the interests of narrative economy which enable a swift and easy communication of the movement of the narrative to take place. 'Narrative markers', he suggests, can be differentiated from the more typically European use of mise en scène detail as symbolic motifs which 'tend to draw attention to feelings or ideas which never come into the plot at all — whether *temps mort* or some "vertical", poetic, overtone or undercurrent'.[27] Indeed, Hitchcock's preference for the American narrative use of detail was picked up by contemporary reviewers. A reviewer in *The Times* commenting on the mise en scène of *Blackmail* suggested that Hitchcock 'knows too the value of details, and how to give details, in this case a glove and a kitchen knife, significance without making them tiresomely symbolic'.[28]

It is possible, however, to discover some quite complex examples of European-style use of the mise en scène for more overtly symbolic reasons in some of Hitchcock's British films. Indeed, *Blackmail* itself provides an example in the jester painting. During the sequence in the artist's studio, Alice is shown glancing out of the window and this is followed by a shot from her point of view of a policeman passing down below in the street. Then there is a sharp cut to a close shot of the face of the jester figure. The camera then draws back and we can see that it is a painting in the artist's studio. At its initial moment of appearance on the screen, however, it is rather like one of the non-diegetic motifs in Eisenstein's *October* (1928) such as the mechanical peacock which is linked to the figure of Kerensky. It arrives unheralded, from nowhere in particular, but it interacts in quite specific ways with the previous images of Alice looking out of the window. The jester figure is shown to be gesturing mockingly at the character in the fiction and, possibly, the spectator in the cinema. The image of the jester is used on five further occasions during the film. After she has stabbed and killed the artist, Alice retrieves her dress which is draped over the painting. As she pulls it away the mocking face of the jester is once again revealed and she grabs at it and rips the canvas. Later, when the police are at the studio investigating the murder, the painting is shown again. At first, it is simply intercut with Frank searching the room but it is then shown a second time just after he had discovered Alice's glove. Again, it can be interpreted as a commentary upon one of the characters in the narrative, upon their plight and predicament. The final appearance of the painting takes place at the end of the film when Alice sees it at the police station just after she has been 'saved' from confessing to the killing. Again, as in the previous sequences, it is shown twice — once to establish its presence at the police station — it is part of the evidence from the artist's studio — and then to exploit its symbolic force in relation to the predicament of the central characters. As Lindsay Anderson has suggested, 'the malevolently smiling jester is used as a sort of dumb commentator on the story'.[29]

Another example of this more complicated manipulation of mise en scène detail, occurs in *The Thirty-Nine Steps*. After Hannay has fallen in with Annabel Smith, the woman agent, they go back to his apartment. The first shot in the apartment is of the hall which is dominated by a large statue of a man with one arm raised to the sky and the other pointing to the window. Although the statue is a striking aspect of the mise en scène it is simply a residual realistic detail at this point in the sequence. Later, however, after Hannay and the woman have retired for the night, the image is shown again. This time the lighting scheme casts ominous shadows, the statue is pointing to the now open window and the curtains are flapping in the breeze. The subsequent shot shows Annabel Smith staggering into Hannay's room crying 'Clear out Hannay ... . They'll get you next'. She then slumps on top of him and we can see that she has been stabbed in the back. The hall image was an expressionist warning, the realist detail of the statue utilised to set the tone of the events which follow and, more generally, to usher in the 'chaos world' into which Hannay is about to descend.

So although narrative economy is an important feature of Hitchcock's mise en scène, it is also possible to find examples of scenic detail being used for more complex symbolic purposes. Also of interest in this context is the frequently detailed attention to surface realism in Hitchcock which, as has already been mentioned,[30] attracted the attention of critics such as John Grierson and Lindsay Anderson. This is not simply a matter of the quasi-documentary sequences which open films such as *The Lodger*, *The Manx-man* and *Blackmail* or the documentary sequences which play an important role in *Rich and Strange*. Rather it was suggested that Hitchcock was skilled in the representation of ordinary everyday life. Lindsay Anderson, although critical of the narrative construction of *Blackmail*, was moved to praise the realism of its mise en scène as follows:

> Much of *Blackmail*, though, is excellent and survives in its own right. The everyday locales — a Corner-House restaurant, the police station, the little tobacconist's shop where the heroine lives with her parents, empty London streets at dawn — are authentic[31]

Hitchcock's early training as a set designer undoubtedly contributes to such a detailed use of the mise en scène to achieve surface realism and one could extend Anderson's comments to many of Hitchcock's British pictures with their detailed reconstructions, particularly of lower middle class households. The Bunting household in *The Lodger*, the Hill's suburban semi in *Rich and Strange*, Verloc's local picture house in *Sabotage* and the crofter's cabin in *The Thirty-Nine Steps* are similarly detailed and authentic in their presentation of socially specific settings.

In the classical system, the details of the mise en scène are motivated by their compositional function in the narrative as 'markers' or they contribute to the surface realism of the diegetic world. In many instances, of course, they perform both functions simultaneously. The presentation of the mise en scène through the cinematography is also governed by rules and conventions in the classical system. As with the mise en scène, these conventions are designed to ensure the subordination of filmic space to narrative progress and to control the potential distractions of cinematographic qualities such as perspective, focus, distance and angle of vision, mobility and so on.

There are some examples of cinematography in Hitchcock which can be seen to stray from the conventions of cinematic classicism. In *The Lodger* and *Blackmail* there are examples of shots taken from a position immediately over a staircase looking straight down on a character descending the stairs. The shot in *The Lodger* occurs when the lodger is going out late at night on one of his searches and in *Blackmail* a similar shot occurs when Alice is leaving the artist's studio after the killing. In neither case can we describe the shot in terms of point-of-view. Although in the example from *The Lodger* the shot is preceded by an image of Mrs Bunting awakened after hearing the lodger on the stairs, the overhead perspective is not signalled as her point-of-view. In *Blackmail* there is no one for whom the shot could be a point-of-view. Such shots fall into the category of the impossible point-of-view, the shot taken from a position which could not be occupied by an observer. Classical cinema tends to avoid such shots which have the effect of drawing attention to themselves as unusual and different and which mark the films with an authorial flourish or directional 'touch'. Ivor Montagu, one of Hitchcock's collaborators, has commented upon his interest in unusual shot perspectives using the following example which does have some affinities with the examples from *The Lodger* and *Blackmail*:

> For example, when he had a scene with the husband and wife and a third party to the triangle, coming back from the theatre and he wanted to show the lover and the wife touching knees in the taxi. He showed the shot from above. But he used the wrong lens and you would have been viewing from a helicopter, if you'd had a helicopter in those days, with no roof on the taxi and to my mind it destroyed the illusion entirely.[32]

The sustaining of the 'illusion' effect in classical cinema depends precisely upon the mise en scène being presented in an undistracting manner with a visual perspective which derives from the diegetic material either as the third person 'objective' view which is not linked to characters in the fictional world or the point-of-view shot which is associated with a character or characters. The latter type of shot is usually clearly marked through optical devices such as the blurring of focus or through the editing when the point-of-view shot is bracketed in between shots of the owner of the view. The 'objective' shot is defined in part by the absence of such marks and partly through its undistracting quality of being the simplest and most efficient way of presenting an event or situation of narrative importance to the spectator. The shots discussed above from *The Lodger* and *Blackmail* resist being explained in terms of narrative motivation and instead might be interpreted as tokens of the film author, marks which establish the formative presence of the artist and examples of the 'exploration of framing in its own right'.[33] Similar examples of 'eccentric' framing can be found throughout Hitchcock's work and one based upon the high overhead shot occurs in *Psycho* (1960). Arbogast, the detective, has just entered the old house and is making his way up the stairs. Suddenly, the spectator is confronted with a very high overhead shot looking straight down on the action as Norman/Mrs Bates comes from the room with knife in hand to attack Arbogast. Again, the perspective is both 'impossible' in

155

point-of-view terms and strikingly unusual and Hitchcock explains its function in the following way:

> Anyway, I used a single shot of Arbogast coming up the stairs, and when he got to the top step, I deliberately placed the camera very high for two reasons. The first was so that I could shoot down on top of the mother, because if I'd shown her back, it might have looked as if I was deliberately concealing her face and the audience would have been leery. I used the high angle in order not to give the impression that I was trying to avoid showing her.
>
> But the main reason for raising the camera so high was to get the contrast between the long shot and the close-up of the big head as the knife came down at him. It was like music you see, the high shot with the violins and suddenly the big head with the brass instruments clashing.[34]

Hitchcock also used the same camera set-up later in the film just before Norman Bates carries his mother down to the cellar although in this case the camera is originally positioned at the foot of the stairs and it travels up to the high overhead position as Norman goes into his mother's room. Hitchcock suggests that the audience in this case would be distracted from what the camera was doing by the 'argument' between Norman and his mother on the sound track. However, the strikingly unconventional quality of the shot which in this case is emphasised by the camera travelling from a more 'objective' position to reach the unusual angle places it within the category of the artistic device which pulls away from the narrative illusion. It is not simply the intrinsic character of the high overhead shot that defines its identity, however, and in *The Thirty-Nine Steps* there is a similar high angled overhead shot when Hannay jumps from the train on the Forth Bridge. On this occasion the shot is securely positioned within the narrative as a point-of-view shot and sandwiched between shots of Hannay clinging to the bridge out of sight of the pursuing policemen and glancing anxiously downwards. The association of the shot with Hannay's viewpoint drains it of artistic significance and narrativises it.

The second example from *Psycho* introduces another feature of Hitchcock's cinematography, the use of mobile framing based on camera movement. It is possible to draw a broad distinction between two types of camera movement. Firstly, there are movements which are determined by movement within the mise en scène usually of the actors; and, secondly, the camera is often moved in order to scan the mise en scène for pertinent narrative detail or to travel through it to a new perspective. Examples of the first type are frequent in classical cinema especially reframing camera movement in which the compositional balance of the image is preserved through minimal camera movements which follow alterations in actor position. Such movements are often 'invisible' but even the more marked travelling shots can be rendered 'invisible' if firmly associated with character movement through the mise en scène.

The second type of movement is more varied in its function and can include, for example, the track or dolly towards characters or a detail in the mise en scène at moment of tension or drama. In *Blackmail* when Frank catches a glimpse of the murdered artist and realises that Alice is probably responsible, the camera travels forward rather quickly towards the prostrate figure on the bed and stresses the moment of shocked realisation experienced by Frank. The movement is associated with Frank's point-of-view and this is a characteristic way in which the marked quality of a camera movement can be anchored in diegetic reality through its links with the subjective perceptions of a character. Hitchcock, of course, is the film maker most celebrated for constructing his films around character point-of-view and camera mobility frequently plays a role in this approach to narrative construction. An early example can be found in *The Lodger* when the central character first sees his room in the Bunting house. He scans the paintings on the walls and the camera moves to reproduce his viewpoint which travels around the room. Although the movement is striking it is linked with character point-of-view and is thus confined within the boundaries of the classical model. In *Rich and Strange* the camera moves to reproduce the movements of the ship at sea as experienced by the passengers. It is the scanning or travelling camera movement that is completely detached from character movement or viewpoint that poses the greatest threat to the seamless surface of classical cinema. In an analysis of *La Règle du Jeu* (Renoir, 1939), André Bazin remarked that 'the camera acts as an invisible guest wandering about the salon and the corridors with a certain curiosity'.[35] It is this independence bestowed upon the camera that tends to foreground the artifice of cinema and poses problems for the illusionism of the classical system of narrative. In Hitchcock the most dramatic example of camera movement which is independent of character occurs in *Young and Innocent* towards the end of the film when the characters are beginning to despair of finding the man responsible for the murder. The camera mounted on a crane begins its journey high above the hotel foyer then travels through to the ballroom and gradually swings around to provide a straight-on view of the band. It continues to travel towards the band and ends up on a very tight close shot of the drummer framed from just below the nose to just above the eyes. He begins to twitch his eyes — the clue that Erica and 'old Bill' have been looking for. In a shot which lasts for more than a minute, the camera has acted as an 'invisible detective' to pick out the vital clue which identifies the murderer yet by 'invisibility' is meant independence from the fictional world. The movement is not invisible in relation to the spectator and it presents itself as another token of the presence of the narrator, a sign of authorial intervention. The motivation for the camera movement is artistic rather than realistic or compositional and is another example of Hitchcock straying from the conventions of classical cinema. Shortly after this shot there is a fast forward travelling shot towards 'old Bill' sitting at a table but in this example the shot mobility represents the drummer's alarmed recognition of the old tramp who can identify him as the murderer. Again the association with character point-of-view keeps the camera movement within the classical convention.

Editing

Hitchcock's own discussions of cinema frequently stress the importance of editing to his own films. In an article written in 1937 he discusses scenic construction in the following terms:

> What I like to do is to photograph just the little bits of a scene that I really need for building up a visual sequence . . . .
> The screen ought to speak its own language, freshly coined, and it can't do that unless it treats an acted scene as a piece of raw material which must be broken up, taken to bits, before it can be woven into an expressive visual pattern.[36]

The terms of the discussion, the stress on fragmentation, the use of the term 'raw material', recall Pudovkin and the Soviet film theorists of the 1920s. In a discussion of the teachings of Lev Kuleshov, Pudovkin wrote:

> He maintained that the film-art does not begin when the artists act and the various scenes are shot — this is only the preparation of the material. Film-art begins from the moment when the director begins to combine and join the various pieces of film.[37]

The scene in Hitchcock's British films that best exemplifies his stress upon editing is the killing of Verloc in *Sabotage*. It begins with a master shot of the Verlocs at the dining table and then proceeds in a series of 30 brief shots — some lasting no longer than two seconds. The entire scene lasts for just under three minutes and consists basically of a series of key details from the master shot. There are a number of close shots of Verloc and his wife and, in addition, some close shots of the empty place where Mrs Verloc's brother Stevie would have been, shots of his pet birds and of the carving knife with which Mrs Verloc eventually kills her husband. The event of the killing is 'constructed', 'assembled' out of these details. The meanings within the sequence are 'alluded' to, to use the Bazinian formulation, although the result of this is a somewhat ambiguous presentation of the actual killing as Truffaut has pointed out.[38] The preparation of this scene followed the pattern of breaking the scene into 'pieces of raw material' and thus differed markedly from the techniques of scenic construction adopted in the American cinema. In the Hollywood style of shooting, as John Russell Taylor has pointed out, 'scenes would be played right through, photographed continuously from first one angle, then another, and cut together afterwards'.[39] Hitchcock's method, by contrast, depended upon a prior selection of details which dictated exactly the images he required for the scene and these could be shot as separate images without the need for the continuous theatrical playing of the entire scene by the actors involved. The American style conceives of the scene as a continuous theatrical entity which is broken down for cinematic presentation and rebuilt according to the demands of dramatic emphasis. Conversely, Hitchcock's approach conceives of the scene as a construction from predetermined detail, as an entity which is built from the dramatic moments. As a shooting method it makes certain assumptions about film acting which de-emphasise performance in favour of what might be called a neutral acting style in which emotion and feeling are created not by acting performance but by the effects of cinematography and editing. As Hitchcock has said:

> When a film is properly staged, it isn't necessary to rely on a player's virtuosity or personality for tension and dramatic effects. In my opinion, the chief requisite for an actor is the ability to do nothing well, which is by no means as easy as it sounds. He should be willing to be utilised and wholly integrated into the picture by the director and the camera. He must allow the camera to determine the proper emphasis and the most effective dramatic highlights.[40]

Hitchcock's position on film acting can again be related to the Soviet film theorists of the 1920s and during the interview with Truffaut he refers to the famous 'Kuleshov experiment' which attempted to 'prove' that emotion in an acting performance could be constructed through the montage and was not necessarily dependent upon what might be termed traditional expressivist acting skills.[41] In a broader sense, the editing develops out of the mise en scène and the cinematography which is carefully designed by a director like Hitchcock to ensure a specific place in the finished film for each individual image. The Hollywood classical approach to editing was developed in the context of a strict division of labour between script-writing and shooting, between shooting and editing, which required a set of guiding principles for editors who might have had no contact with the production process until the editing stage. The business of shooting and reshooting scenes from different camera set-ups with variations of the angle, height and distance, provides the film editor with a variety of possible shot combinations for the reconstruction of a scene and the continuity editing rules (180 degree rule, the cut on action etc.) control that variety. The editing takes place at the editing stage in the classical system in so far as there is some degree of choice possible within the conventional framework whereas Hitchcock 'edited in the writing of the script and carried out that editing process in filming'.[42] The main effect of the highly codified rules of scenic construction through the editing in the classical cinema is the 'containment' of stylistic effect and the achievement of what is often referred to as 'invisible' editing, shot transitions which have the appearance of inevitability. The style of the editing in the stabbing scene in *Sabotage* works to stress the editing, to emphasise the moment of shot transition, to overlay the scene in its imaginary unity (as it would be if acted on the stage) with a clear form of discourse which, as in the case of the marked camera movements and bizarre camera angles, functions as a sign of the author. As if to stress the highly constructed nature of the sequence, Hitchcock closes it with a lengthy shot lasting over 20 seconds in which the camera, placed almost at ground level, incorporates a view of Verloc's feet as he lies dead after the stabbing and of Mrs Verloc gradually moving away from the camera into the depth of the scenic space to sit down in another room at some distance from the camera but still within its view. The striking use of staging in depth in this shot contrasts with the highly edited sequence of somewhat flat images that precedes it. The shot suggests the style of shooting favoured by André Bazin in which the unities of scenic space and time are paralleled in cinematic techniques. Bazin favoured the use of deep space, the continuous image and camera movement, over editing, partly because such techniques brought the natural ambiguities of appearance to the cinematic image and offered a certain amount of interpretive freedom to the spectator. He further argued that 'the nature and essence of editing is such that it stands in the way of the expression of ambiguity'.[43] Yet, as has been suggested above, this particular scene from *Sabotage* with its highly edited format nevertheless does yield a certain amount of ambiguity concerning Mrs Verloc's intentions during the incident. *Sabotage* also contains another example of the highly deliberate use of editing in the sequence where Stevie, the young boy, is killed while he is on the bus carrying the bomb to Piccadilly Circus. The pattern of cutting in this example is geared to the generation of suspense with images of the boy being intercut with images of clocks whilst the time advances towards a quarter to two, the time set for the explosion. The device of cross-cutting between distinct spaces for reasons of suspense is, however, a conventional figure in classical cinema despite its evident discontinuity and obtrusiveness, and can be traced back to early chase films and the work of D.W. Griffith. The cutting back and forth between Stevie and the clocks is governed by the concerns of the narrative as the spectator has already been informed about the time that the bomb is primed to explode. *Secret Agent* also contains an example of distinctive cross-cutting between radically different spaces although one in which the causal links between the two sets of images are less clear. Ashenden has mistakenly identified the Englishman, Caypor, as the enemy agent who is to be killed and he arranges a mountain walk which will provide opportunity and a convenient cover (a climbing accident) for Caypor's murder. The images of Ashenden, the Mexican and Caypor on the mountain walk are alternated with images of Caypor's wife with Elsa Carrington back at their hotel. The focus in these latter images is upon Caypor's small dog who becomes increasingly agitated during the course of the sequence. His frenzied barking and scratching at the door parallel the increasing tension in the mountain images in which the moment of murder gradually draws closer and closer. The climax of the sequence is the very distant shot of Caypor as he is pushed over the mountain's edge by the Mexican which is immediately followed by a shot of the dog whining mournfully.

Sound

The avoidance of stylistic effect that obtrudes over the narrative line in the classical system also applied to the manipulation of the sound track. The arrival of the sound picture in the late 1920s was greeted with some dismay by critics and theorists whose aesthetic of cinema had been formulated in response to the silent film. Yet it was not long before such writers developed a set of perspectives on the additional material of expression delivered by the sound track. Such perspectives tended to lament the introduction of speech and dialogue, whilst recognising that the other types of sound, especially music, had been part of the misleadingly termed 'silent cinema' from its earliest days. As Paul Rotha put it, 'the appeal of the film lies absolutely in the vision of the images on the screen, soothed and emphasised by a musical accompaniment'.[44] A proper relationship between musical sound and image had evolved during the 'silent' era but speech and sound effects posed new problems and Rotha argued that 'a film in which the speech and sound effects are perfectly synchronised and coincide with their visual images on the screen is absolutely contrary to the aim of cinema'.[45] Rotha and others recommended asynchronous sound and the technique of aural counterpointing as the correct method of integrating sound with the highly developed art of the silent film and, as we have seen in Chapter 2, Hitchcock provided an early example of counterpointing sound and image for psychological-expressive purposes in the celebrated 'knife' sequence in Blackmail.[46] Non-synchronous sound, however, can be seen as a distraction from the narrative line, an obtrusion of stylistic effect and the classical cinema soon developed conventions for the control of this potentially disruptive element. The basic aim of the classical sound track is 'to create synchronisation of sound and image — a totality that masks the split between the two'.[47] 'Photographs of people talking', to use Hitchcock's own words, or the synchronisation of dialogue and sound effects with the visual image, is the clearest expression of this aim in the classical film but given the variety of sonic material available to film makers a system of conventions was necessary to preserve the sound/image unity. Although the sound track can be made up of several different kinds of sound material including noise and music, the dialogue has the position of central importance in the classical system. As Kristin Thompson puts it:

dialogue is given primary consideration, with its volume level determining the levels of other sounds. The intelligibility of the dialogue takes precedence over canons of realism: volume will rise and fall according to the audience's need to hear rather than in relation to the situation of the scene.[48]

The avoidance of abrupt transitions between different and sharply contrasting sounds, repetitive sounds and silence itself, the tendency to avoid cutting the sound track at the same time as the image track, the secure anchoring of diegetic sound to its diegetic source even if it is displaced in the narrative, are amongst the other conventions which ensure that sound as a stylistic element is subordinated to the progress of the narrative line.

Hitchcock's British films contain numerous examples of the orthodox use of the sound track in the presentation of dialogue. Indeed, *Blackmail*, for example, contains many sequences in which we simply have 'photographs of people talking' and dialogue synchronised with the image in an uncomplicated manner. *Blackmail*, of course also contains the 'knife' sequence much admired for its innovatory distortions of the dialogue track yet because of the expressionist intention behind the technique and its relevance to the narrative line, it can be argued that the sequence remains within the classical style. *Murder!* Hitchcock's third sound feature, also contains an unusual manipulation of the dialogue track in the 'interior monologue' sequence. Sir John Menier, the central character in the film, is mulling over the details of the jury discussion after the trial and the spectator is presented with images of him whilst shaving and a sound track which presents his thoughts. There is also a musical element on the sound track — a performance of Wagner coming from the radio. Hitchcock has said of this sequence:

Anyway, we had to reveal his inner thoughts, and since I hate to introduce a useless character in a story, I used a stream-of-consciousness monologue. At this time, this was regarded as an extraordinary novelty, although it had been done for ages in the theatre, beginning with Shakespeare. But here we adapted the idea to the techniques of sound.[49]

There are many examples from other Hitchcock pictures of the 1930s which indicate quite clearly the special attention that the director paid to the sound elements in his films. His cinematic formation belongs to the silent period and this is reflected in the strong attention to the visualisation of narrative and an aversion to the 'excessive reliance on dialogue'.[50] Yet he clearly welcomed the possibilities for cinema created by the other elements on the sound track, sound effects and music, and strove continuously to develop new ways of relating sound,. including speech, to the images of his films. For example, the sequence in the open air cafe in *Secret Agent* where Ashenden and Elsa are sitting shortly after the killing of Caypor contains a further example of the use of sound to convey the interior feelings of a character. The singers are spinning coins in bowls and creating a sustained monotonous high pitched sound which is signalled as a mesmeric correlate for Elsa's somewhat shell-shocked state of mind after she has learnt the fate of the unfortunate Caypor. In *The Thirty-Nine Steps*, just after the killing of Annabel Smith, the sound track replays some of her earlier warnings to Hannay to indicate his realisation that she was telling the truth about the spy plot earlier on. Again sound is used to project the interior life of a character although this time it is displaced diegetic sound which is given the status of memory. Innovatory as these uses of sound may have been, they can be located within the classical cinema in so far as they are strongly linked to the narrative line through their association with the consciousness of specific characters.

There are, however, other examples of the use of sound in Hitchcock which might pose problems for the classical model. In *Blackmail*, after Alice has killed the artist, she wanders through the streets of London at dawn towards her home. As she walks she comes across a tramp lying in a doorway. We are shown an image of his hand lying in a position which echoes the image of the hand of the artist just after he has been stabbed. Alice starts back and opens her mouth. Then there is a cut to a shot of the landlady discovering the dead artist and she screams. Alice opens her mouth but the scream is elsewhere. There is a variant on this in *The Thirty-Nine Steps* when the landlady discovers the murdered Annabel Smith in Hannay's apartment. The camera is positioned behind her as she opens the door to the apartment and she then turns, opening her mouth. The sound that we hear, however, is the shrill whistle of a train and there is a swift cut to a train emerging from a tunnel to 'claim' the sound. Fidelity of sound to source is a strong convention of classical cinema and here Hitchcock deviates from it in order to provide a 'striking transition' between two disparate images.[51] A somewhat more complicated play with sound occurs in *Secret Agent* at the climax to the sequence in which Caypor is pushed off the mountain. I have already described the alternating montage structure which shows scenes of Caypor on the mountain intercut with scenes back at the hotel and gradually as the sequence develops to its macabre conclusion the sounds of the dog barking and scratching at the door are overlaid on the images from the mountain. As Ashenden looks through the telescope at Caypor and the Mexican on the edge of the mountain we hear the dog's agitated barking and whining on the sound track. When Caypor is eventually pushed to his death the plaintive whine of the dog which falls to a whimper constitutes a kind of aural 'objective correlative' of his actual fall to death as well as evoking sympathy for his plight. These are examples of quite experimental uses of sound in the context of classical cinema which draw attention to themselves and emphasise the actual split between image and sound which the conventions of classical cinema seek to mask.

There is one more typical Hitchcockian sound device which also depends on a very clear separation between sound and image. As Elisabeth Weis puts it:

his soundtrack is also distinctively contrapuntal to the visuals. That is to say, the sounds and images rarely duplicate and often contrast with each other. During a Hitchcock film we are typically looking at one thing or person while listening to another.[52]

Hitchcock puts it somewhat more prosaically as 'the sound-track says one thing while the image says something else' but he also talks of this approach to the sound/image relationship as 'a fundamental of film production'.[53] There are two examples of this in *The Thirty-Nine Steps*. At the crofter's cabin whilst he is saying the blessing before they have supper, the images show his wife glancing furtively at the newspaper headline which incriminates Hannay, and then anxiously at Hannay himself. Later in the film when Hannay seeks refuge from the police in Professor Jordan's home we see him sitting with the professor and we hear an off-screen conversation about the fugitive Portland Mansion murderer. The examples differ in so far as the former scene places its emphasis for narrative purposes on the images with the off-screen sound less significant whilst the latter scene depends very much on the importance of the content of the off-screen conversation. Both, however, create their tension through a 'contrapuntal' relationship between sound and image.

Hitchcock — A Classical Film Maker?

In so far as the classical cinema can be equated with the commercial cinema in Britain during the 1930s then Hitchcock, as a professional film maker working within the commercial entertainment cinema of the time, was required to produce films which corresponded in form, style and content to the classical Hollywood films which constituted the normal film fare for British audiences. Hitchcock's films circulated through the same cinemas that showed classical Hollywood films and would have been read by audiences in the context of the classical conventions of such cinema. The trade paper reviews tended to stress the entertainment qualities of Hitchcock's films, positioning them in the main within the classical entertainment film industry and confirming, at the institutional level at least, that Hitchcock was indeed a 'classical film maker'. However, we have noted that the influential distributor, C.M. Woolf, had nurtured a suspicion of Hitchcock's artistic qualities since the production of *The Lodger* in the mid-1920s.[54] Although Woolf's antipathy to Hitchcock has been explained in terms of studio politics it may be that he was aware of the tendencies within the films which took them away from mainstream conventions, from the classical norms. *Kine Weekly* also noted that a film like *Secret Agent* had a treatment which was 'artistic and subtle'[55] and thus somewhat different from the conventional espionage drama, although the reviewer did not see this as an obstacle to box-office success. The difference of Hitchcock was also marked by a limited alternative circulation for his films so that, for example, extracts of his films were screened at the Film Society and *Blackmail* was revived at the Everyman cinema during the 1930s. As a corollary of this there was also some grudging discussion of his films by highbrow critics in the more artistically oriented film journals and magazines of the period. This suggests at least a complicated relationship between Hitchcock's films and the classical system of conventions which dominate entertainment narrative film making in the 1930s and this point has been elaborated by many contemporary critics and theorists. In an important essay on classical Hollywood cinema, Thomas Elsaessar isolates Hitchcock along with Fritz Lang and Orson Welles as directors whose films lie outside the mainstream classical tradition to the extent that they display 'a far more explicitly intellectual, analytic approach to the medium, in which the tradition is reflected only obliquely, or reformulated altogether'.[56] Raymond Bellour has written of Hitchcock's cinema as providing 'both an eccentric and examplary version'[57] of classical narrative film making, and Michael Renov has suggested that 'it is the Hitchcock film which tests the limits of ... (classical cinema) ... through the continuous manipulation of the most disruptive elements of classical cinema (the radical close-up, the montage sequence, the zoom and especially the point-of-view shot)'.[58] Now, writers such as Elsaesser, Bellour and Renov address themselves primarily to Hitchcock's American films yet their comments seem to be applicable to the British films also. I have indicated some examples of the ways in which films such as *The Lodger, Blackmail, Sabotage* and *Secret Agent* can be seen to work at the limits of classical cinema depending upon the disruptive formal elements identified by Renov and displaying intellectual and analytic qualities which the classical tradition usually discourages. Such qualities of self-consciousness are at odds with the anonymity associated with the tradition of classical film making and a final point to make in this context is that that most familiar mark of Hitchcock's personalisation of his films, his own appearances, began in his British films with *The Lodger.*

Notes

1. D. Bordwell, *The Films of Carl-Theodor Dreyer* (University of California Press, London, 1981), p. 4.
2. Ibid., p. 4.
3. S. Heath, 'Narrative Space', *Screen*, vol. 17, no. 3 (1976).
4. K. Reisz and G. Millar, *The Technique of Film Editing* (Focal Press, London, 1968).
5. A succinct account of the features of the classical narrative system is contained in Bordwell and Thompson's *Film Art An Introduction* (Addison-Wesley, Reading, Mass., 1979) esp. Chs. 3, 6 and 9.
6. J. Bergstrom, 'Alternation, Segmentation, Hypnosis: Interview with Raymond Bellour', *Camera Obscura*, 3-4 (1979), p. 88.
7. This remark is mentioned by Robin Wood in 'Fear of Spying', *American Film*, Nov. 1983, p. 30.
8. See Chapter 6, pp. 138-9.

9. Bordwell and Thompson, *Film Art*, p. 52.
10. Ibid.
11. See C. Metz, *Film Language* (Oxford University Press, London, 1974), Ch. 5.
12. Bordwell and Thompson, *Film Art*, p. 59.
13. R. Bellour, 'Psychosis, Neurosis, Perversion', *Camera Obscura* 3-4 (1979), p. 105.
14. Bordwell and Thompson, *Film Art*, p. 74.
15. J. Staiger, 'Dividing Labour for Production Control', *Cinema Journal*, vol. XVIII, no. 2 (1979), p. 19.
16. J. Ellis, *Visible Fictions* (Routledge and Kegan Paul, London, 1982), p. 63.
17. Bordwell, *Dreyer*, p. 5.
18. N. Burch, 'Fritz Lang' in R. Roud (ed.), *A Critical Dictionary of Cinema* (Secker and Warburg, London, 1980), p. 585.
19. See A. Bazin, 'The Evolution of Film Language' in P. Graham (ed.) *The New Wave* (Secker and Warburg, London, 1968).
20. Bordwell, *Dreyer*, p. 32.
21. See Note 13.
22. Bordwell and Thompson, *Film Art*, p. 56.
23. Bordwell, *Dreyer*, p. 37.
24. Ibid.
25. See Chapter 2, p. 26.
26. R. Durgnat, *The Strange Case of Alfred Hitchcock* (Faber and Faber, London, 1974), p. 80.
27. Ibid.
28. *The Times*, 25 May 1936 (review of a revival of the film at the Everyman Cinema, London).
29. L. Anderson, 'Alfred Hitchcock', *Sequence*, no. 9 (1949), p. 116.
30. See Chapter 2, p. 28.
31. Anderson, 'Hitchcock', p. 116.
32. I. Montagu, 'Interview: Ivor Montagu', *Screen*, vol. 13, no. 2 (1972), p. 80.
33. Bordwell and Thompson, *Film Art*, p. 121.
34. Truffaut, *Hitchcock*, pp. 343-6.
35. A. Bazin, *Jean Renoir* (Simon and Shuster, New York, 1973), p. 87.
36. A. Hitchcock, 'Direction' in C. Davy (ed.) *Footnotes to the Film* (Lovat Dickson and Thompson, London, 1937), p. 7.
37. V.I. Pudovkin, *Film Technique and Film Acting* (Vision, London, 1958), pp. 166-7.
38. Truffaut, *Hitchcock*, p. 120.
39. J. R. Taylor, *Hitch* (Faber and Faber, London, 1978), p. 140.
40. Truffaut, *Hitchcock*, p. 126.
41. Ibid., p. 265.
42. Montagu, 'Interview', p. 89.
43. Bazin, 'Evolution', p. 46.
44. P. Rotha, *The Film Till Now*, 4th edn (Spring Books, London, 1967), p. 404.
45. Ibid., p. 408.
46. See Chapter 2, p. 29.
47. K. Thompson, *Eisenstein's Ivan the Terrible* (Princeton University Press, Princeton, New Jersey, 1981), p. 55.
48. Ibid., pp. 55-6.
49. Truffaut, *Hitchcock*, pp. 81-2.
50. E. Weis, 'The Sound of One Wing Flapping', *Film Comment*, vol. 14, no. 5, (1978), p. 42.
51. Bordwell and Thompson, *Film Art*, p. 198.
52. Weis, 'The Sound of One Wing Flapping', p. 44.
53. Truffaut, *Hitchcock*, p. 25.
54. See Chapter 5, p. 88.
55. *Kine Weekly*, 14 May 1936.

56. T. Elsaesser, 'The American Cinema 2. Why Hollywood', *Monogram*, no. 1 (1971), p. 5.

57. R. Bellour, 'Psychosis, Neurosis, Perversion', *Camera Obscura*, 3/4, Summer 1979, p. 106.

58. M. Renov, 'From Identification to Ideology: The Male System of Hitchcock's *Notorious*', *Wide Angle*, vol. 4, no. 1 (1980), p. 30.

Chapter Eight

Conclusion –
Hitchcock's British Films

Although the primary context for an analysis of Hitchcock's career in Britain is the entertainment film industry of the period, the links between his films and various aspects of the film culture which lie outside the commercial industry have to be taken into consideration. The growth of an intellectual approach to the cinema, the minority film culture of the Film Society, the development of the specialised film journal, the 'art' cinemas of Europe which sprang into being in the 1920s and the British document-ary film movement of the 1930s together constitute a formidable and relevant background to the films which Hitchcock made in the somewhat different circumstances of the commercial film industry of the interwar period. Although films such as *Blackmail, The Thirty-Nine Steps* and *Secret Agent* can be fitted comfortably into the context of British entertainment cinema as genre pieces drawing upon traditions familiar to the cinema of the period, they also can be situated in relation to these other aspects of the overall film culture. Hitchcock is a particularly striking example of a professional film maker working within the commercial film industry but with a set of interests and concerns which intersect with areas of the film culture that implicitly rejected the commercial cinema. He was not the only such figure, however, and it is worth drawing attention to some other film makers of the period who straddled the worlds of the majority and minority film cultures in a similar way. Anthony Asquith's film *A Cottage on Dart-moor* (1930) with its montage pyrotechnics and its complicated narrative structure suggests a detailed knowledge of the 'art' cinemas of the twenties whilst Thorold Dickinson's close involvement with the artistic culture of the Film Society is possibly betrayed in the unlikely context of the opening montage sequence of Basil Dean's *Sing As We Go,* a Gracie Fields vehicle on which Dickinson worked as editor. Although leading figures from the minority film culture such as Rotha and the *Close Up* writers drew a rather rigid evaluative distinction between popular cinema and the emergent 'art' and documentary cinemas of Europe, there does seem to have been a limited amount of interchange between the two sectors of the film culture in terms of personnel. Barry Salt has suggested that the fast cutting style in

169

British feature films of the 1930s may be linked to the fact that film directors and editors from the commercial sector attended the Film Society screenings and, in particular, fell under the influence of the Soviet cinema of the 1920s often featured in Society's programmes.[1]

Hitchcock and the Entertainment Cinema

We have already noted that, despite the economic depression of the 1930s and the decline of the older heavy industries such as coal and steel, a number of industries, particularly those linked to the growing consumer goods area, actually developed and flourished during the decade.[2] The entertainment industries expanded and cinema exhibition was a major beneficiary of the more diversified leisure patterns that were a feature of the period. Through the course of the decade the number of cinemas in Britain increased from 3,300 in 1929 to 4,967 in 1938.[3] This increase in exhibition venues represents the consolidation of cinema-going as a staple form of entertainment for the mass of the British people during the period and it has been suggested that some 40 per cent of the population went to the cinema once a week and 25 per cent went twice a week or more.[4] The cinema was a cheap form of entertainment and its influence reached across all sections of British society including the least well off and the unemployed. The cinema-going habit and the popularity of film as entertainment were based upon the American cinema rather than the British cinema of the time. The expansion that took place during the 1930s was geared to the Hollywood production industry with its massive output of between 400 and 500 films a year and its evident ability to cater to the tastes of the British popular audience. Although, as has been noted earlier, there has been some recent speculation about the relative popularity of American films and their British counterparts during the 1930s, it is clear that British audiences did massively approve of the gangster films, the musicals and the melodramas which the Hollywood studios turned out regularly and consistently.[5] In 1937, *World Film News* published summaries of a symposium on box office appeal which was based upon the questioning of a range of exhibitors. These summaries indicated that the exhibitors were broadly satisfied with the kinds of films coming from Hollywood but that they regarded British films as unsuitable for the substantial working class element of their audiences. However, the article did go on to suggest that the middle class elements of their audiences were more appreciative of the indigenous product and suggested that British pictures were, in fact, 'the type most in demand (especially in places like Bournemouth, Dorking, the Isle of Wight etc.)'.[6] The enthusiasm for British pictures in the Home Counties and on the South Coast is, perhaps, unsurprising given the character of the British cinema of the time and this aspect of the investigation contrasts sharply with the comments of an exhibitor from a very different part of the country. A Scottish cinema operator suggested that 'British films' was a misnomer as the domestic industry, in fact, produced 'English films in a particularly parochial sense' and that these were 'more foreign to his audience than the products of Hollywood, over 6,000 miles away'.[7]

The prospects of the British film industry dislodging Hollywood from its position of international supremacy and dominance of the British cinema screen were never very bright; yet it was with the Hollywood industry that many British companies sought to compete in quite a direct manner. Gaumont British and Korda's London Film Productions were two of the prominent concerns that attempted to compete with the major American companies both for a significant presence in the British market and, a rather more difficult proposition, a presence in the American market. The two spheres of competition were, in fact, interrelated as far as the British production industry was concerned for although the Quota Act of 1927 had provided British film producers with a guaranteed share of the home market, the British audience was not large enough to generate a return on production costs for films which moved out of the minimal budget category. Overseas and particularly American distribution was necessary to guarantee the greater production finance required for British films to be able to display the lavish production values — the big stars, the spectacular settings, costumes and so on — of their Hollywood counterparts. The American industry, by contrast, had access to a vast domestic market which enabled it to recover its production costs in the home market alone. Such an advantage over the smaller film industries of the European countries meant that Hollywood could concentrate upon production for the American market and also be in a position to market its films overseas at prices which its competitors could not hope to match. Such a situation was inevitably testing for the British film industry which had declined to a point of near collapse in the mid-1920s. On the one hand, British film makers were engaged in an artistic and ideological struggle to construct a distinctively British cinema, a cinema of national identity which would strike a chord with British cinemagoers; on the other hand, British film makers were also attempting to make films for an international market and particularly films which would appeal to an American audience. British film makers, in a sense, were trapped within a paradox, a mesh of contradictory demands. British audiences, in the main, had become attuned to American films and had formed their notions of cinema on the basis of Hollywood genre film making. Yet, if British film makers were to follow the example of other European countries in the construction of a distinctive national cinema, this implied a departure from the form and content of the American film. And such a departure might then pose problems for a cinema which wished to appeal to the American audience. It might be argued that the British cinema mistakenly opted for such a paradox in its attempt to produce an imitation of the American cinema instead of trying to develop an indigenous cinema based upon national characteristics and marketed on the basis of its distinctiveness. The 'art' cinema route, for a variety of reasons, was not part of the thinking of the time in the industry. British producers concentrated either on the low budget 'quickie' end of the market or sought to make prestigious 'quality' pictures along Hollywood lines.

Critical opinion has been very hard on the British cinema of the 1930s. Verdicts of failure have been consistently delivered both in terms of the apparent inability of the industry to develop a distinctively British cinema and the unpopularity with the bulk of the British audience of the films actually produced. It is true that certain films did manage to win audience approval, notably the regional comedies with music hall stars such as Gracie Fields and George Formby, but such films did not win critical approval and, it is argued, they remained resolutely parochial in their appeal. The British cinema had also gained a very poor reputation from the development of the 'quota quickie' and this hindered the other ambition of the industry to produce prestigious films for the international market. There were intermittent successes in America such as the Korda spectacular historical pictures and the more modestly budgeted Hitchcock thrillers but the industry failed to build up that sustained success which would have provided the British cinema with a consistent access to the lucrative American market. In fact, the concerted attempt to break into the American market during the middle years of the decade ended in the production crisis of 1937. Although this period was marked by the availability of production finance on an unprecedented scale, the underlying problems of the industry, its precarious infrastructure and its lack of managerial expertise led to the closing down of many production units towards the end of the decade.

Yet despite the unpromising prospects of the British cinema in the face of American domination, it was within the entertainment film industry that Hitchcock was to build a successful career. In one respect, it was no surprise that Hitchcock should enter the commercial film industry, given his professed admiration for the American popular cinema. It might also be argued that his specific class background and formative influences made it more likely that he would gravitate towards the industry rather than towards the artistic sectors of the film culture of the time. Yet, he did share the artistic interests of the university educated upper middle class intellectuals who began their film careers in the 1920s and early 1930s but who tended to opt for the state-sponsored documentary movement rather than the commercial film industry.

Hitchcock's career can be charted in terms of a conventional commercial trajectory through the film industry of the 1920s and 1930s. He worked with the major British stars of the day such as Betty Balfour (*Champagne*), Ivor Novello (*The Lodger, Downhill*) and the Danish actor Carl Brisson (*The Ring, The Manxman*). During the thirties he was to work with leading female stars such as Jessie Matthews (*Waltzes from Vienna*) and Madeleine Carroll (*The Thirty-Nine Steps, Secret Agent*), Margaret Lockwood, the rising star of the late thirties (*The Lady Vanishes*) and the

172

leading British male actor of the period, Robert Donat (*The Thirty-Nine Steps*). He worked at Gaumont British during its 'internationalist' phase of the mid-1930s and directed a number of the imported American stars such as Robert Young (*Secret Agent*) and Sylvia Sidney (*Sabotage*). He was also to work with many of the foreign technical personnel who flocked into the British film industry in the years following the Quota Act of 1927. For instance, he worked on three occasions with Alfred Junge, the German art director who had settled in Britain after working on a number of German silent films in the 1920s. Hitchcock was a thoroughgoing professional in the sense that he interested himself in all aspects of the production of a film including the preparation of the scenario, the art direction, the cinematography, the editing and the sound as well as the actual business of film direction on the studio floor or on location.

His attitude towards the marketing and publicity dimensions of the industry also suggests a business-oriented professional. We have noted that Hitchcock was especially attentive to the role that film reviewers and critics could play in the successful selling of a film to the public, an attitude that probably derives from the critical acclaim of *The Lodger*, a consolidation point in his early career as a director. It is in this early period, indeed, that the role of publicity in establishing his position within the industry must have been crucial. The article by Cedric Belfrage in *Picturegoer* which presented Hitchcock in glowing terms as 'the world's youngest film director' was written around the time that his first feature — *The Pleasure Garden* — was given a press screening and before the massive critical acclaim of *The Lodger* which was not screened until later in the year. Neither of the films was shown to the public until the following year yet by that time Hitchcock had signed a lucrative contract with British National Pictures and had become the most prominent and most highly paid director of the time. That Hitchcock ended up at John Maxwell's commercially-oriented British International Pictures is not surprising given his somewhat hard-nosed professional approach. He worked at BIP as a conventional contract director on a series of assignments which derived from the general production policies of the studio. Although his first picture for the studio — *The Ring* — was a personally initiated project, it failed at the box-office and Hitchcock subsequently worked to a more orthodox production schedule based upon adaptations of proven literary and dramatic successes for the screen. Even *Blackmail*, regarded by many critics as the most successful and personal of Hitchcock's BIP films, was based upon a stage success. One point to note about Hitchcock's period at BIP is that despite sustained critical support during this time, the films were not consistent box-office successes which casts some doubt upon the link between critical and commercial success supposed by the publicity conscious director to exist. Hitchcock's professional experience at BIP was undoubtedly affected by the general problems of the industry during the period from the passage of the Quota Act in 1927 to the early 1930s. Firstly, the industry faced the substantial problems involved in the adjustment from the conditions of piecemeal production which obtained in the early 1920s to the demands of mass production following the quota legislation. In addition to this, the industry was also faced with the massive adjustment to the sound picture which necessitated substantial re-equipping of both film studios and cinemas as well as the aesthetic implications of the newly developed technology. In the midst of these massive transformations the problems of constructing a cinema of national identity remained and the answer at BIP from the point of view of studio policy seemed to be a mixture of middle-brow theatrical and literary adaptations and low budget programme pictures. In such a context Hitchcock, the ambitious professional, meandered through a number of such adaptations and ended up producing a 'quota quickie' — *Lord Camber's Ladies*. His own judgement on his period at BIP is often harsh and dismissive with comments like 'lowest ebb of my career' and 'creative decline' summing up his unhappy memories of the time.

By the time he renewed his professional association with Michael Balcon, the climate in the British cinema had become more settled and more conducive to the emergence of Hitchcock the specialist genre director with a distinctive and stable identity as a film maker. A kind of generic constellation had begun to crystallise with crime films, comedies and musicals dominating the production schedules of most British companies. The commercial imperatives of mass production, the logic of standardisation in the commercial film industry, had generated the beginnings of distinctive traditions in the British cinema and some of these, notably the crime pictures and the comedies, were drawing upon well established popular cultural forms such as crime literature and the music hall. The period at Gaumont British, the period of the highly successful thriller sextet, was also a time of plentiful finance for production and in the improved economic climate many companies moved away from the 'quickie' policies of the early thirties. Although Hitchcock's films were not as lavishly financed as the Korda spectaculars he did undoubtedly benefit from the more generous approach to film financing in the middle of the decade in terms of his access to bigger stars such as Carroll and Donat and the general improvement in production values evident in the thrillers when compared with the BIP pictures. Despite his early prominence and critical acclaim, despite the accolade of 'Alfred the Great', Hitchcock, the professional film director, was very much at the mercy of the general shifts in the industry of the time. His career in the late 1920s and early 1930s parallels the struggles of the nascent British film industry to establish itself in the face of the superior resources and capacities of the American film industry. Both Hitchcock and the film industry were struggling to find a role and an identity at this time. His most sustained period of commercial sucess was with the thriller cycle of the mid-thirties which also provided him with a specific identity as a film maker, one which he carried through to his Hollywood career. The years of the sextet — 1934 to 1937 — were also the years when the British film industry enjoyed a measure of success and stability although this was short-lived and a severe production crisis followed towards the end of the decade. The expansion of production had been built upon precarious foundations and unwarranted expectations, and the failure to penetrate the crucial American market with any degree of consistency created substantial problems for even the largest of British companies. Gaumont British, Hitchcock's own studio, closed down its Shepherd's Bush studio in 1937, reduced its production programme and placed the distribution of its films in the hands of General Film Distributors — the renting arm of the embryonic Rank Organisation which eventually was to absorb Gaumont British in the early forties. For Hitchcock the late nineteen-thirties were a time of decision. Hollywood was clearly interested in the leading British director of the day and the *Variety* reviews though varying in their overall judgements on his pictures usually singled out the directorial contribution for special praise. However, a profile in the *New Yorker* written just after Hitchcock had signed for the independent producer David O. Selznick, suggests that Hitchcock's films had a certain limited coterie appeal for American audiences:

> The vogue for Alfred Hitchcock's cinema melodramas is mainly a local phenomenon. 'The Thirty-Nine Steps', his best-known job of direction, has, in the past three years, has been revived thirty-one times by various theatres on Manhattan Island, and is to be shown again this month ...
> ... Hitchcock has become the chief support of that sizable group of defeated cinema-goers who attend a new production with the mistrust born of much disillusionment and who would rather go to see one of their old favorites again. These people count it a poor month in which New York doesn't offer them at least one Hitchcock revival.[8]

The future of production in Britain was uncertain, Hitchcock had probably exhausted the possibilities of working in British studios with the thriller cycle and it is not surprising that his professional approach to film making drew him to the entertainment film capital of the world. He, of course, had long admired the American cinema and the move to Hollywood with its superior studio facilities and its array of international film talent would offer him greater opportunities than were available in the crisis-ridden British film industry of the late thirties.

Hitchcock, Art and Documentary

Despite Hitchcock's admiration of American cinema, it has been demonstrated that films such as *The Lodger* and *Blackmail* bear the imprint of the international 'art' cinemas of the twenties.[9] Hitchcock's experience of working in Germany, the centre of 'art' cinema in the 1920s, his attendance at Film Society screenings and his personal and professional relationships with leading figures in the minority film culture provided the director with a number of routes towards the alternative and oppositional film styles that were being developed in response to the aesthetic hegemony of the classical American film. Against Hitchcock 'the professional' film director working for a large commercial studio, we need to set Hitchcock 'the aesthete', the film maker very much aware of the artistic development of film form and style during the crucial experimental years of the 1920s. Indeed, as has already been noted, it was the characterisation of Hitchcock as artist, intellectual and highbrow by businessmen such as C.M. Woolf and John Maxwell which led to a number of problems for Hitchcock in his commercial career.

It is possible, to a limited extent, to relate Hitchcock's films to the European cinema on the basis of theme and narrative concern. The philosophical cast of the German cinema, its macabre themes and Gothic elements, are present in films such as *The Lodger, Blackmail* and *Sabotage* whilst the stress on the subjective psychological narrative in the work of the French Impressionist film makers is a central feature of Hitchcockian cinema. However, the strongest link between Hitchcock and the 'art' cinemas of the period is in terms of form and style rather than content and subject matter. Hitchcock's films have strong affinities with the Soviet montage films of the twenties with their stress on editing but there is little trace in Hitchcock of the political and social dimensions of films such as *Battleship Potemkin* and *Mother*. The emphasis on design in the *mise en scène* of German cinema, the French Impressionist development of subjective camera techniques, and the cutting styles of the Soviet film makers became harnessed to the Hitchcockian narrative style which blends progressive experimental techniques with the demands of the classical narrative.

Many of the British intellectuals who shared Hitchcock's interest in the new European cinemas of the period moved into the documentary movement as film makers in the late 1920s and early 1930s. They took with them the formal and political influences of the Soviet film makers in terms of an adherence to montage cutting styles and left-wing social commitments together with some of the philosophical and artistic presuppositions of the 'art' cinema. As Alan Lovell has suggested, it was the documentary movement under the general direction of John Grierson that captured the interest in film as an art form which was developing in Britain during the 1920s. This had important consequences for the commercial entertainment cinema in so far as it generated within British film culture 'a bias against the commercial, fiction cinema, except where that cinema has adopted documentary modes'.[10] It was not a route that one would have expected Hitchcock to follow given his commitment to entertainment cinema and to the American popular cinema in particular. Also, the class background of the documentary film makers was very different to that of a figure like Hitchcock. In fact, the earliest stirrings of an intellectual interest in the cinema had been in the university film societies during the early 1920s and Grierson has suggested that 'there was a time when we used to say that you couldn't get into documentary unless you had a double first, and from Cambridge too'.[11] The upper middle class university educated milieu of the documentary movement and, indeed, of the minority film culture itself, was quite at odds with the lower middle class background of shopkeepers from which Hitchcock had come.

Despite all this, the strands of 'realism' in Hitchcock's films demonstrated to the documentary minded critics that although he worked primarily upon melodramatic material, he had considerable skills in the methods of 'realist' presentation. It is fascinating to note that John Grierson, himself, was an admirer of Hitchcock — albeit a qualified one — referring to him in one breath as 'the best director, the slickest craftsman, the sharpest observer and the finest master of detail in all England' and, in the next breath, as 'the world's best director of unimportant pictures'.[12] Lindsay Anderson writing some time after Grierson also picked up the 'realist' elements in Hitchcock's British films referring particularly to the authenticity of the 'everyday locales' and the 'authentic minor characters, maids, policemen, shopkeepers, and commercial travellers'[13] populating the films. We have already drawn attention to the semi-documentary opening sequences of *The Lodger, The Ring, The Manxman* and *Blackmail*[14] but many of the later thrillers also contain social vignettes and cameos which impressed critics with a disposition towards 'documentary modes'. Anderson draws attention to 'realist' everyday locales such as 'the Corner House Restaurant', 'the little tobacconist's shop' in *Blackmail,* the 'drab little nonconformist chapel' in *The Man Who Knew Too Much*, the 'solidly respectable country house' in *The Thirty-Nine Steps*, Verloc's 'unpretentious suburban cinema' in *Sabotage* and the '*thé dansant* at the seaside hotel' in *Young and Innocent.*[15] The pinpointing of what might be called a middle or lower middle class iconography intersects in an interesting way with some comments that Hitchcock himself made in an article for *Kine Weekly* written in 1937. Hitchcock argues that the British cinema has neglected 'that vital central stratum of British humanity, the middle class'[16] and he continues:

I am trying to get this stratum of England on the screen. I am fighting against a hard enemy, the film of chromium plating, dress-shirts, cocktails and Oxford accents which is being continually made with the idea that it shows English life. Soon I hope we shall do unto America what they have done unto us, and make the cheerful man and girl of our middle class as colourful and dramatic to them as their ordinary everyday citizens are to the audiences of England.[17]

Here Hitchcock presents himself as the aspirant documentary poet of the middle classes speaking in a vein of 'realism' which is at odds with much of his other discussion of his film making practices.

In fact, it is necessary to disentangle the 'realism' of a Hitchcock picture from the 'realism' of the documentarists with its specific social commitment and purpose. Indeed, Hitchcock himself has frequently disavowed 'realism' as an aesthetic base. As he said to Truffaut:

> I don't want to film 'a slice of life' because people can get that at home, in the street or even in front of the movie theatre. They don't have to pay money to see a slice of life.[18]

He also delivered what amounts to a guarded rebuke to the traditions of documentary and the class bound nature of the 'realist' aesthetic in the following comment, also to Truffaut:

> You must remember also that British intellectuals traditionally spend their holidays on the continent. They go into the slums of Naples to take pictures of starving kids. They love to look at the washing hanging out between the tenements, the donkeys in the cobblestone streets. It's all so picturesque![19]

Clearly, to call Hitchcock a 'realist' director, to situate him within the traditions of cinematic 'realism' is incorrect; yet, there remains in his pictures a careful attention to surface detail, a 'realism' of sorts and this has to be placed within the Hitchcockian aesthetic. One way to account for such a dimension of Hitchcock's work is to see it as a pointed and dramatic contrast to the unreal twists and turns of the narrative action which are characteristic of many of his films. As Lindsay Anderson puts it, 'these films gain a particular excitement from their concern with ordinary people (or ordinary-looking people) who are plunged into extraordinary happenings in the most ordinary places'.[20] The 'realist' features of Hitchcock's cinema such as the meticulousness of detail in the mise en scène and the careful attention to the gamut of minor characters, construct an authentic context for the thematic plunge into the extraordinary — 'the chaos world' — which is a central feature of the 'Hitchcockian universe'. The 'realist' elements do not relate to a specific social or political concern but rather have a compositional function in the overall logic of the narrative. It can be argued, however, that historical and political readings of the spy thrillers, in particular, are available in the context of the growing international tensions of the period and that they contain oblique comments on the rise of Fascism in Europe and the impending war. As Raymond Durgnat has observed in relation to the thematic shifts in Hitchcock's British films, the 'stress on secret agents appears only with the escalation of the Nazi threat in Europe'[21] and he discusses *The Lady Vanishes* in terms of 'its resonance with the mood of Munich'.[22] The volatile world of international politics which is a necessary aspect of the spy thriller genre provides the films of the 'classic sextet' (apart from *Young and Innocent*) with some link to contemporary actuality. One other explanation of the 'realist' elements in Hitchcock's films has to do with the prestige of the documentary movement within the overall film culture. Alan Lovell has suggested that the 'entertainment cinema has always been rather overawed by the document-ary movement and paid tribute to it by adopting documentary modes'.[23] Despite Hitchcock's disavowal of the documentary spirit and his repudia-tion of any 'realist' intentions, his films do contain many sequences which indicate a mastery of 'documentary modes', and a clear awareness of this hegemonic current in British film culture.

Hitchcock's Cinematic Identity

The cinematic identity that Hitchcock defined during his British period does not derive from the middlebrow literary and dramatic adaptations which dominate his early years but rather from the thriller sextet which drew upon the very different traditions of British popular culture. The thriller cycle can be located within a strand of popular culture which has its roots in Gothic literature, the nineteenth century crime novel, the spy thrillers of Buchan and 'Sapper', the fascination with sexual murder drawn from the world of the popular Sunday newspaper and the figure of 'Jack the Ripper' on which *The Lodger* — 'the first Hitchcockian picture'[24] — was based. The '*News of the World* culture'[25] with its emphasis on sexuality and violence is a central component of the 'strong under-life'[26] of British cinema which runs counter to the 'cinema of good taste, characterised by restraint, understatement and sophistication'[27] preferred by the orthodox film culture and it is to the subversive counter-current that Hitchcock's British films relate.

In Hitchcock's British films, the convergence of sexuality and violent crime is central to such films as *The Pleasure Garden, The Lodger, Blackmail* and *Murder!* and explorations of sexuality form significant elements of many other films from this period. *The Thirty-Nine Steps*, for example, is at one level a fast paced thriller with the constraints of the genre propelling the narrative forward at breakneck speed, piling incident upon incident in Hannay's interwoven flight from capture and pursuit of the spy ring. Yet, the film is also marked by the eruption of sexuality. The headlong flight of the narrative itself is arrested by the sequence in the crofter's cabin where Hannay spends the night, with its stark depiction of a cruel and repressive marriage and the victimised woman who is trapped within it. It is a detain-ing sequence which generates a surplus over and above its specific contribu-tion to the progress of the narrative, a kind of *Brief Encounter* in miniature in which the crofter's wife is offered a glimpse of freedom from her repres-sion through her chance encounter with Hannay. Sexuality is taken up rather more explicitly later in the film and, indeed, is conjoined with violence when Pamela is handcuffed to Hannay and they spend the night together in the remote Highland inn. The couple are placed in that position of 'enforced intimacy' which occurs in a number of Hitchcock's films from this period, weaving the themes of sexuality and the couple into the adven-ture-laden world of the thriller. Elsa Carrington and Ashenden are thrown together early in *Secret Agent* in the intimate circumstances of a fictional marriage devised as a cover for their espionage activities and during their initial encounter she is dressed only in a towel. Erica is drawn into a close relatinship with Robert in *Young and Innocent* as he flees from the police and Gilbert's first encounter with Iris in *The Lady Vanishes* occurs when he camps in her hotel bedroom for the night. Violence, sexuality and the heterosexual couple are elements which are present either overtly or in more covert fashion in many of these early Hitchcock films and such films are thrown into more prominent relief when reviewed in the light of later American films such as *Strangers on a Train, Rear window, Vertigo* and *Psycho* in which such a thematic constellation becomes paramount. In 1965, Robin Wood wrote, 'Look carefully at almost any recent Hitchcock film and you will see that its core, the axis around which it is constructed, is invariably a man-woman relationship: it is never a matter of some arbitrary "love interest", but of essential subject matter.'[28] It might be suggested that this key summary of the central quality of films such as *Vertigo* and *North by Northwest* is also relevant to many of Hitchcock's British films, even those which are ostensibly quite precise genre pieces such as *The Thirty-Nine Steps.*

The other related and equally central thematic element of the films is the 'chaos-world' which lies just beneath the surface of normality in the fictional universe of Hitchcock. The nightmare world suggested by the lodger's apparently furtive activities, the bizarre voyage undertaken by the Hills in their attempts to break free of the constrictions of suburban life in *Rich and Strange,* and the plunge into adventure and mystery occasioned by Hannay's visit to the music hall in *The Thirty-Nine Steps* offer a series of variations on the precarious character of the civilised world of order. Just as the convergence of the themes of sexuality and violence in Hitchcock has its roots in broader traditions of cultural practice such as crime and horror literature, so the theme of the 'chaos-world' can be related to other cultural strands. Indeed, the Argentinian critic, Jorge Luis Borges, writing about G.K. Chesterton, describes his fictional world in terms that apply equally well to the 'Hitchcockian universe':

the powerful work of Chesterton, the prototype of physical and moral sanity, is always on the verge of becoming a nightmare. The diabolical and the horrible lie in wait on his pages; the most innocuous subject can assume the forms of terror.[29]

This is another example of Hitchcock drawing strength from the popular interests and obsessions which find a number of different cultural and artistic outlets at a variety of levels in literature and the visual arts. Taking up this particular theme, Peter Wollen has described Hitchcock's cinema as being constituted by 'the rhetoric of the unconscious, the world which surges up beneath the thin protection offered us by civilisation'.[30] He formulates Hitchcock's distinctiveness in terms of the psychoanalytical concerns which turn on the human activity of watching and gazing — voyeurism, exhibitionism and so on. 'The act of watching', suggests Wollen, 'dominates his films, both in the narration and the narrative, in his style and in the relations between the *dramatis personae*'.[31] Indeed, the very genre so closely associated with Hitchcock — the thriller — with its stress on looking, watching, spying allows a full play to such concerns. As Steve Neale has written:

> Think of individual scenes in any number of detective films and thrillers in which the central protagonist is engaged simply in secretive looking. It is worth noting in this context that the many celebrated instances of voyeurism, exhibitionism and fetishism in the films of Alfred Hitchcock are, partly at least, a function of the fact that Hitchcock makes thrillers: the thriller is a genre that consists of the elaboration of a narrative under the sign of these three drives, they are part — and arguably the dominant part — of the conditions of existence of the genre.[32]

With this psychoanalytical dimension in Hitchcock's cinema we return to the prurient world of 'the *News of the World* culture' cited earlier although with Hitchcock we are discussing an exploration rather than an exploitation of the dynamic under-life of civilised order.

Such dimensions of Hitchcock's work suggest a considerable indebtedness to certain traditions in British popular culture and one which feeds through into his American work despite the very different contexts of Hollywood and American popular culture. Alan Lovell has pointed out that Hitchcock's formation within a specifically British culture and his attachment to British life and interests is an important component of his American films although one that has been neglected by critical debates which frequently seek to weigh one phase of his career against the other. Lovell draws attention to a number of features of the American films which betray Hitchcock's British origins. Six of the films are set in Britain (*Rebecca, Suspicion, The Paradine Case, Stage Fright, Dial M For Murder, Frenzy*) whilst major sections of *Foreign Correspondent* and the 1956 version of *The Man Who Knew Too Much* are set in Britain. *Under Capricorn* is set in Australia under British colonial rule and four films are based upon British plays or novels with the settings changed to America (*Rope, The Trouble with Harry, The Birds* and *Marnie*). In addition to this, a number of Hitchcock pictures, whilst set in America or elsewhere outside Britain, contain sequences which evoke British life as in the horse-riding episode in *Notorious* and in the rather more fully developed English ambience of the Rutland home in *Marnie* with its afternoon tea ritual and its fox hunt in traditional costume. One further aspect of Hitchcock's American films which Lovell related to the Britishness of the director is the centrality of the blonde heroine in so many films, especially those of the fifties. What Truffaut refers to as the 'icy sexuality'[33] of actresses such as Grace Kelly, Kim Novak and Tippi Hedren can be related to a particular

English sexual stereotype summed up by Hitchcock as 'the drawing room type, the real ladies, who becomes whores once they're in the bedroom'.[34] Madeleine Carroll, from the British period, might be regarded as the antecedent of the blonde heroines of the fifties American films especially with her performance in *The Thirty-Nine Steps*.[35]

The literary critic Bernard Bergonzi has written that 'the text is a field of force ... its whirling constituents come from many possible sources as well as the author's creative brain and imagination'.[36] Certainly, Hitchcock's films despite the formidable personality of the author can be related to a number of sources. Although the films remain examples of the commercial entertainment cinema in Britain during the interwar years, they frequently betray radically different cinematic affiliations. The films can be linked to the minority film culture of the period and the intellectual interest in cinema signalled by the Film Society, journals such as *Close Up* and writers such as Paul Rotha and John Grierson. The films of the twenties, in particular, can be discussed in the context of the diverse artistic currents to be found in the experimental cinemas of Germany, France and the Soviet Union. Although the primary formal and stylistic influence on Hitchcock was the classical American cinema, the experimental qualities in his films which link them to the 'art' cinemas of Europe, make for an off-centred relationship between them and mainstream classical cinema. To this complex artistic inheritance must be added the substantial influence of the popular culture of crime and sexuality which Hitchcock was to filter through the aesthetics of the European avant-garde. Such an assembly of 'whirling constituents', as many critics have pointed out, positions Hitchcock both as a popular showman film maker producing a cinema with mass appeal drawing upon strong and potentially subversive traditions of popular culture, and as a serious 'highbrow' artist comparable to film makers such as Murnau and Eisenstein[37] and attracting the attention of highly sophisticated critics and theoreticians. This is not a recent phenomenon and we have drawn attention to the interest of the *Close Up* critics in certain aspects of his work and the somewhat grudging praise that films such as *Blackmail* and *Murder!* received from Rotha and Grierson. This somewhat grudging character of the highbrow interest in Hitchcock is in itself testimony to the complex quality of his work, standing as it does somewhere between the supposed poles of 'art' and 'entertainment'. The minority film culture with which Hitchcock has some affinities found its principal cinematic outlet in the documentary movement of the 1930s, a cinema to which Hitchcock was opposed in a number of respects. His central interest was in entertainment — 'Some films are slices of life. Mine are slices of cake' — and his class origins, which may explain his interest in popular cinema and popular culture, were very different to those of the upper middle class university types who dominated the minority film culture. Hitchcock's lower middle class origins drew him into the world of the popular film yet he possessed the kind of analytical grasp of the potential of film as an art form which was more readily associated with the documentary cinema and its intellectual adherents.

Hitchcock's commercial and business orientation, his flair for self-advertisement and publicity, are somewhat it odds with his evident artistic interests and this makes it difficult to pin him down in terms of identity as a film maker. Although it seems natural to locate him within the sphere of entertainment cinema, his strong links with the 'art' cinemas of the day frequently impose themselves at the level of his textual practice. Yet he cannot be treated as a film artist without taking account of his commitment to entertainment cinema and his immersion in the traditions of popular culture. Within the context of what was a stratified film culture in Britain during the interwar years, Hitchcock can be seen as a marooned figure, too businesslike and commercial to be an 'artist', yet too 'artistic' to be fitted comfortably into the British entertainment cinema of the time.

Notes

1. B. Salt, *Film Style and Technology: History and Analysis* (Starword, London, 1983), p. 284.
2. See Chapter 3, pp. 33-5.
3. N. Branson and M. Heinemann, *Britain in the Nineteen Thirties* (Panther, St Albans, 1973), p. 275.
4. Ibid.
5. See Chapter 4, p. 80.
6. *World Film News*, Feb, 1937, p. 6.
7. Ibid.
8. R. Maloney, 'Alfred Joseph Hitchcock', *New Yorker*, 10 Sept. 1938, p. 28.
9. Chapter 2, pp. 24-30.
10. A. Lovell and J. Hillier, *Studies in Documentary* (Secker and Warburg, London, 1972), p. 35.
11. E. Sussex, *The Rise and Fall of British Documentary* (University of California Press, California, 1975), p. 21.
12. F. Hardy (ed.), *Grierson on Documentary* (Faber and Faber, London, 1966), pp. 71-2.
13. L. Anderson, 'Alfred Hitchcock', *Sequence*, no. 9 (1949), p. 118.
14. See Chapter 2, p. 28.
15. Anderson, '*Alfred Hitchcock*', pp. 117-8.
16. A. Hitchcock, 'More Cabbages, Fewer Kings', *Kine Weekly*, 14 Jan. 1937, p. 30.
17. Ibid.
18. F. Truffaut, *Hitchcock* (Panther, London, 1969), p. 112.
19. Ibid., p. 141.
20. Anderson, 'Alfred Hitchcock', p. 117.
21. R. Durgnat, *The Strange Case of Alfred Hitchcock* (Faber and Faber, London, 1974), p. 126.
22. Ibid., p. 142.
23. A. Lovell, 'The British Cinema — The Unknown Cinema', British Film Institute seminar paper (1967), p. 7.
24. Truffaut, *Hitchcock*, p. 54.
25. In unpublished manuscript notes on Hitchcock.
26. C. Barr, 'A Conundrum for England', *Monthly Film Bulletin*, Aug. 1984, p. 235.
27. Lovell, 'The British Cinema', p. 7.
28. R. Wood, *Hitchcock's Films* (Zwemmer, London, 1965), pp. 20-21.
29. J.L. Borges, *Other Inquisitions* (Souvenir Press, New York, 1977), p. 81.

30. P. Wollen, 'Hitchcock's Vision', *Cinema* (UK) no. 3 (1969), p. 4.

31. Ibid., p. 2.

32. S. Neale, *Genre* (British Film Institute, London, 1980), p. 43.

33. Truffaut, *Hitchcock*, p. 279.

34. Ibid., p. 278.

35. This paragraph is based upon unpublished manuscript notes on Hitchcock written by Alan Lovell.

36. B. Bergonzi, *Reading the Thirties* (MacMillan, London, 1978), p. 5.

37. 'Only Eisenstein and Murnau can sustain comparison with him when it comes to form'. E. Rohmer and C. Chabrol, *Hitchcock*, trans. S. Hochman (Frederick Ungar Publishing, New York, 1979), p. 152.

Filmography

The filmography contains details of the 23 feature films directed by Hitchcock during the period from 1925 to 1939, in chronological order indicating the production company, the studio and the date of production. Where the release date for a film varies from the date of production this is included in parentheses.

Gainsborough-Emelka

The Pleasure Garden	Emelka Geiselgasteig, Munich	1925 (1927)
The Mountain Eagle	Emelka Geiselgasteig, Munich	1925 (1927)

Gainsborough

The Lodger	Islington	1926 (1927)
Downhill	Islington	1927
Easy Virtue	Islington	1927

British International Pictures

The Ring	Elstree	1927
The Farmer's Wife	Elstree	1927 (1928)
Champagne	Elstree	1928
The Manxman	Elstree	1928 (1929)
Blackmail	Elstree	1929
Juno and the Paycock	Elstree	1930
Murder!	Elstree	1930
The Skin Game	Elstree	1930-1 (1931)
Number Seventeen	Elstree	1931 (1932)
Rich and Strange	Elstree	1932

Tom Arnold

Waltzes from Vienna	Shepherd's Bush	1933

Gaumont British

The Man Who Knew Too Much	Shepherd's Bush	1934
The Thirty-Nine Steps	Shepherd's Bush	1935
Secret Agent	Shepherd's Bush	1935 (1936)
Sabotage	Shepherd's Bush	1936

Gaumont British (Gainsborough)

Young and Innocent	Shepherd's Bush, Pinewood	1937 (1938)
The Lady Vanishes	Islington	1937 (1938)

Mayflower

Jamaica Inn	Elstree	1938 (1939)

Select Bibliography

Anderson, L., 'Alfred Hitchcock', *Sequence*, no. 9 (1949), pp. 113-24
Armes, R., *A Critical History of British Cinema* (Secker and Warburg, London, 1978)
Balcon, M., *A Lifetime in Films* (Hutchinson, London, 1969)
Barr, C., *Ealing Studios* (Cameron and Tayleur, London, 1977)
—, 'Blackmail: Silent and Sound', *Sight and Sound*, vol. 52, no. 2 (1983), pp. 122-6
—, 'A Conundrum for England', *Monthly Film Bulletin*, vol. 51, no. 607 (1984), pp. 234-5
Bogdanovich, P., *The Cinema of Alfred Hitchcock* (Museum of Modern Art, New York, 1963)
Bordwell, D. and Thompson, K., *Film Art — An Introduction* (Addison-Wesley, Reading, Mass., 1979)
Brown, G., *Launder and Gilliat* (British Film Institute, London, 1977)
Brunel, A., *Nice Work* (Forbes Robertson, London, 1949)
Cawelti, J., *Adventure, Mystery and Romance* (University of Chicago Press, Chicago, 1976)
Curran, J. and Porter, V. (eds.), *British Cinema History* (Weidenfeld and Nicolson, London, 1983)
Davy, C. (ed.), *Footnotes to the Film* (Lovat Dickson and Thompson, London, 1937)
Dean, B., *Mind's Eye* (Hutchinson, London, 1973)
Durgnat, R. *The Strange Case of Alfred Hitchcock* (Faber and Faber, London, 1974)
Dyer, P.J., 'Young and Innocent', *Sight and Sound*, vol. 30, no. 2 (1961), pp. 80-4
The Film Society Programmes (Arno Press, New York, 1972)
Gifford, D., *The British National Film Catalogue 1895-1970* (David and Charles, Newton Abbot 1973)
Greene, G., *The Pleasure Dome* (Secker and Warburg, London, 1972)
Hardy, F. (ed.), *Grierson on Documentary* (Faber and Faber, London, 1966)
Higson, A. and Neale, S., 'Introduction: Components of the National Film Culture', *Screen*, vol. 26, no. 1 (1985). pp. 3-8
Klingender, F. and Legg, S., *Money Behind the Screen* (Lawrence and Wishart, London, 1937)
Lovell, A., 'The British Cinema — The Unknown Cinema', British Film Institute seminar paper (1967)
—, 'Notes on British Film Culture', *Screen*, vol. 13, no. 2 (1972), pp. 5-15
— and Hillier, J., *Studies in Documentary* (Secker and Warburg, London, 1972)
Low, R., *The History of the British Film 1918-1929* (Allen and Unwin, London, 1971)
Manvell, R., *Film*, 3rd edn (Penguin, London, 1950)
Montagu, I., 'Interview: Ivor Montagu', *Screen*, vol. 13, no. 3 (1972), pp. 71-113
Palmer, J., *Thrillers* (Edward Arnold, London, 1978)
Perry, G., *The Great British Picture Show* (Paladin, St. Albans, 1975)
Political and Economic Planning, *The British Film Industry* (PEP, London, 1952)
Richards, J., *The Age of the Dream Palace* (Routledge and Kegan Paul, London, 1984)
Rohmer, E. and Chabrol, C., *Hitchcock*, trans. S. Hochman (Frederick Ungar Publishing, New York, 1979)

Additional bibliography

Barr, C., *All Our Yesterdays* (British Film Institute, London, 1986)

Brill, L., *The Hitchcock Romance* (Princeton University Press, New Jersey, 1988)

Deutelbaum, M. and Poague, L. (eds), *A Hitchcock Reader* (Iowa State University Press, Ames, 1986)

Eyüboglu, S., 'The authorial text and postmodernism: Hitchcock's *Blackmail*', *Screen*, Vol. 32, No. 1 (1991), pp. 58-78

Higson, A., *Waving the Flag*, (Clarendon Press, Oxford, 1995)

Kapsis, R., *Hitchcock The Making of a Reputation* (The University of Chicago Press, Chicago, 1992)

Landy, M., *British Genres Cinema and Society, 1930-1960* (Princeton University Press, New Jersey, 1991)

Leff, L., *Hitchcock and Selznick* (Weidenfeld and Nicolson, New York, 1987)

Low, R., *Film Making in 1930s Britain* (Allen & Unwin, London, 1985)

Modleski, T., *The Women Who Knew Too Much* (Methuen, London, 1988)

Price, T., *Hitchcock and Homosexuality* (The Scarecrow Press, Metuchen N.J., 1992)

Ryall, T., *Blackmail* (British Film Institute, London, 1993)

Sloan, J. E., *Alfred Hitchcock a filmography and bibliography* (University of California Press, Berkeley, 1995)

Sterritt, D., *The Films of Alfred Hitchcock* (Cambridge University Press, Cambridge, 1993)

Wood, R., *Hitchcock's Films Revisited* (Columbia University Press, New York, 1989)

Index